Ruling Pine Ridge

Department of Interior sign welcoming visitors to Pine Ridge reservation, 1940s.
Courtesy National Archives, photo no. RG 75-N PR-Misc.

Ruling Pine Ridge

Oglala Lakota Politics from the IRA to Wounded Knee

Akim D. Reinhardt

Foreword by Clara Sue Kidwell

Texas Tech University Press

This book is typeset in Plantin. The paper used in this book meets the minimum requirements of ANSI/NISO Z39.48–1992 (R1997).

Library of Congress Cataloging-in-Publication Data
Reinhardt, Akim D.
Ruling Pine Ridge : Oglala Lakota politics from the IRA to Wounded Knee / Akim D. Reinhardt ; foreword by Clara Sue Kidwell.
p. cm. — (Plains histories)
Includes bibliographical references and index.
ISBN-13: 978-0-89672-601-7 (hardcover : alk. paper)
ISBN-10: 0-89672-601-0 (hardcover : alk. paper) 1. Oglala Indians—South Dakota—Pine Ridge Indian Reservation—Government relations. 2. Oglala Indians—South Dakota—Pine Ridge Indian Reservation—Politics and government—20th century. 3. Pine Ridge Indian Reservation (S.D.)—History—20th century. 4. United States. Office of Indian Affairs. Pine Ridge Agency—History—20th century. I. Title.
E99.O3R45 2007
323.1197'5244—dc22   2006026609

Printed in the United States of America
07   08   09   10   11   12   13   14   15 / 9   8   7   6   5   4   3   2   1
T S

Texas Tech University Press   Box 41037   Lubbock, Texas 79409–1037 USA
800.832.4042   ttup@ttu.edu   www.ttup.ttu.edu

For my Grandparents
One by one, they are no longer here, but never
will they leave me

Contents

Contents

Illustrations

Photos following page 105

Pine Ridge school children
Oglala woman plastering cabin
Reservation food distribution
Oglala Sioux Tribal Court
John Collier
Benjamin Reifel
Jake Herman and Ben Chief
James Red Cloud

MAPS

Tables

Foreword

FROM TIME IMMEMORIAL (history having a different meaning for people who lived on this continent long before Europeans arrived and who gauged time by the repetitive cycles of seasons), Indian nations governed themselves. Kinship created networks of mutual obligation and responsibility that shaped social relationships. Men and sometimes women were publicly recognized as leaders. Among the Iroquois Nations in the Northeast and the Natchez in the Southeast, men who governed were descendents of female lineages and were chosen by women. On the Great Plains, men assumed positions of leadership because they gained the respect of their followers through demonstrated wisdom in making decisions, or personal charisma, or demonstrations of bravery in battle. One role of such chiefs was to provide for those members of the community who could not provide for themselves—widows, orphans, the elderly. The people known today as the Sioux, who formerly ranged over most of what now constitutes the states of North and South Dakota, Montana, Nebraska, Colorado, and Wyoming, followed this style of governance. The Pine Ridge Reservation in the state of South Dakota is a vestige of this former territory, and it is the home of the Oglala Lakota, a band of the great Sioux Nation.

In 1973, Pine Ridge erupted in a violent confrontation between Indians and agents of the United States government, including the F.B.I. It took four decades of a functioning colonial regime to reach this point. The Oglala ostensibly governed themselves under a constitution formulated by the Bureau of Indian Affairs and approved by the reservation residents in

1936 under the terms of the Indian Reorganization Act of 1934. The IRA was passed by the U.S. Congress under the guise of giving Indian tribes self-governance and economic self-sufficiency.[1] The Bureau, however, continued to exercise oppressive control over the affairs of Lakota people, and officials elected under the constitutional system were seen more as puppets of the BIA than as legitimate Lakota leaders. On Pine Ridge, Dick Wilson, elected as chairman of the Oglala Lakota Sioux Council in 1972, became a symbol of autocratic power. The Bureau of Indian Affairs upheld his election in the face of protests against his administration, and he appointed what amounted to his own private police force to enforce his sense of law and order on the reservation.

The confrontation between Wilson's opponents and federal agents at the town of Wounded Knee in 1973 was a critical point in the emergence of a national Indian consciousness and antigovernment activism. That consciousness was fostered by the general political tenor that characterized American society in the early 1970s. The Civil Rights movement and anti–Vietnam War sentiments created the atmosphere in which the American Indian Movement (AIM) could emerge in opposition to the BIA. The new Indian political consciousness sparked a modern notion of tribal sovereignty. Just as the original massacre of a band of Minneconjou Sioux in 1890 at Wounded Knee Creek had been a symbol of the destruction of Indian nationhood, the Indian takeover of a long-established, non-Indian-owned trading post in the town of Wounded Knee came to symbolize a rebirth of Indian power.[2]

The standoff at Wounded Knee resulted in the deaths of two Lakota men and the arrest and trials of a number of the American Indian Movement members. It lasted more than two months in the bitter winter of 1973 until negotiations finally ended the federal seige. AIM's failure to force the ouster of Dick Wilson demonstrated the futility of violent confrontation as a tactic to break the hold of the Bureau of Indian Affairs on the reservation government. It did, however, pave the way for new tribal leadership and ultimately for changing the relationship between Indian tribes and the U.S. government.

Tribal sovereignty is a much more complex concept in the early twenty-first century than it was in the 1970s. The basis of sovereignty is not only that Indian nations exercise self-government, but also that they operate on a government-to-government relationship with other entities. It is a historical fact that representatives of Indian nations signed treaties with agents of European nations and later with the American government. Although this premise of a government-to-government relationship was largely denied in federal Indian policy throughout much of the twentieth century, treaty rights are still cited as the basis for tribal relationships with the U.S. government.[3]

The history of Pine Ridge demonstrates a number of key points that underlie contemporary tribal sovereignty. One is that Indian identity has become a matter of politics as much as it is a matter of blood. Intermarriage between white settlers and traders and Indian women created divisions within Indian societies. Full bloods and mixed bloods constituted political factions. Full bloods were associated with ongoing cultural values, language, and ceremonies, while mixed bloods, because of their white parentage, were perceived to reject those ways in favor of assimilation into American society. The distinctions were not hard and fast, however. The terms became associated at Pine Ridge with political conservatism or progressivism. They did not necessarily correlate with biology but rather with ideology.

A second point emerges from the work of Steven Cornell, a sociologist who has studied a number of reservation communities to determine effective patterns of governance. Cornell has asserted that the more closely a tribal government follows cultural patterns of leadership, the more effective and more stable it will be.[4] The story of Pine Ridge again shows how the imposition of a hierarchical form of governance (an elected official heading an elected group of councilmen exercising power to make decisions, pass laws, and administer justice) disrupts relationships in a society where there are strong cultural values of individual autonomy, and social relationships are determined largely by family obligations and responsibilities rather than higher authority. A strongly centralized form of government goes against a sense of the autonomy of family groups and individuals to govern themselves. The IRA government at Pine Ridge was a complete mismatch with the cultural values and traditional governing structures of the community. The result was internal conflict.

A third point is that when tribal communities are dependent upon the federal government for their economic base and social services, they are susceptible to in-fighting and social disruption. For the Lakota, social controls resided in family groups, and Lakota people still value the *tiospeya*, or extended family lineage, as the source of their personal identity. Communal events such as the spring buffalo hunt and Sun Dance brought these groups together into the larger sense of tribal identity and bonded family groups through sharing of goods and through intermarriage. When these communal events and ceremonies were no longer possible, family allegiance began to take precedence over tribal allegiance, creating fracture points within the community. At Pine Ridge, the Oglala Sioux Tribal Council was dependent upon the Bureau of Indian Affairs for funding social services to tribal members, and jobs on the reservation were usually with the BIA or other federal programs. Federally funded programs became sources of political power for members of the tribal council who could control hiring. Kinship obligations translated into contemporary bureaucratic terms of nepotism and favoritism, creating factions within the community. Dick Wilson's government seized political and economic power from outside the community in ways that contravened communal interests, and in doing so tore the Pine Ridge community apart.

In the twenty-first century, tribal governments are still faced with a difficult situation. They must both provide social services to their citizens and run businesses that generate tribal income to cover the expenses of government. They must choose between maximizing employment in tribal businesses to provide jobs for the greatest number of tribal members and minimizing labor costs by cutting jobs to generate the greatest profit so they can fund social services.

With little or no private-sector economy on Indian reservations, tribal governments have no tax base to support social services. At Pine Ridge, the tribal council consolidated financial power from sources outside the community (i.e., federally funded programs and the Bureau of Indian Affairs) and used it selectively within the community in the hiring and firing of tribal employees, as was the case with the director of the Head Start program in 1968. Because tribal jobs and salaries were a major source of income on the reservation, the situation became explosive.

In 1969, a Cherokee anthropologist, Robert K. Thomas, wrote an article in a little-known journal, *New University Thought*, published by the University of Chicago. The title was "Colonialism: Classic and Internal," and in it Thomas compares Indian reservations to the colonized native populations of the British empire and likens the Bureau of Indian Affairs to a colonial administration determined to keep Indian reservations subordinate and exploit their resources.[5] In *Ruling Pine Ridge*, Dick Wilson can be seen as the ultimate agent of a colonial government, a Native man devoted to carrying out the will of the Bureau of Indian Affairs, and Pine Ridge as the exemplar of Thomas's "internal colony"—a poverty-stricken reservation population, marginalized in American society and subject to the often arbitrary decisions of a bureaucratic government as to what was in its best interests.

Wounded Knee has, however, become the symbol of a rebirth of Indian identity, political activism, and emergent tribal sovereignty. *Ruling Pine Ridge* reveals the complex forces that have shaped contemporary Indian identity on several levels—blood, politics, culture, and nationalism. The confrontation focused the attention of the American nation on the deprivation and oppression of Indian people. It also revealed the failure of federal policy to absorb Indians into American society. Dick Wilson, in his own blatant self-interest and grasping after power, came to represent the corrosive influence that federal policy had exercised on the community life and cultural integrity of the Pine Ridge community. The American Indian Movement represented freedom and self-determination for Indian people.

The Oglala Lakota of Pine Ridge are still a proud people with a strong sense of their own identity. The recent history of their reservation is instructive for other tribal governments. Although events on Pine Ridge certainly have their own unique character, the situations reveal broader structural issues in the operations of tribal governments as sovereign entities and how they must transcend the results of years of colonial oppression by the United States government. By demonstrating the sources and results of colonialism, *Ruling Pine Ridge* can provide strategies for the future that will help Indian nations achieve greater degrees of self-determination and sovereignty.

CLARA SUE KIDWELL
Norman, Oklahoma, 2007

Acknowledgments

IF YOU'VE READ acknowledgments in other books that in a prior incarnation were dissertations, then you're probably already familiar with the string of clichés about how long and arduous that transformation can be. Rest assured that all of those clichés are true. Consequently, all of the words that follow are very heartfelt.

First and foremost, I must acknowledge my family. Their encouragement has helped carry me through the years. My Eastern European refugee maternal grandparents were unflagging in their encouragement of my schooling and professional development. My mother, the retired high-school English teacher, has not only supported me in any countless number of ways (far too many to mention here), but she even went the extra mile of helping me proof the manuscript, a department in which I can always use extra help. Despite having muddied American waters for some three centuries, it's my understanding that my cousin and I are the first Reinhardts of our line to earn college degrees. However, you might not have known that given my father's attitude. The North Carolina farm boy turned Bronx general contractor, who was familiar with Russian literature and Japanese film, simply expected me to graduate from college. His moral support continues to be unwavering. And even though she's my kid sister, Megan still leads by example.

John R. Wunder flawlessly shepherded the earlier dissertation at the University of Nebraska. In the years since, his ongoing guidance has continued to be vital and irreplaceable. It is because of him that I am a professional. Without theirs and the efforts of Dolores Greenberg, my master's adviser at Hunter College CUNY, I would be little more than a hack.

I know that I speak for almost all of the historians I have met over the years when I say that archivists and librarians are truly among the most helpful and generous professionals in academia. It is with eagerness and a permanent sense of gratitude that I would like to mention some from among their ranks who have given me invaluable aide: Leonard Brugier and Joseph J. Kafka at the South Dakota Oral History Center, University of South Dakota; Julie Lakota and Barbara Means-Adams at Oglala Lakota College, Pine Ridge Reservation; and Marilyn Fink at the National Archives Regional Administration in Kansas City. All were grace personified. Without these archival wizards, I'd still be chasing my tail.

Judith Keeling and the rest of the TTU Press staff did a wonderful job of editing this project, right down to these very acknowledgments. Pat Guiberson constructed the beautiful maps contained herein. As someone who cannot draw a straight line without a ruler and a stiff drink, I am indebted to him for his generous work, expertise, and friendship.

Several people have read parts of this manuscript in one form or another, and they have offered me solid advice that has helped broaden my perspective and improve this final draft. In addition to those mentioned above, they include Parks Coble, David Wishart, Ken Winkle, Tim Mahoney, Pat Romero, Todd Kerstetter, Matt Bokovoy, Margaret Connell Szasz, Barbara Krauthamer, David Rich Lewis, Tim Hanson, and Kathy Fernstrom. Also thanks to Mark Blyth, a liberal artist masquerading as a social scientist, for his professional council, intellectual stimulation, and friendship.

In academia I've been very lucky to find myself repeatedly in pleasant situations. Therefore I would be remiss if I did not mention my fine colleagues in Towson University's Department of History. They are an intellectually vibrant and personally friendly group, and they help make it enjoyable to go to work each day, which is a great help when you're trying to write a book. Equally important, from Jeri Cunningham to Emily Daugherty, I've had the tremendously good fortune to work for secretaries with joyous dispositions and overwhelming competence.

I would like to acknowledge two sources that helped to underwrite some of my expenses: The Towson University Academy of Scholars and the University of Nebraska history department's Addison E. Sheldon Fellowship in Great Plains Studies.

WHEN I WAS A SMALL BOY, from time to time my grandfather would ask, "Akim, whadda you wanna be when you grow up?" More out of deference and/or laziness than any instinctive affinity for the Socratic method, I would typically respond, "What do you think I should be, Grandpa?" "Whatever you want," he always told me. "Just be good at it." Though he is gone, I have always remembered his sage advice. This book is one of the many things that I am. I hope it lives up to his words.

A Note on Terminology

THE WORD "SIOUX" is popular English vernacular to describe a wide-ranging but related group of peoples whose reservations today spread across the central part of the northern Great Plains. The word that the "Sioux" use for themselves is "Dakota." Dakota is simultaneously the name of the people and their language, and it loosely translates into English as "Allies."

The Dakota language is in the Siouan language family and has three dialects, each pronouncing the "d" syllable differently. Some pronounce it as a soft English "d" (as in the word, "bedding"), some as an "n," and some as an "l." Consequently, the three dialects are known as Dakota, Nakota, and Lakota. The people discussed in this volume are the Lakotas. The word "Sioux" will not be used unless it is in reference to someone else's usage of the word.

On March 11, 1824, the United States established the Indian Bureau (also known as the Indian Office or Indian Service) and placed it within the War Department. In 1849, the Interior Department was formed, and the Indian Bureau was moved there. By the turn of the twentieth century, the Indian Bureau was commonly known as the Office of Indian Affairs (OIA). In 1949, it was officially re-named the Bureau of Indian Affairs (BIA). Both of these terms are used in this volume, as appropriate to the period referenced.

The Office of Indian Affairs also had (and continues to have) an executive appointee for each reservation. Before the advent of the Indian Reorganization Act (IRA) in 1934, he was known as the Reservation Agent. Since the IRA, the agent is now known as the Reservation Superintendent. Again, either term will be used when relevant to the time period referenced.

The reservation-based institution primarily studied in this work is the tribal council system. The Oglala Sioux Tribal Council (OSTC) was set up on the Pine Ridge Reservation in 1936. Like all tribal councils on reservations around the country, it features an executive head. This chief executive on Pine Ridge has two titles: Chairman and President. The terms are interchangeable, and both will be used in this work. The reader should not try to espy any meaning from the use of either title.

As the anthropologist Morton Fried pointed out many years ago, it is problematic when Europeans and their descendants apply the word "tribe" to non-Europeans and their descendants; the biblical etymology of the word is a mess, and the racist and ethnocentric connotations of applying the word to non-European "Others" can be profound. If this non-Indian had his druthers, the word would be relegated to descriptions of the ancient Hebraic tribes from which I am partly descended. However, as is often the case, we cannot completely escape the missteps of our forbears. The word "tribe" has now firmly established itself in both the English vernacular and the arcane lexicon of the U.S. legal system. With regard to the former, most people, including Indians themselves, continue to use the word casually. With regard to the latter, "tribe" is a specific legal term in American Indian law. Consequently, it is with a great deal of frustration that I will use the word from time to time in this book. However, I will also refer to, with more conviction, and I believe more rightly, Indian *nations*.

Scholars have recently renewed the debate over what is the best proper noun for the people native to this hemisphere who have historically been called "Indians." In my experience, the first preference of most Indian people is to refer to their social or linguistic affiliation. In the case of this book, that would be Oglala Lakota, which I use. However, from time to time, it is necessary to write about all people, regardless of their affiliations. As someone who is not "Indian," I do not feel comfortable making any proclamations about what the best term might be. Though it is a legacy of Columbus's ignorance and arrogance, many Indian people continue to use the word "Indian" quite unself-consciously. "Native American" or simply the capitalized "Native" has also gained currency over the last several decades. And more recently, "Indigenous" as a proper noun, not a mere adjective, has taken its place among the others. I have elected to use all three in this book, and do so interchangeably.

A Note on Methodology and Sources

THE CORE IDEAL driving this study is the effort, wherever possible, to use Lakota sources to discuss the issues in question. This is not to the exclusion of non-Lakota or non-Indian sources, which at times are vitally important. However, too often the academic study of Native American history (particularly politics) has been a top-down, outside-in affair. In other words, authors have frequently been more concerned with federal Indian policies than the actual workings of Indian governments, and they have likewise relied heavily on source material generated by federal, state, and local government policy makers and outside observers. While these sources can be very valuable at times, when they become the primary wellspring of information, they fundamentally alter the focus of the work. A simple example might help to illustrate the point.

Imagine a book that purported to be a study of U.S. political history but for its documentation turned first and foremost to records of the French foreign ministry, the journals of French diplomats in the United States, and the reporting of the French press. While the quality of scholarship might very well be outstanding, the perspective of the work would probably make it very difficult to seriously categorize it as American political history. The classification of American diplomatic history (at best), the history of American-French relations (more likely), or perhaps even French history (quite possibly) would probably be more appropriate.

However, many studies of Native American history have been undertaken in a similar vein. While some of them are excellent works, many are simply not Native history as such. More often, they should be properly labeled as Indian-U.S. history or even simply as American diplomatic (or perhaps political) history.

Of course, the raising of these issues is not new. The recent efforts by many scholars to utilize Native oral history in their work reflects the larger, long overdue trend in American Indian history to begin making Native agents and sources central to Native history. Since the chronology of this volume follows the mid-twentieth century, I have had the good fortune of being able to cull a wide array of Native sources, including letters, newspapers, autobiographies, tribal council records, and the forementioned oral history.

To that end, this book uses a wide variety of Indigenous primary sources in an effort to construct a modern, academic American Indian history. Some may deem it ironic that the majority of these primary sources are *not* oral history (though oral history sources are indeed present throughout). However, given the study's chronology, this should not come as a surprise. Lakotas, after all, have been generating written documents (in both English and Lakota) since long before the temporal boundaries of this book.

However, while I am eager to emphasize Native historical agency, in no way am I attempting to relay history through the people's voice, as it were. The Lakota people are quite capable of speaking for themselves, and I would not be so presumptuous as to speak for them. Rather, this is simply a monograph that synthesizes their words, documents, and actions, along with numerous other sources, to produce an academic history. Relying primarily on Native sources and focusing on mid-twentieth-century political developments, this book seeks to outline Oglala Lakota political history by building a bridge to clarify the connection between two major events on Pine Ridge Reservation that are separated by nearly forty years.

At this time, I would like to ask the forgiveness of Lakota elders for any misstatements, inaccuracies, misinterpretations, or other errors that may follow. Pilamayaye.

Part I

1 9 3 4 – 1 9 4 6

1

Introduction

Hopscotching the Past

FOR SEVENTY-ONE DAYS on Pine Ridge Reservation in early 1973, as the blinding white winds of a northern Great Plains winter receded into the flutter and warmth of spring, the tiny hamlet of Wounded Knee seemed to be the very center of the world. In late February some of the Oglala Lakota people who lived on the reservation decided they had simply had enough. They had had enough of their tribal chairman, the rambunctious and autocratic Dick Wilson; their nearly successful attempt to impeach him was proof of that. Indeed, they had had enough of the entire tribal council system of government, which federal officials had pressured them into accepting back in 1936. And now their frustration reached a boiling point. They defied Chairman Wilson and members of the council, they defied the Bureau of Indian Affairs administrators and police force, they defied the menacing FBI and U.S. Marshal agents who had come at Wilson's request, and they made their stand at Wounded Knee.[1]

But what had begun as a local political dispute quickly grew into something of national and even international proportions. It was soon evident that control was slipping away from the local protestors whose occupation had been truly spontaneous; affairs inside the besieged perimeter were being managed by their allies from the American Indian Movement (AIM). Furthermore, the protestors were not merely up against Wilson and his private, local paramilitary, a group so free about using intimidation and violence that both sides openly referred them as the GOON Squad. Within hours of taking over the small village, the Wounded Knee occupiers were also facing down the M-16s of federal forces, soon to be augmented by aircraft, armored personnel carriers, and artillery.

As the event erupted into an epic showdown, media from around the world took notice and flocked to the reservation. Reporters and commentators from major television and radio outlets, newspapers, and magazines were complemented by representatives of the underground press and various observers. Pretty soon celebrities like Marlon Brando were voicing their support of the occupiers. Others, like writer Angela Davis, were even showing up in person.[2]

As the predictable arc of media coverage peeked and descended, tales of the ongoing siege drifted from front covers to back pages, and the mushrooming Watergate scandal soon eclipsed Wounded Knee in the national consciousness. When the occupation finally ended in early May, the little town was empty and broken. Buildings were stained with graffiti and pockmarked with bullet holes, most of them destined to be razed after nearly two and a half months of violence and protest.

As the world's attention began to wane, the people of Pine Ridge were left to pick up the pieces and to continue their very local political struggle. The immediate origin had been the divisiveness arising from Dick Wilson's contentious reservation presidency. But as the conflict had grown, it tapped into deep rifts on Pine Ridge. It widened social and cultural fissures that were as old as the reservation itself. And it went to the very heart of Oglala politics, raising questions that had frustrated many Lakotas for just as long: What kind of government could the Oglala people have? What kind did they want? What was the nature of Oglala sovereignty? What would be the future of Oyate kin?[3]

THE PEOPLE REACT TO WOUNDED KNEE

By Wednesday April 4, 1973, the siege was well past its first month. That day, a local Oglala woman sympathetic to the protestors gave an interview, openly voicing her opinions about what had gone wrong with her reservation's government. This was no small task. She had been active in opposing the Wilson administration, and she knew that by speaking out publicly against the chairman and the tribal council system, she was putting herself in grave danger. Indeed, she had only agreed to the interview reluctantly and with an important condition: her name would remain a secret. The interviewer could record it for posterity and bring that information back to the archive at the University of South Dakota, located far at the other end of the state in the town of Vermillion. But in the meantime, her identity would remain anonymous; people who accessed her interview would not be allowed to name her publicly. With this caveat established, she spoke into the interviewer's microphone as children played nearby, and she said what she believed.[4]

She criticized the tribal council. She felt that many of the reservation's elected officials seemed "to forget the reason why they're there. And they get the idea that they have the power to do as they please. . . . They're in it for themselves and they forget the people are out there." And she was clear about the direct connection between the discontent with tribal government and the protests against Wilson, which had culminated in the occupation of Wounded Knee. Of the protest, she said, "I think the Indian people are using their voice because of such people being elected to office."[5]

She was intimately familiar with the workings and policies of the reservation's government, the Oglala Sioux Tribal Council, and to her this was nothing short of a crisis in tribal politics. And the roots were deep. "I think it's been like that [in a state of crisis] maybe for the past ten years or so." But she also realized just how much damage the current administration had done. She accused Wilson of being corrupt and concentrating power. She blamed the council for allowing him to act that way and the people of the reservation for electing him in the first place. She accused Wilson of intimidating his opponents and using fear to keep them from checking his power.[6]

What did she feel was the solution? She espoused a restructuring of the reservation's government. She advocated a decentralized, community-based system in line with Oglala Lakota social values and political culture. She wanted a system that would preclude centralized power, a system that would act more directly on the will of the people. She approved of local people making their own decisions for their local districts. And when the interviewer asked if she believed that the current council had abused its powers, she calmly answered, "Yes."[7]

By Tuesday, July 17, the ashes of Wounded Knee were cold. The summer was full and the siege's final day was more than two months past. Pine

Ridge Chairman Dick Wilson was now telling his side of the story to a sympathetic interviewer. He sported a fresh crew cut and was full of tough talk. His voice had the soft and measured tones of a man who had been burned by the media and was now attentive to finding an outlet to get his views across. He was confident and defiant.[8]

He was also condescending and dismissive of those who yearned to indigenize the reservation's government by incorporating traditional cultural values. He derided those who advocated restoring Lakota sovereignty as outlined in the 1868 Second Treaty of Fort Laramie. "As far as I'm concerned, them few who wanna go back to the 1868, they damn well sure can," he scoffed, "'cause I'm not going to."[9]

In part, Wilson was able to be patronizing because he was also in denial about the depth of opposition he faced from a large contingency of his own people. From the start, he painted the Wounded Knee occupation as an AIM stunt, challenging the idea that the Movement or the siege ever had much local support. He denied AIM even the most minuscule percentage of local favor, granting them perhaps "one-half of one-half percent." He claimed that AIM had targeted Pine Ridge because his own vice president, David Long, had been an AIM sympathizer. In Wilson's opinion, the impeachment hearing against him had not been the work of his own disaffected people, but was nothing more than AIM's attempt to bring about an effective coup and take over the reservation.[10]

In trying to downplay local opposition, he derided the very existence of a competing Indigenous political culture. "There is [sic] no traditional chiefs or headsmen on this reservation," he asserted despite their ongoing existence. He labeled those who claimed to be such as pretenders and he staunchly supported the tribal council system that he governed, which had been created under the Indian Reorganization Act of 1934. "You gotta understand that we're operating under the Reorganization Act of 1934, and this in effect done away with the chiefs and whatnot. And by no means is [Frank] Fools Crow a traditional chief. He's Fools People is what his name should be." Wilson even went so far as to question the elder's Lakota heritage, wondering aloud if Fools Crow was even really an Oglala.[11]

Of course, even the tribal chairman had to admit that there were some traditional leaders who could not be brushed aside with bad puns about their names and questions about their lineage. "If there's anybody that comes close to being a traditional chief, it would be Charlie Red Cloud, although that has never been bestowed upon him. It is an honorary thing. So there's no traditional chiefs."[12]

Wilson's conviction that AIM was the true source of local opposition to his presidency and the real force behind the occupation led the chairman to harshly criticize all who opposed him. Steeped in Cold War culture, he even criticized local churches that supported his opponents as being "militant" and "communist oriented." Which ones? "All of them. My own church, I'm Episcopal. I don't go anymore because of this. I believe in the good Lord, but I don't believe in some of them clowns that carry his message."[13]

As the president of Pine Ridge, he vigorously supported the federal system of tribal council governments of which his office was part. He viewed the siege of Wounded Knee not as a local political dispute, but as a defense of the tribal council system against attacks by outside agitators. And he fell back on dubious but prevalent Cold War theory to explain it. "I think the stand that I and my tribal government took has strengthened tribal governments, not only here, but nationwide. . . . Had we folded here, it would have been like dominos then."[14]

Wilson's catharsis lasted for nearly an hour. During the interview he ran a gamut of emotions. At times he was openly hostile to those who opposed him, even threatening to "take a swing" at AIM leader Russell Means. At other moments he was genuinely remorseful for the suffering that people had endured and the deteriorating situation on the reservation. And he was periodically discomfited by the reality that federal authorities had run roughshod over him during the siege, shunting him to the side as they managed the situation directly; he even agreed with the interviewer's description of Pine Ridge as a "police state" in light of the ongoing heavy concentration of federal officials and law enforcement. From start to finish, Wilson's frustration was palpable.[15]

"I just get pissed off when I talk about Wounded Knee."[16]

The very next day, Wednesday, July 18, a press conference took place on Pine Ridge Reservation. Sitting at the table, fielding questions from the media, was Secretary of the Interior Rogers Morton. Because the Oglala Sioux Tribal Council was under the authority of the Bureau of Indian Affairs (BIA), which was part of Interior Department, Morton was second only to the president of the United States as the highest-ranking federal executive on Indian affairs. Sitting alongside Morton were several assistants and Pine Ridge Chairman Dick Wilson.[17]

Morton established his presence and exuded authority throughout the conference, addressing the media's various queries in the polished manner of a presidential cabinet member. No, he had never felt much was to be gained from armed occupations like what had taken place at Wounded Knee. Yes, he believed that the basic motivation of AIM leaders was to help the Indian community. No, in his view the occupation had been completely unnecessary.[18]

Chairman Wilson sat there quietly. Throughout the press conference, from start to finish, he barely spoke. There was very little that the national media wanted to ask him. And there was none of the previous day's bravado. On the few occasions that he did address those present, he sounded cowed; his speech was quiet, hesitant, and at times stuttering. Listening to the audio recording of the press conference, one can almost imagine Morton and his staff prepping the outspoken and impolitic Wilson beforehand, firmly telling the infamously volatile chairman that when they met the press he should sit there quietly, be seen and not heard. This clearly was not his show.[19]

POLITICAL CULTURES

Prior to contact with Europeans, there is no written source material concerning Lakota history. Therefore, we must rely on a combination of oral history and archaeology in our attempt to see the shape of the Lakota nation through time's translucent gaze. Archaeological records have established their earliest verifiable residence in modern-day Minnesota at the headwaters of the Mississippi River. Oral tradition has it that the Lakota-speaking Tetonwan people held one of the seven council fires that comprised the Oceti Sakowin. The Oceti was a loose regional confederacy whose members spoke the Lakota, Nakota, and Dakota dialects. The Nakota-speaking Ihanktunwan held two of the council fires, and the Dakota-speaking Isanti held the remaining four. While details are foggy, and some scholars argue that the council may never have even actually existed, what remains clear is that each of the closely related groups retained substantial autonomy. It is also very unlikely that arbitrary power was vested in any political office.[20]

By the mid-1600s, the Lakotas were beginning to emigrate westward, soon to be followed by the Nakotas. This movement further stretched the political bonds between the council fires. Adopting the horse, eventually forsaking agriculture, and basing their economy on hunting (particularly bison) and commerce, the Lakota nation saw a rapid rise in its wealth, prestige, and power during the eighteenth and early nineteenth centuries. Befitting the oyate's mobile settlement pattern and burgeoning strength, Lakota political structure during this period was decentralized and imperial. Domestic matters were influenced by political leaders who earned their positions through achievement; authority was flexible and distributed through a complex and localized meritocracy. On the international front, Lakota leaders became used to wielding substantial influence as other Indigenous and European nations alike yielded to their expansion.[21]

This period of nearly unbridled growth began to end in the mid-nineteenth century, when the Tetonwan Oyate ran headlong into another expansive empire: the United States. Military encounters between the two powers brought mixed results. However, the United States eventually asserted its dominance by strangling the Lakota economy; U.S. policies hastened the destruction of the bison herds upon which the Lakota economy rested and fostered a trade imbalance between the two sides that emphasized Lakota exports of raw materials and imports of U.S. finished goods. The trade imbalance led Lakotas into cycles of debt and dependence on U.S. imports of manufactured products such as guns and ammunition, and in some cases even clothing; for those deeply in debt, bison robes could not be used as attire for they were too valuable as a trade item. By the end of the century, the entire Lakota populace had been rounded up onto reservations that represented a mere fraction of prior Tetonwan land holdings, and they were now under the imperial jurisdiction of the United States. In the aftermath of Lakota capitulation, "reservation" was little more than a euphemism for "prison camp." What followed was more than half a century of direct colonial rule. U.S. federal authorities employed draconian measures to subordinate Tetonwan political institutions.[22]

Pine Ridge Reservation is the modern homeland of the Oglala people, who comprise one of the seven subdivisions of the Lakota nation.[23] The concern of this book is the reservation's mid-twentieth-century politics, and as such its primary contribution is in the realm of Lakota political history. Its chronology commences with the establishment of the Oglala Sioux Tribe (OST) in 1936 under the auspices of the 1934 Indian Reorganization Act (IRA), which led to an upheaval in the political landscape of Pine

Ridge. In 1935, under the terms of this federal legislation, members of the reservation narrowly voted to establish a new government as outlined by the IRA's provisions. Also known as the Wheeler-Howard Act for its congressional sponsors, the IRA marked a major shift in the way the federal government would now conduct business with all Native nations. And for those nations such as the Oglala Lakotas of Pine Ridge, which agreed to reorganize under the IRA, it also meant important changes in the local politics of their reservations. Reorganization meant (among other things) that tribal governments would be restructured to conform to a U.S. cookie-cutter model and that the federal government would now recognize these new bodies politic as the only legitimate Indian governments on their reservations.[24]

The IRA's federal architects designed the tribal council system as part of an adaptation to the changing nature of the United States' colonial subjugation of Indigenous peoples. When the designers of the IRA took up their self-appointed task in the 1930s, the final stages of military conquest over Native nations were several decades in the past. During the intervening period of direct colonialism, U.S. federal policy toward and rule over Indian reservations had been authoritarian and shaped by overt cultural hostility. The time was now ripe for change. That change came during Franklin Roosevelt's administration in the form of the Indian New Deal, the centerpiece of which was the IRA legislation. The Indian Reorganization Act ushered in the transition from direct colonial rule to a policy of indirect colonialism. Through the new tribal councils, Indians would begin to manage some of the day-to-day business of running their reservations. But the federal government would still have final say on all important matters. Thus, the advent of tribal councils in no way represented a restoration of full sovereignty. Rather, it was a loosening of the reigns, an opportunity for limited self-government within the context of ongoing subordination to federal authority.

There already exists some scholarly discourse on the nature of Pine Ridge politics during the tribal council era. Some academics, such as anthropologists Marla Powers and Paul Robertson and literary scholar Elizabeth Cook-Lynn, have emphasized the diminished Native sovereignty that is a consequence of the IRA; the continued subordination of the OST to the U.S. government results in a council that is locally elected, but whose members often behave more like federal authorities than the people's true representatives. Others, such as anthropologists William Farber and Ernest Schusky and political scientist Tom Holm, have stressed cultural problems in the system. They have maintained that the IRA is conceptually flawed and destined to fail on Pine Ridge; the OST's governing body, the Oglala Sioux Tribal Council (OSTC), coupled with its Oglala constituency, is tantamount to round pegs and square holes. The council's administrative apparatus is so completely foreign to the Lakota political culture that the two are inherently incompatible and this admixture has led to chronic dysfunction.[25]

These explanations are not as divergent as they may at first seem. For one, both interpretations agree on the failure of the IRA system on Pine Ridge. Beyond that, they are certainly not mutually exclusive, and both are in fact crucial to understanding the failures, shortcomings, and tumult surrounding the Oglala Sioux Tribe since 1934.

Indeed, the Oglala Sioux Tribal Council's structure is utterly foreign to Lakota politics. Furthermore, a combination of this disparity and the ongoing suspicion and doubt among many Oglalas about the OST's subordination to Washington, D.C., has led to a large measure of Indigenous apathy, resistance, and tribal council dysfunction.

However, as is abundantly evidenced in the chapters that follow, the IRA certainly has its supporters, on Pine Ridge Reservation and elsewhere. This support is understandable, as some important and positive accomplishments have stemmed from the Indian New Deal. Nonetheless, the IRA's flaws, deep and indelible, are undeniably amplified on Pine Ridge.[26]

PLACE

Perhaps it is the relatively large size of their nation. Perhaps it is their eighteenth- and nineteenth-century martial, bison-hunting horse culture, which continues to fascinate many outsiders. Perhaps it is their history, so punctuated with dramatic episodes, both triumphant and heartbreaking. Whatever the reason, the Lakota nation, particularly the Oglalas, has always drawn much attention from writers, academic and otherwise.

Recent scholarship on Oglala Lakota politics has begun to strengthen our understanding of the subject's historical development. Catherine Price has offered a detailed treatment of Oglala politics during the mid-nineteenth century. In so doing, she has helped elucidate the decentralized and complex nature of Lakota government in the twilight of its imperial phase. More recently, historian Jeffrey Ostler has brought colonial theory to bear in his reassessment of nineteenth-century Lakota international relations. Two anthropologists, first Thomas Biolsi and then Paul Robertson, have each considered the latter period of direct U.S. colonial rule and the transition to the indirect colonialism of the IRA tribal council era. Biolsi has emphasized the continued, behind-the-scenes authority of the Office of Indian Affairs during the early IRA era, while Robertson has employed colonial theory to suggest that the early Oglala Sioux Tribal Council was a political medium for the local, mixed-blood colonial elite to enhance themselves at the expense of Pine Ridge's full-blood community.[27]

Political studies of Pine Ridge featuring post-1934 topics have typically trained their lenses on the turbulence of the early 1970s and have often focused as much if not more on the American Indian Movement than on the politics of the Oglala Sioux Tribe. Historian Rolland Dewing covered all involved parties in his exhaustive chronology of the occupation and siege, but AIM members and federal authorities often take center stage in his narrative. English professor Robert Warrior and writer Paul Smith teamed up to explore the Red Power movement of the late 1960s and early 1970s. In so doing, they paid attention to Pine Ridge politics and were more critical of the Wilson regime than Dewing had been. But their examination of Lakota politics was always secondary to their primary investigations concerning Indian activism. In addition to scholarly output, there has also been a string of primary accounts published by participants in the events of the 1970s. However, most of these have been composed by members and allies of AIM and who uniformly subscribe to an AIM-centered narrative and an interpretation that is highly favorable of AIM's role on the reservation.[28]

The focus on Wounded Knee is understandable. The 1973 occupation and ensuing seventy-one-day siege are arguably the most explosive political events, both literally and figuratively, in Indian Country since the end of U.S.–Indian warfare. By the time the standoff ended on May 8, 1973, four of the besieged were wounded, two had been shot dead, one U.S. marshal was paralyzed, the small town of Wounded Knee was virtually destroyed, and more than 200 people were arrested. During the siege, protestors were supported by allies from the vocal, attention-grabbing AIM leadership, whereas the tribal government was backed by federal forces including the

U.S. Marshals, the Federal Bureau of Investigation, and the Bureau of Indian Affairs. Consequently, this episode is usually viewed as a final, pyrotechnical chapter in the heyday of Red Power activism.

But what is lacking in these accounts is an understanding of the event within its local context. Academics, autobiographers, journalists, and other writers have consistently downplayed this aspect of the story, at times even ignoring it altogether. This may have partially resulted from the discretion of intimidated participants, like the anonymous woman quoted earlier in this chapter who withheld her name for fear of the retribution that might rain down upon her for openly critiquing the Wilson administration. Part of the answer also undoubtedly lies in the strong media presence of AIM and the federal government; in contrast, the press was far less interested in the tribal council and the local Lakotas of the rural reservation, portraying them in muted tones, when at all.

No matter the reason, however, the occupation was in fact the direct result of a sizeable contingent of Pine Ridge Oglalas being dissatisfied with and protesting against their own IRA-sponsored tribal government. The siege itself was simultaneously the culmination of a grassroots political protest on Pine Ridge and the beginning of a three-year Lakota civil war that witnessed political corruption, repression, and a torrent of politically motivated violence, including dozens of murders.

Resting upon a bedrock of Indigenous source material that other scholars have not yet examined in any detail, including tribal council records, tribal newspapers, and local oral history, this book corrects that emphasis. The Oglala Lakota people and the Oglala Sioux Tribe are the centerpiece of the story of Pine Ridge's twentieth-century political history.[29] The establishment of the IRA tribal council government on Pine Ridge in 1936 and the occupation and siege of Wounded Knee in 1973 frame this work. These two events are more than just convenient chronological bookends. They are the defining chapters in the mid-twentieth-century political history of Pine Ridge Reservation. Furthermore, they are intimately related to each other, despite the nearly forty years separating them. Both events have already been the subject of academic studies. However, no one has yet done any substantial research to connect and relate them within the context of domestic Oglala politics. Though some scholars note a link, their discussions are brief and usually stem from an analysis of one episode or the other. That is to say, scholars either study the IRA and project forward or study the siege of Wounded Knee and extrapolate backward. This book seeks to bridge that gap by studying Pine Ridge politics during the mid-twentieth century. In essence, it is the ligature that binds together these two momentous developments.

With regard to interpreting the connection between these two seminal events, there is already some debate. One school of thought among scholars accepts that the establishment of an IRA government on the Pine Ridge Reservation in 1936 was one of the major historical catalysts for the later occupation of Wounded Knee. Historian Lawrence Hauptman has said, "The road to Wounded Knee in 1973 was blazed by the paradoxes and inconsistencies of the Indian Reorganization Act."[30] This sentiment has been echoed by a number of scholars and other observers associated with Native politics and affairs. They declare the failure of the IRA system on Pine Ridge and generally support the notion that the initial occupation of Wounded Knee in 1973 was directly tied to an effort to remove Pine Ridge OST president Richard "Dick" Wilson from office and then escalated into a movement to purge the entire system from the reservation. That is to say, nearly forty years of discontent with the system finally bubbled over during the contentious Wilson administration. However, there is an opposing view.[31]

The argument laid down by Dick Wilson and his supporters, endorsed by the federal government at the time and parroted by some scholars, is as follows. The siege of Wounded Knee was instigated and propagated by outsiders, particularly members of AIM and their allies, many of them non-Indian, and the uprising did not reflect the actual sentiments of the Oglala people living on Pine Ridge. Rather, the argument continues, it was the work of urban Indians and others who chose the site of Wounded Knee for its historic symbolism (as the site of the 1890 massacre). These people had no legitimate claim to represent the residents of Pine Ridge Reservation or their interests. This interpretation clearly de-emphasizes any connection between the siege of Wounded Knee and the establishment of an IRA government on Pine Ridge. Those who champion this interpretation draw strength from the official stance of the Wilson regime and the federal government, and from the fact that the siege deeply divided the reservation. Many of its residents were opposed to it.[32]

Nevertheless, the Wilsonian interpretation rings hollow. It was obviously self-serving for the chairman to downplay local outrage against his administration by blaming outside agitators, and it was likewise self-serving for the federal government to divert attention away from Indian discontent with the federally sanctioned tribal council system. But the Wilsonian view is also problematic on a deeper level. To argue that the occupation of Wounded Knee was the result of historical forces emanating from outside the reservation (namely urban Indian activism) is to deny the historical agency of Pine Ridge Oglalas. It is simply unacceptable to leave the people of Pine Ridge out of the story of their reservation. It is undeniable that there were many Oglalas who opposed the occupation, just as there were many who supported it and many who were conflicted. And while AIM did play an important role in the siege, the initial occupation was an outgrowth of local Oglalas protesting against the larger IRA system in general and Dick Wilson's chairmanship in particular.

Of course, both the advent of the IRA and the occupation of Wounded Knee, while locally important, also had national implications. The IRA was indeed a creation from without, one that affected every reservation in the United States, not just Pine Ridge. However, the occupation of Wounded Knee stemmed from domestic factors within Pine Ridge Reservation, many of them connected directly to the IRA-sponsored Oglala Sioux Tribe. The siege reverberated throughout the country, transcending its local roots and achieving a level of national (and some would argue, international) importance. In effect, Pine Ridge Reservation was a percolator into which the IRA was poured in 1934, adding to the existing political brew. The mixture bubbled and boiled for nearly four decades and then exploded back onto the national scene in the form of the occupation and siege of Wounded Knee in 1973.

This book charts the major political developments on Pine Ridge Reservation in the years following reorganization and leading up to Wounded Knee. In so doing, it offers substantial research that settles once and for all that there is indeed a strong connection between the establishment of an IRA government on Pine Ridge and the siege of Wounded Knee, as well as the exact nature of that connection: the two events together represent major bookmarks in the history of the Pine Ridge Reservation that need to be studied in conjunction with one another in order to gain a fuller appreciation of the reservation's political history during the mid-twentieth century.

The historical record indicates that a large proportion of the Oglala people did not want to reorganize from the start. After reorganizing, many

Oglalas were unhappy with the new government, which was at times ineffective and even worked to the detriment of much of its constituency. During its first decade, the IRA-sponsored tribal council was to a large extent
nullified by the continued domination of the federal government through
its colonial organ, the Office of Indian Affairs (OIA). But by the 1960s the
OSTC, while still subservient to the federal government, had substantially
increased it powers. When in 1972 the council came under the control of
Chairman Dick Wilson, a corrupt ruler with overtly violent and autocratic
tendencies, Oglala sentiments were mobilized into active protests, which
eventually climaxed in the occupation of Wounded Knee. The ten-week
siege that followed the occupation was in fact dominated to some degree by
the American Indian Movement, but the initial occupation itself was a culmination of local political protests against the IRA government.

A NOTE ON STRUCTURE

This work is composed of two parts. The first deals with the specifications
of the Indian Reorganization Act and the ten years following its establishment on Pine Ridge in an attempt to understand the changed (and
unchanged) flow of power under the IRA's new political equation and the
subsequent implications for and reactions by Oglala Lakota people. The
second part looks at Pine Ridge politics during the late 1960s and early
1970s, challenging the ahistorical Wilsonian/federal "invasion" theory of
Wounded Knee. By analyzing local political and historical framework, it
ties the founding of the OST definitively to the 1973 siege.

Chapter 2 discusses the advent of the Indian Reorganization Act on
Pine Ridge Reservation. In so doing, it places Commissioner of Indian
Affairs John Collier's IRA vision and goals within the context of colonialism; the IRA is understood less as a dramatic sea change in Indian affairs
and more as a shift in colonial administrative policy. The chapter discusses
both Oglala support of and resistance to reorganization. The reservation
was greatly divided over the issue of whether or not to reorganize, and that
difference of opinion was in part driven by, and certainly exacerbated,
existing social, political, and cultural divisions. Reorganization's eventual
victory did not work to heal those divisions, nor did it establish a successful
model for Oglala political revival. To the contrary, it set in motion a history
of ongoing political discontent and dysfunction.

Chapter 3 examines the immediate political consequences of reorganization on Pine Ridge Reservation. It shows that despite the Collier administration's propaganda, Pine Ridge's new governing body, the Oglala Sioux Tribal Council, was not immediately endowed with substantial political power. Rather, the arm of federal dominance over Indian peoples, the Office of Indian Affairs, maintained its tight grip on the reservation, exercising its control through a variety of mechanisms. By contrast, the OSTC was rather impotent, as evidenced by its inability to exercise the most basic practices of sovereignty. The chapter then looks at Oglala reaction to reorganization. It becomes clear that the people of Pine Ridge understood very well the political equations being played out on the reservation. They correctly perceived the OIA's continued position of dominance as well as the OSTC's weakness, and they acted accordingly.

While not approaching the status of a sovereign power, the OSTC did nonetheless hold some political authority. Chapter 4 considers more specifically the role of the council during its first decade. Growing out of the reservation divisions outlined in chapter 2, the new OSTC often descended into constituent politics, representing the interests of its supporters to the detriment of the opposition. Ironically, this brought the OSTC into conflict not only with the people it represented, but also the reservation's true hegemon, the Office of Indian Affairs. When the council's actions contradicted the OIA's presumptions on how the OSTC should be acting, discord often arose. Thus, after creating and promoting the implementation of what turned out to be a contentious political scenario, the federal government was frequently drawn into the ensuing political strife.

Opening part II, chapter 5 fast forwards to the late 1960s, updating political events on Pine Ridge. The economic situation remained destitute and federally dominated, and the OSTC continued to be plagued by constituent politics. However, unlike its Depression-era incarnation, it now flexed considerably more political muscle. While the federal government had not eschewed the colonial hierarchy of power that kept reservations subordinate (and still has not), changes in federal policy had allowed the council more leeway in its decision making and authority over the reservation's day-to-day affairs. Given the OSTC's problematic dynamics, the uneasy status quo of the council's constituent politics was in danger of careening out of control. Two factors quickly helped make this a reality: the emergence of a strong civil rights movement on Pine Ridge and the election of dictatorial and antagonistic tribal president Dick Wilson. Under these conditions, genuine political revolt was soon in the offing.

Chapter 6 explores the brewing political storm on Pine Ridge during the early 1970s. At the same time that the Wilson administration was alienating many people on the reservation, AIM began to involve itself in the growing Indian civil rights movement of the northern Great Plains. As Wilson's opponents naturally gravitated toward an alliance with AIM, Wilson leaned more heavily on his sponsors in the federal government for support. In this atmosphere, the long simmering frustrations of many Oglalas spilled over. At the same time, Wilson and his federal allies used AIM's involvement as an excuse to disregard complaints against themselves, centralize their political power, and cast the Movement as outside agitators stirring up trouble.

As the political situation worsened, it escalated into violence. The Wilson regime was ruthless in its efforts to quash dissent, while the chairman's opponents were relentless in their criticism of him. The matter eventually culminated in a failed impeachment hearing against the tribal president, which is the subject of chapter 7. With Wilson still in office and the reservation now occupied by armed federal officers as well as the chairman's own private army, political tension and frustrations on the reservation had no productive outlet. The result was the occupation and siege of Wounded Knee.

Chapter 8 concludes by adding various levels of historical depth to Wounded Knee. The site of the occupation was not chosen spontaneously; the locale was symbolic for reasons that went far beyond its irrefutable connection to the 1890 massacre and included more recent historical developments that embodied Oglala frustration and discontent with a century's worth of colonial exploitation. On the eve of the 1973 occupation, Wounded Knee already held many important meanings.

In the last quarter-century, more and more academic research has focused on reservation-based politics.[33] Hopefully this work will assume a place in that growing pantheon and serve as a contribution to Indigenous Studies. However, this book is not a comparative study between reservations; rather, it represents a neglected piece of the political history of the Lakota people.

2

Indirect Colonialism

The Indian Reorganization Act

THE COMING OF THE IRA

THE FEDERAL INDIAN AGENCY at Pine Ridge was established in 1878, when the Oglala Lakota leader Mahpia Luta (Red Cloud) settled there with many of his followers. The small agency was originally an indelible piece of the larger Lakota landholding called the Great Sioux Reservation. Outlined in the 1868 Second Treaty of Fort Laramie, its boundaries initially encompassed the entire western half of South Dakota. The treaty also stipulated that Lakotas held title to additional territory covering parts of North Dakota, Montana, Wyoming, and Nebraska. But in 1889, the federal government unilaterally stripped the Great Sioux Reservation of eleven million acres and broke up the remainder into six smaller reservations (see map 1).[1] The second largest of the six diminished reservations that were left, Pine Ridge is located in the southwestern corner of South Dakota.[2]

Then in 1910, the federal government continued its dispossession of Lakota lands when it amputated Pine Ridge's southeastern quadrant, opening it to non-Indian settlement that year and allowing South Dakota to officially organize it as Bennett County in 1912. The remaining three-fourths of the reservation were within the parameters of Washington

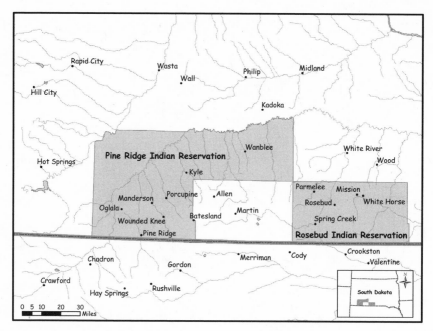

Pine Ridge Reservation and the Surrounding Area

(northwestern quadrant), Washabaugh (northeastern), and Shannon (south-western) counties. Washington county would eventually be subsumed into an expanded Shannon County in 1942, while Washabaugh County remained in the East (see map 2).[3]

As the federally sanctioned home for the Oglala Lakota nation, Pine Ridge at the turn of the early twentieth century was no different than any other reservation in one important aspect. Its Indian residents, the Oglala Lakotas, were a politically marginalized people, having capitulated to the United States after a series of military engagements. For nearly the first sixty years of the reservation's existence, Pine Ridge's Indigenous inhabitants were subject to the direct colonial authority of the United States. The administration of Indian reservations was handled by the Office of Indian Affairs (OIA), a branch of the Interior Department. At the head of the OIA was the commissioner of Indian affairs (CIA), a presidential appointee who reported directly to the secretary of the interior.[4] The chief colonial administrator on a reservation was an OIA official known as the reservation agent. Required to acquiesce only to the CIA and superior federal officials, the reservation agent was a de facto autocrat whose word was law, a reality that

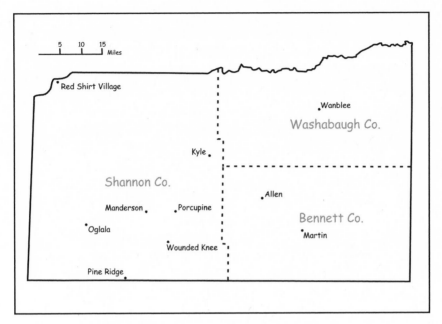

South Dakota Counties in Pine Ridge Reservation

Indians and non-Indians alike readily observed at the time. Indeed, in the aftermath of the United States' conquest, American Indians throughout America were often not even allowed to leave their reservations without the permission of the local OIA agent.[5]

The official manner and extent to which Native peoples were allowed to govern themselves was largely left to the agents' discretion, and official avenues of recourse for Indians were minimal. It was not until 1912 that Congress agreed to recognize the input of Indian people in even selecting an agent, and it was not until 1916 that Congress allowed Indian people to impeach and remove an agent. This, of course, is not to deny the historical agency of Native people who were able to resist colonial authority in any number of ways, especially on a large, far-flung reservation like Pine Ridge. Nonetheless, one of the results of military conquest was the severe mitigation of any official Lakota body politic.[6]

However, with Franklin Roosevelt's ascendancy to the presidency in 1933, this approach to Indian affairs began to give way. Roosevelt selected John Collier to serve as the new CIA, and it was Collier who envisioned a new federal Indian policy that would forever alter the relationship between

American Indians and the U.S. government. Broadly known as the Indian New Deal, the central and enduring thrust of the policy would be outlined the following year in a piece of congressional legislation called the Indian Reorganization Act (IRA). Collier, with the help of his assistants, designed IRA, and he would prove to be its driving force during Roosevelt's long reign.

John Collier was born in 1893 to an elite Southern family. Prior to the Civil War, his mother grew up on a plantation with 113 slaves, and during his childhood, his father served as mayor of Atlanta. Collier began his professional career as an urban reformer, seeking to improve the living conditions of immigrants in the slums of New York City during the Progressive Era before briefly moving his family to California to take a job in education. But in 1920, while visiting noted socialite Mabel Dodge in New Mexico, he had the opportunity to journey to the Taos Pueblo. This encounter began his lifelong fascination with Native American cultures. Like many people living in the wake of and disillusioned by World War I, he reveled in a modernist celebration of the "primitive," questioning the Victorian view of civilization's linear progression and ascent through history. He was also relatively young and naive, and he quickly developed a highly romanticized and stereotyped, if well-meaning, view of Native Americans. Given to speaking in platitudes that might be seen as harbingers for a misguided New Age tradition (for example, as late as 1951 Collier made the rather ludicrous assertion that the "Pueblos of the Southwest . . . are the most representative survivors of pre-Columbian civilization"), he reoriented his career according to his new interests. He spent the next thirteen years in Washington, D.C., working as a political advocate for Indian issues.[7]

Although Collier was a veteran of federal Indian affairs by the time he took over as CIA, he was still burdened by his stereotypical views of Indian peoples. Tied to FDR's unprecedented four presidential electoral victories, Collier's tenure (1933–1945) would prove to be by far the longest in the history of the office. In many ways, it would also be the most influential.

Riding the coattails of Roosevelt's sweeping legislative and executive initiatives, Collier was ready to harness the power of the New Deal in order implement a variety of innovative policies. The new commissioner's aim was nothing short of completely overturning the prior longstanding federal policy of assimilation. With its roots in the earliest colonial times, assimilation had been the dominant federal policy since the presidency of

Ulysses S. Grant. Its goal was cultural genocide. Consequently, the government had waged wholesale attacks on most aspects of Indian cultures and societies, seeking to exterminate many Indigenous religions, languages, architectures, economic models, family patterns, spatial relationships, educational practices, and moral conventions, among others.[8]

Collier rightly despised the assimilation policy as an unwarranted and morally repugnant attack on Native cultures, and he sought to reverse the decades of damage it had wrought on Native societies and psyches. And to his credit, Collier remained firm in his efforts to eradicate the central tenet of assimilation: American society's (and by extension the federal government's) overtly hostile stance toward Native cultures. Instead, he believed that Native cultures should be revered and encouraged.

However, this does not mean that Collier was likewise ready to oversee the lifting of the colonial yoke from Native nations in favor of recognizing and promoting their independence and sovereignty. To the contrary, on the political front, Collier was not adamant in his promotion of the Indigenous. The new CIA sought to maintain U.S. colonial rule over Native nations; he wanted to refashion it, but he had no intention of dispensing with it altogether. Collier recognized that American Indians were still laboring under the oppression of direct colonial control, a system in which the OIA ruled and micromanaged with varying degrees of heavy-handedness from reservation to reservation. He believed that his greatest contribution would be to usher Indian peoples into a new era of indirect colonialism in which their Indigenous cultures would be celebrated, but Indigenous political institutions would be forever banished and replaced with a watered-down version of American republican democracy. Collier's goal was to more fully incorporate American Indian reservations into the American political system, assuming a role akin to a junior partnership with the United States. So, although he worked against assimilation, his policies are perhaps best described not as the abolition of colonialism, but rather as kind-hearted modifications to colonial rule. As with all of the CIAs who had preceded him, Collier was a high colonial official, and he willingly and knowingly accepted this role.[9]

Collier's own words explicitly illustrate his colonial ideology. As the commissioner later recounted in his 1963 autobiography, he first became familiar with the terms, concepts, and theories of "indirect administration" and "indirect rule" during the early twentieth century while reading about

British colonial domination of the Pacific island of Fiji. Subsequent studies made him aware of similar British efforts in the African colonies of Nigeria, the Gold Coast, and later in Tanganyika. He was enamored with the concept, even referring to indirect rule as an "art." His devotion to these ideas continued throughout his career. Early on, he contacted British colonial officials who had been involved in implementing indirect rule, and he incorporated their ideas and experiences. In 1944, toward the end of his term in office, Collier would even bring British colonial administrator Dr. Victor McGusty to Chicago to act as a consultant to OIA employees. Collier's recollections of McGusty still shone brightly years later as he spiritedly lauded the British imperial official's "experience and creativity" in applying indirect colonialism. He deemed these techniques ideal for application to the entire aboriginal population of the Americas. "The whole of the Indian world south of the Rio Grande needed Dr. McGusty," Collier later proclaimed. Apparently, the former commissioner had found the white man capable of bearing the burden. It is no wonder then that during the years following his commissionership, Collier would continue his attempts to refine the system of indirect colonialism and trumpet its supposed virtues. In 1947, he would even publish a study to that effect in Britain titled *America's Colonial Record*.[10]

Collier was also a personal acquaintance of H. A. C. Dobbs of the British Colonial Office and an Oxford University lecturer on colonial administration. The two men originally became familiar through each other's work, and when Collier visited England in 1946, shortly after his tenure as CIA had ended, the two men met in London and Oxford and engaged in substantial discussions about indirect colonialism. In Collier's words, they "found a common understanding of many things." And in the early 1950s, Dobbs would receive a Commonwealth Fellowship to travel to the United States for a year's worth of observation and study of U.S. Indian policy and administration.[11]

Though Collier developed these relationships with British colonial officials several years after he had pushed through the Indian Reorganization Act, they speak to his ongoing commitment to indirect colonial rule, and they reinforce his open allegiance to its ideals. It is not surprising that Collier would eventually seek out Dobbs and McGusty when the opportunity presented itself. They were, in his eyes, men of his own stripe: government workers who had likewise dedicated their efforts to implementing a system of indirect colonial rule and administration over subjugated populations. Collier was thoroughly convinced that this was the most effective strategy for ruling a subject people. In his autobiography, Collier would make the following observation:

> [I]n my prolonged examination of the white man's dealings with Indians of the Americas, I discovered that *direct rule* by white governments over United States Indians had brought disaster each time of the hundreds of times; while *indirect rule, indirect administration,* when faithfully applied in the few cases where it had been applied, had brought mutuality between the races, peace to the Indian's heart, and the conservation of ancient Indian values through planting within them new hopes and new practical goals. Most impressive was this contrast between direct rule and indirect rule in the Untied States Indian record. Enough to point out here that the generations of multitudinous disaster for Indians were generations of direct rule by the Untied States; while the radical, methodical shift in the Indian New Deal–a shift to indirect rule or, better, indirect administration–changed Indian disaster to Indian victory. [12]

Collier's historical interpretations are so sweeping and ideological as to render them meaningless, but more importantly, the above quote shows that it is difficult to overstate his devotion to the tenets of indirect colonialism. To him, it was not simply a better mousetrap; it was the only suitable way to govern a subjugated population. And in no way did he consider his goal to be the full restoration of Indian sovereignty. The United States would continue to govern Native Americans.

Interestingly though, within the framework of his conceptions, this brand of colonialism was not incompatible with democracy. To the contrary, he saw it as democracy's evolution in the right direction. "By *indirect rule,* the sovereign aims toward a mutual, an organic relationship with the people being governed," he asserted. "Ultimately, it means a genuine and ever-deepening, ever more precise democracy, within a total field of forces in which the alien ruler is a minor and, ideally, a disappearing part." Thus, when Collier first assumed the commissionership in 1933, his actions and ideas proved to be consistent with those he would espouse later in his career. [13]

Upon assuming the commissionership, John Collier was ready to implement his ideas, but he also perceived an important political reality: as an executive appointee, his policies could be easily overturned by whoever succeeded him in office. If his policies were going to last, they would have to be codified into legislation, approved by Congress, and signed into law. After taking office, he immediately set about composing the bill that would be the cornerstone of his administration: the Indian Reorganization Act. Aided by Interior Department Solicitor Nathan Margold and the head of Margold's legal staff, attorney Felix S. Cohen, the commissioner quickly produced the first draft of the IRA in 1934.[14]

Originally submitted to Congress on June 12, the IRA had four major provisions. One called for the fostering of Indian cultures and traditions. Prohibitions on Indigenous religious activities and various cultural practices, which had been a mainstay of assimilation, would be repealed. Programs to nurture Indigenous languages and traditional arts and crafts would be offered, and vocational education would be subsidized. The second provision proposed placing reservation lands owned by individual Indians into tribal ownership to be held in common by the tribes. A third provision sought to create a Court of Indian Affairs comparable to federal district courts to hear matters between Indians.[15]

But the IRA's centerpiece was a new system of tribal government that was an attack on the direct colonialism of the assimilation era. Reservations would no longer be ruled by autocratic agents. Instead, they would be administered by Indian tribal councils under the jurisdiction of the OIA. On each reservation, Indians would democratically elect their leaders from among their own ranks. These politicians would then serve on a tribal council whose structure was modeled after a corporate board of directors. The agent (henceforth renamed the superintendent), while retaining substantial authority, including veto power over all tribal council decisions, would in theory now serve mostly in a supervisory capacity. A tribe could then write a constitution, charter itself as a tax-exempt corporation, and take advantage of certain economic development programs, such as low-interest federal loans. Furthermore, once in place, the new tribal councils would be the only form of government on a reservation that the United States would recognize as legitimate. It was a template for indirect colonialism. Much of the day-to-day affairs on reservations would be handled by local Indian leaders, but their very offices were created by the United

States, and the federal government would in no way relinquish its ultimate authority over the reservations and their populations.[16]

Senator Burton K. Wheeler of Montana and Representative Edgar Howard of Nebraska, both Democrats, sponsored the IRA in Congress. The Wheeler-Howard Act was predictably attacked in Congress for both budgetary and ideological reasons, but more pointedly it also suffered the slings of Indian critics. And while expecting a battle in Congress, Collier was caught off guard by Native criticism. That the commissioner was surprised by Native discontent serves to illustrate his paternalism. Even more indicative, however, was one of the primary complaints voiced by many American Indians: they had not been consulted about this comprehensive, far-reaching piece of federal legislation that was going to affect many aspects of their lives. John Collier was sympathetic to Indians, but he was a colonial administrator at heart, and he had betrayed those sentiments in not seeking Native input. It would seem that Collier was not only prepared to remove the weights that oppressed Indians, but he also contrived to personally remedy their injustices in the manner that he saw fit. Furthermore, and emblematic of his paternalism, he was generally surprised and even suspicious when Indians, whom he considered the beneficiaries of his work, dared to criticize him. His arrogance backfired, and early opposition came especially from the Indians of Oklahoma and New York, where the Five Nations and the Haudenosaunee Confederacy, respectively,[17] each had a long history of dealing directly with the federal government on sophisticated legal issues. There was also discontent in the Dakotas, where the memories of wars of independence were still fresh.[18]

Two main issues incurred the wrath of many reservation residents. One was that the IRA called for the reversal of the allotment policy. Most reservations, some of which entire tribes had once held communally, had since been divided into allotments and parceled out to individual Indians during the era of assimilation. Indians also lost much of their reservation acreage when the federal government auctioned off "excess" allotments to settlers, and when Indian owners subsequently lost their allotments through tax defaults, sales, fraud, and corruption. Collier recognized that, among other things, the policy of allotment had diminished a tribe's economic potential by fragmenting its land base. He wanted to restore all allotments to tribal control. This upset many Indians who had successfully managed their privately owned land during the decades since receiving allotments. It also represented Collier's naive interpretation of traditional Native attitudes toward ownership. Titles and deeds might be specific to European culture, but the concept of private ownership clearly is not; and while some Native nations in preconquest times held their lands in common, many did not, and all of them had a firm conception of private ownership in one form or another. Thus was Collier's proposal not only a complete reversal of a half-century of land policy to which some (though certainly not all) people had comfortably adjusted but also a harkening back to a past that was in some ways mythical and nonexistent.[19]

For many Native Americans, the second source of unhappiness with the IRA was the proposal to establish new tribal council governments. Even under the assimilative strictures of direct colonialism, traditional forms of government had not been specifically outlawed in most cases; they had simply been marginalized by agents who ruled reservations with virtually unfettered control. That is to say, on many reservations Indigenous governments had remained in form, though their power and authority had been gutted. Although mostly symbolic in governmental terms, they were nevertheless an important symbol for those people who maintained the hope of one day restoring Native sovereignty. They were also vital cultural institutions. Thus, Indians who advocated traditional Native governments did not always initially discern the rather subtle shift in colonial styles that the IRA represented; to many of them, the IRA appeared to be further undermining what little remained of their sovereignty by usurping their indigenous political institutions and imposing foreign ones. In many ways, they were right, and they did not welcome this new form of government that Commissioner Collier was prepared to foist upon them.[20]

The fact that some of the early Indigenous critics of the IRA were concerned with the welfare of Native cultures (i.e., Native political institutions), while others were concerned with issues of personal wealth management (i.e., individual land ownership) is not an irrelevant discrepancy. Many of those who profited from individual land holdings were not only advocating a departure from various traditional Indian cultural institutions instead of a return, but they also frequently (but not always) had some formal education and sophistication in dealing with broader American culture and U.S. politicians. Those who championed Native national sovereignty very often (but not always) did not. The consequences were predictable.

Old dealers

Congressional concerns over such a dramatic policy change were also widespread. The bill endured revisions in the House and Senate for the benefit of congressional and Native critics. When those revisions were complete, the IRA featured some major changes. The mandatory transfer of allotted lands back to the tribes was made voluntary and thereby effectively annulled. A statement promoting the preservation and augmentation of Indian cultures was deleted. The proposal for a Court of Indian Affairs, which would have enabled tribal governments to circumvent federal and state courts, was eliminated. The new system of tribal government was retained, but many of its self-governing powers were removed, and its authority was made subject to the secretary of the interior. All of Alaska's Natives, 95,000 of Oklahoma's Natives, and any Indian not a member of a federally recognized tribe were excluded altogether, although the Alaskans and Oklahomans would eventually be covered by similar, subsequent, separate legislation. Any Indian with less than 50 percent blood quantum was ineligible. And, at Representative Howard's insistence, reservations would have an opportunity to opt out of reorganization; each Native nation would hold a referendum in which they could avoid having the IRA imposed upon them. This revised version of the Indian Reorganization Act became law on June 18, 1934.[21]

The next step was setting up referenda on reservations to decide whether they would accept political reorganization. These reservation referenda, however, were tricky pieces of juxtaposed democracy, and an early indication of the lengths to which Collier would go in order to bring his vision to fruition. Indians were not voting to approve the bill. Rather, Congress had already voted to approve the IRA for them. But because of Howard's clause, they now had the means to avoid having reorganization unilaterally bestowed upon them. In other words, a referendum would be a tribe's only chance to reject the IRA and its mandate to reorganize. So, for example, the fourteen tribes that ultimately failed to hold elections during the proscribed time period were simply subjected to reorganization by default. Furthermore, unlike a standard democratic election, initial plans for these referenda were for abstentions to be counted as votes to approve reorganization. Amazingly, a simple majority of actual votes cast on a reservation would not be sufficient to reject reorganization. Instead, a majority of all eligible voters, regardless of how many actually showed up at the polls (provided there was a 30 percent quorum), would have to vote to reject reorganization in order to prevent its implementation. So, for example, if 51 percent of the eligible voters on a reservation did not vote, reorganization would pass automatically, even if 100 percent of the actual voters were against it. Though the plan to count abstentions as "yes" votes was ultimately overturned in the face of voluminous Indian protest, it nonetheless speaks to the determination of the Collier administration to manifest the commissioner's vision. Despite this loaded scenario, there was still stiff opposition throughout Indian country, including Pine Ridge Reservation.[22]

Of 97,000 eligible Indian voters on reservations across the United States, barely one-third (38,000) actually voted to reorganize. A similar number (35,000) never showed up at the polls, and 24,000 voted to reject it. In the end, it was accepted on 174 reservations and rejected on 78, including the most populated reservation in the United States (Dine, a.k.a. Navajo), some of the oldest (all of the Haudenosaunee), and several Siouan reservations in close proximity to Pine Ridge: Fort Peck (eastern Montana), Devil's Lake (North Dakota), and Sisseton (South Dakota). Of the 174 reservations that accepted the IRA, only 92 of them (including Pine Ridge) chose to make constitutions and even fewer wrote charters and incorporated. In terms of the Native populace, only 116,000 American Indians had new constitutions, while 194,000 did not. One reservation that voted to accept the IRA (though it remained unincorporated and without a charter), albeit under tumultuous circumstances, was Pine Ridge.[23]

The years 1933–1934 had been hard ones due to a drought. With the browning grasses of the high plains as a backdrop, the debate over acceptance of the IRA on Pine Ridge from 1934–1935 was contentious. There was already a longstanding political dispute with cultural overtones between Oglalas. On one side were those who advocated traditional forms of government and looked to the 1868 treaty of Fort Laramie[24] between the United States and Lakota (as well as Nakota and Dakota) people as the ultimate arbiter in nation-to-nation negotiations. These people had tended to hold on to their lands after allotment and generally rejected those aspects of American culture that clashed with their own. They have occasionally been called "traditionals," "full bloods," or "treaty Indians." They tended to oppose the IRA. On the other side were those sometimes known as "progressives" for their tendency to refute pre-conquest Lakota culture and embrace American ways, or as "mixed bloods" since many (but certainly not all) had mixed Euro-American/Indigenous ancestry. These people tended to eschew those elements of traditional Lakota cultural that had been the focus of American persecution during the assimilation era, including many political, social, and religious institutions.[25]

According to oral history, this division was also evident on other Lakota reservations in South Dakota at this time and likewise colored the debate over reorganization. Hunkpapa Lakota Floyd Taylor, originally from Standing Rock Reservation, later worked for the federal government's Office of Economic Opportunity on the nearby Crow Creek and Lower Brule Reservations in the 1960s. While Lower Brule readily accepted reorganization, neighboring Crow Creek resisted it, rejecting the IRA altogether and not setting up a tribal council until the 1940s. Taylor maintained that this was because in the 1930s Lower Brule had a larger population of "verbal" and "aggressive" mixed bloods who gravitated to the new American system of representational government, while Crow Creek had more full-blood supporters of traditional Lakota government.[26]

On Pine Ridge, the debate over reorganization often divided along these lines. One of the historical factors contributing to the divisiveness was the relatively high Lakota/Euro-American intermarriage rate and subsequent growth of a mixed-blood class, which had been ongoing on the reservation for some time. White Americans, men in particular, had been coming to settle on the Pine Ridge Reservation since shortly after its establishment in the late nineteenth century. Many of them were of French descent, with surnames like Amiotte, Larvie, Pourier, and Bisonette. Some of them were descended from French traders who came from as far away as New Orleans. One of the reasons for this development on Pine Ridge was economic gains available for the immigrants: after arriving, many of them took Oglala wives, and through this union obtained reservation land. For their part, Oglala women could often obtain some measure of financial security amidst the desperate economic conditions of the postconquest era. And with new marriage patterns came new settlement patterns. While Lakota families often wanted their land located along the creeks, where they could obtain water and wood more easily as when they were free, the white men tended to settle their families by the meadows. There were few Indians by the meadows and plenty of grazing land for cattle.[27]

During the early twentieth century, the intermarriage rate on Pine Ridge skyrocketed as white men increasingly took Oglala wives. Full-blood Lakotas often looked upon these marriages cynically, believing that many of them were the result of crass opportunism by white men who married Lakota women "as a trick to get in on the government programs" that were ostensibly designed to benefit Indians. Some full bloods derisively labeled the newcomers as "squaw men." They frequently viewed these white husbands as disingenuous interlopers who were not to be trusted for the most part. While some of the white men marrying Lakota women may have been genuine in their marital intentions, Lakota skepticism was not conspiratorial paranoia. Some of the newcomers openly admitted to marrying Lakota women in order to claim their new wives' reservation lands. The results were stunning. In 1888, the ratio of the full-blood-to-mixed-blood population on Pine Ridge was better than 9:1. By 1925 it was less than 2:1. The Lakota word for the offspring from mixed Lakota/non-Lakota marriages is *iyeshka* (or *ieshka*). This is a later linguistic adaptation of an existing word that originally referred to a person's fluency in language and ability to interpret. Beyond the word's initial reference to bilingualism, biculturality also became relevant to its newer, expanded meaning. The dramatic increase in the mixed-blood population contributed to a widening social rift on the reservation.[28]

Compounding these sociocultural divisions were the consequences of the allotment policy, which had been one of the central mechanisms of assimilation. Once the process of parceling up land on Pine Ridge had begun, numerous mixed bloods who did not live on the reservation began applying for allotments, some of them moving to Pine Ridge afterward, some simply selling the land off immediately to speculators. An initial twenty-five-year moratorium on sales of and taxes on individual allotments had been put in place as a way to allow Indian landowners to adapt to the new world of titles, deeds, and the cash economy. However, reservation agents often prematurely stripped mixed-blood allotees of this protection. Mixed-blood landowners themselves frequently requested an early lifting of the moratorium, which would enable them to sell to speculators. Sometimes reservation agents unilaterally cut the twenty-five-year period short, in which case landowners frequently lost their lucrative allotments through sale, tax default, and even fraud, the land almost always falling into white hands. Furthermore, often acting with the encouragement of non-Indians eager to claim Pine Ridge Reservation land, many mixed bloods had played a pivotal role in the opening of Bennett County to American settlement in

1910. All of this was still fresh in many memories, and now the debate on Pine Ridge over whether to accept the IRA further polarized these two groups.[29]

Numerous Pine Ridge participants and subsequent scholars of the event have noted the following dynamic with relation to the debate over reorganization. On Pine Ridge, many of those who advocated the IRA were landless, mixed-blood proponents of assimilation into American culture while many who opposed it were full bloods who had held on to their land and supported traditional forms of Lakota government. Additionally, many landed advocates of traditional government were fearful that some of the landless, pro-IRA class would use the new system of government to control their lands, or possibly even divest them of their lands. Thus, the initial debate on Pine Ridge over reorganization quickly aggravated existing reservation divisions.[30]

True to form, as the referendum dates drew near, John Collier campaigned around the country in favor of the IRA. In an attempt to persuade Indians on the Northern Plains, the commissioner held a meeting on March 2–5, 1934, in Rapid City, South Dakota, just west of Pine Ridge Reservation. At the meeting, he was accompanied by (among others) an assistant named Henry Roe Cloud, who was a Ho Chunk (Winnebego) and one of the few Indians in the United States at the time to hold a doctorate. One of the several women taking dictation was Agnes Riegert. A secretary for Superintendent James H. McGregor, she was a mixed-blood Anishinaabe (Ojibwa) who had moved to Pine Ridge in 1924.[31]

At the meeting, Collier regaled the Native people in attendance with glowing reports on the virtues of reorganization. Nearly a half-century later, Riegert (then known by her married name, Agnes Gildersleeve) vividly remembered the scene. "Even now I can see him marching up and down that stage." The commissioner took to sitting on the floor with his back against the wall when fatigue would set in during the two-day marathon meeting. But despite all his salesmanship, his proposals were not generally well received. "Collier was on the stage and oh my gosh, and those Indians booed him, almost booed him right off," Riergert reminisced. "[T]hey'd say what they thought, alright. . . . And they didn't like something he said to them, and they just booed him on that stage and so he backed up." Emblematic of this, after Roe Cloud explained part of the bill, an Oglala Congregationalist minister, the Reverend Joe Eagle Hawk, accused him of being a "Judas Goat" who led the Indians to a metaphorical slaughter.[32]

A young Lakota named Benjamin Reifel was in attendance that night. He was college-educated and years later would go on to become a Pine Ridge Reservation superintendent himself, as well as a congressman from South Dakota, and eventually commissioner of Indian Affairs. He was taken with the IRA, despite the criticism, and after the Rapid City meeting he asked Collier if he could help out by explaining the bill to Indian people. Collier approved, but betrayed his paternalism and true priorities by adding, "I do not mind the little red school houses so long as they are not red on the inside." In other words, Reifel was free to use Lakota language and cultural references to explain the IRA; but in no way was reorganization going to be watered down by Oglala desires to revive their Indigenous political institutions. By July, Reifel would be head of the Northern Plains Region of the Indian Organization Division, a group charged with assisting tribes to reorganize under the IRA.[33]

Undeterred by Native opposition, Collier sent Roe Cloud to Pine Ridge the following month in an effort to increase support for his bill. And later that summer, the Office of Indian Affairs funded and organized campaigns on the reservation to explain the IRA in a positive light. Men like James White Bull, Vance Fielder, and Charlie Brooks, Oglalas on the OIA payroll, took to the field. They attended meetings at all corners of the reservation, explaining the provisions of the IRA as best they could wherever they went. Even Christian churches got into the act of translating and explaining the bill. But despite government and private efforts, staunch opposition remained. "I know the Indians were not accepting of it," Riegert recollected. "They didn't take too kindly to it." Leading the opposition were those who supported traditional Lakota government. Among them were respected Oglala leaders of several generations, including a number of widely respected elders such as American Horse, the famed Oglala veteran of the Battle of Greasy Grass Creek (The Little Big Horn). "That was a hard-fought battle," Pine Ridge Lakota Mildred Young recalled more than thirty years after the referendum. Apparently many Indians were more interested in regaining true autonomy than they were in the most recent policy emanating from Washington, D.C.[34]

The election to refute or accept reorganization on Pine Ridge took place on December 14, 1935. There were 4,075 eligible voters on the reservation. The IRA was approved by the narrow margin of seventy-four votes (1,169–1,095).[35] But perhaps more importantly, over 44 percent of the electorate did not vote at all. Within the context of Lakota culture, many of the abstentions might have counted as de facto votes against the IRA. This interpretation is derived from the fact that in Lakota culture, abstention is frequently a sign of disapproval; if one disagrees with the nature of the proceedings, one votes with his or her feet, maintaining integrity and showing displeasure by refusing to take part in the proceedings. And in a less strident form, apathetic voters simply do not vote. Thus, among the nearly 2,000 eligible voters who stayed home, it is probable that quite a number of them did so as a way of showing their antipathy toward the entire process. And in fact, almost from the outset, many Oglala Lakotas have maintained that this was the case.[36]

While campaigning, Collier had met with two Pine Ridge full bloods: Frank Fools Crow and Charles Red Cloud. The full-blood people of Pine Ridge's Porcupine district (see maps 3 and 4) had appointed Fools Crow as their traditional chief in 1925. Red Cloud was the grandson of his famous namesake and soon to be a traditional chief himself. Although dubious about Collier's plans for reorganization, the two men felt resigned. The federal government had unilaterally imposed policies on them since the beginning of the reservation era. Collier spoke of an election, but the commissioner was a federal authority vested with a tremendous amount of power over the reservation, and he was very clear on how he wanted them to vote. From their point of view, grounded in well over a half-century of economic dependence and direct colonial rule following military defeat, bucking Washington could draw serious reprisals. Of course they could vote "no," but did they really want to find out what would happen if they did? "We all had little choice but to go along with Mr. Collier," Fools Crow later reminisced.[37]

The sense of resignation that Red Cloud, Fools Crow, and other Lakotas felt was not based merely on history or deference to authority. The OIA had subjected them and other Indians to very real and undue pressure, something which Congress eventually acknowledged. By 1937, some U. S. senators were even contending that the OIA had indulged in a campaign of retribution against outspoken Indian opponents of reorganization, having gone so far as to cut off their depression-era relief payments. A congressional investigation followed. The findings appeared in a 1940 report, which concluded that the OIA had spent an unjustifiably exorbitant amount of money in promoting the IRA to Indians; the OIA had coerced, threatened, and otherwise intimidated Indian opponents; and the OIA had made disingenuous promises to Indians about nearly unlimited loans that would supposedly be available to those reservations that chose to reorganize. It was a scathing indictment that tainted the results on many reservations, and certainly anywhere the results had been as hotly contested as Pine Ridge.[38]

Nonetheless, as far as the OIA was concerned, Pine Ridge had accepted the IRA regardless of any complicating or obfuscating factors, and Secretary of the Interior Harold Ickes approved those results on January 15, 1936. Henceforth, the new Oglala Sioux Tribal Council would be the only Pine Ridge government recognized by the United States.[39]

THE ESTABLISHMENT OF THE IRA

Prior to reorganization, the Oglala people of Pine Ridge Reservation had maintained their political culture and manifested what remained of their sovereignty through a governing body known as the Oglala Council. Established in 1891, the Oglala Council utilized many facets of traditional Lakota government while also incorporating certain aspects of American government. For example, under the leadership of Council President James H. Red Cloud, it ratified its own constitution and bylaws in 1921. But whenever the Oglala Council assumed mechanisms and ideas from the United States, it usually did so willingly. As such, it was very much an Indigenous form of government, an institution that manifested the dynamic nature of Lakota culture. However, as with all reservation governments during the direct colonialism of the assimilation era, the extent to which it could actually govern was at the mercy of a succession of OIA agents, who themselves were appointees of, and answerable to, the commissioner of Indian affairs. During the more than four decades between its founding and when it was supplanted by the IRA, the Oglala Council was alternately tolerated and attacked by various agents. In fact, Agent McGregor had even banished the Oglala Council altogether in December of 1928, replacing it with a less-traditional form of government more to his liking. Then, just as arbitrarily, he allowed the old Oglala Council to return in 1931. Clearly, the

Oglala Council's powers were in a permanent state of eclipse, overshadowed by federal authority in the form of the agent, who was the de facto colonial autocrat. But beyond its diminished role as a governing body, it also served as a potent Indigenous institution for Pine Ridge advocates of Lakota sovereignty and political culture.[40]

The IRA affected both the Oglala Council and the position of reservation agent. The totalitarian agent would be renamed superintendent, and he would now, at least in theory, serve largely in an advisory capacity. He would still be the official representative of the secretary of the interior, subordinate to the commissioner of Indian affairs, and he would still retain a tremendous amount of power. But the IRA now directed him to rein in that power for, as Collier paternalistically phrased his well-meaning intentions, "Indian tribes ought to be permitted to make their own mistakes." As for the Oglala Council, the all-encompassing political prerogative of the IRA would no longer allow it to exist. The new Oglala Sioux Tribal Council (OSTC) would henceforth be the only tribal governing body that the United States would recognize as legitimate.[41]

The first step was to write a constitution that would usurp the one ratified by the Oglala Council in 1921. Those Indians who had believed that the IRA would bring them real self-government and a substantial restoration of sovereignty grew disillusioned as the creeping paternalism of Collier's administration began to show itself as this process got under way. During 1935, Lakotas offered several proposals and drafts for the new constitution. The OIA largely disregarded them. To begin with, the government was concerned that the documents be written in proper legalese. But federal input went beyond ensuring technicalities. While visiting Pine Ridge in 1935, Felix Cohen and OIA representative Fred Daiker made substantial revisions to the draft sponsored by the Oglala Council. These changes concerned land tenure, increases in the new OSTC's powers, and the introduction of a new legal system for the reservation.[42]

Beyond the basic content, core values can also be seen in the language itself. The tone of the 1921 constitution's preamble, which had been written by Lakotas, is substantially different from the IRA constitution's preamble, which was largely written by OIA officials. The latter not only sounds like it is aping the U. S. Constitution, but it also keenly reflects the values of the Collier administration; it even uses the phrase "home rule," a key element in the philosophy of indirect colonialism (see appendix A).[43]

The outgoing Council was skeptical of the new document and resisted endorsing it, but the OIA responded with pressure throughout Pine Ridge and from all quarters of its organization. Even teachers at government schools praised and endorsed the new document. Federal representatives held meetings with reservation denizens. Their goals were to encourage the passage of the constitution and to attempt to demystify its legalistic terminology, much of which was jargon that did not translate readily into the Lakota language; Lakota was still the first (and sometimes only) language of many Oglalas. In fact, as he toured the reservation in his effort to explain the IRA to fellow Lakotas, Benjamin Reifel even took to supplementing his Lakota translations with his own ad hoc representational drawings for words and concepts that were outside the boundaries of the Lakota language. But despite his innovative pedagogy, Reifel often met with skepticism from many full bloods who now saw him as an "OIA Indian" whose ultimate allegiance was in question. Then in November, John Collier himself visited the reservation to campaign for the new constitution. During his visit, he urged Lakotas to move swiftly in ratifying the new constitution, and he hinted that voting the wrong way or even hesitating to vote "yes" would have a price. The commissioner strongly implied that the longer Oglalas waited to ratify the new constitution, the less money would be available to Pine Ridge after the fact. The OIA was setting up new credit programs to stimulate economic development on reservations, and Collier disingenuously suggested that they would be available on a first-come first-served basis to tribes with new constitutions when this was not actually the case. He was leveraging threats of decreased funding against the people of an impoverished, economically dependent reservation. And he was lying about it. Despite substantial debate and protest by Lakotas, federal pressure paid off. The constitution passed in another close public referendum on December 14 by the count of 1,348–1,041. The secretary of the interior approved the results on January 15, 1936.[44]

As was the case on most reorganized reservations around the country, Pine Ridge's new constitution was more of a Felix Cohen–authored template than it was an original document reflecting Indigenous political structures. Anthropologist Thomas Biolsi has rather aptly critiqued the process that led to the constitution's creation: "The constitution and bylaws of the . . . Oglala Sioux Tribe were not drafted by, nor do they represent the intentions of, the Lakota constitution committees, the tribal councils, or the grassroots. Rather, they were drafted in conformity with the OIA mode of Indian self-government." Biolsi goes on to assert that "[i]t would not be inaccurate to say that the Lakota[s] were presented with boilerplate constitutions and allowed to fill in the blanks." He was not alone in his assessment. Even though Benjamin Reifel was an avid supporter of the IRA, he nonetheless readily admitted that the constitutional documents on reservations around the United States were so similar in their design that they amounted to little more than "blanket constitution[s]."[45]

With its ratification, the new constitution and its attendant bylaws bestowed upon Pine Ridge's new political entity the official name of the Oglala Sioux Tribe (OST).[46] The next step in Pine Ridge's reorganization was to supplant the old Oglala Council with the new Oglala Sioux Tribal Council. The new council would prove to be an odd blend of parliamentary, corporate, and republican structures that, taken as a whole, was foreign to both the Lakota people and the American form of government it was supposedly emulating. The council itself is a legislative body that governs by majority vote, which is antithetical to the Lakota tradition of governing by consensus. Its members are democratically elected to give proportional representation to the initially seven and eventually nine districts into which the reservation would eventually be divided. The head of the council is called president, or chairman, and although elected (along with the vice president) by the entire reservation every two years, he (more recently, she) is not the head of a separate executive branch. Instead, the chairman is a non-voting (except as a tie-breaker), *ex officio* member of the legislative council, whose meetings he or she calls to order and oversees. In fact, there is no separate executive branch at all, as the Council is charged with executing its own legislation. Furthermore, the judicial branch falls under the authority of the Council instead of being equal to it. Thus, there are no substantial separation of powers or checks and balances upon which American democracy so prides itself. Instead there is a pyramidic structure in which the president of the United States sits at the top, above the secretary of the interior and then the commissioner of Indian affairs. Beneath the commissioner is the reservation superintendent, then finally the Tribal Council, which includes the chief executive (the chairman) and holds jurisdiction over the judiciary.[47]

In the presence of OIA official George M. Nyce, the Oglala Council met as a federally recognized organization for the last time in January of

1936 at the town of Wanblee on the eastern edge of the reservation. Among those in attendance at the meeting were several people who would come to serve in the upcoming IRA-sponsored Oglala Sioux Tribal Council, including the man who would preside as the first OSTC chairman, Frank G. Wilson.[48]

The meeting, which focused on grazing permit and land lease matters, also served as a segue from one era to the next. Outgoing Chairman Robert Bad Wound opened the meeting by noting that in light of the passage of the IRA, the Oglala Council had agreed not to act on the issues at hand until the new council was organized. But two important harbingers appeared during the proceedings of the two-day meeting. One is that Frank Wilson proved himself to be a cantankerous member who was more in tune with Robert's Rules of Order than he was with Lakota social codes of conduct. After two members spoke in Lakota (no transcript given), Wilson, himself fluent in Lakota, demanded that the stenographer record in the minutes that the procedure of the meeting was irregular and out of order because English was not in exclusive use. Apparently, the old Council did not think much of Wilson either. When they formed a delegation to represent their interests in an upcoming trip to Washington, D.C., seven men, including Wilson, ran for four positions. A total of 119 votes were cast for the seven candidates. Wilson received a total of two votes.[49]

The second precedent was more far reaching and had implications that were far longer lasting than Frank Wilson's caustic personality. Despite earlier government rhetoric, the IRA was first and foremost a doctrine of indirect colonialism. It would afford Indians limited self-government or home rule. Now the nature of those limits was becoming apparent. The secretary of the interior still had the final say over all tribal council decisions. And although Collier had preached that Indians should be "permitted to make their own mistakes," it was becoming apparent that the OIA would occasionally still throw its weight around in order to influence the new tribal councils, and that assimilation-era paternalism and condescending attitudes would not disappear overnight.

OIA representative George Nyce addressed the Oglala Council on the pressing issue of soon-to-expire leases that allowed non-Indian sheep ranchers to graze on Pine Ridge land at well below market prices. A number of Lakotas at the meeting expressed consternation over these ranchers and voiced the opinion that their leases should not be renewed. Nyce implored the Council to renew all of the grazing permits for a one-year period and then give "these sheep men plenty of time to get off the reservation." He supported his suggestion with an anecdote about the Blackfeet Reservation in Montana, where the hasty expulsion of sheep ranchers had created logistical problems that forced the OIA to assume temporary responsibility for the sheep and incur unforeseen costs. But Nyce seemingly felt that the story was not sufficient persuasion. He insisted on invoking the approval of the commissioner of Indian affairs in a manner that was reminiscent of a teacher warning schoolchildren about their parents: "I know that the Commissioner is going to ask me when I get in there just what the attitude of the council is here and I want to be able to say to him that the council used judgement under the present conditions and are trying to cooperate with him in every way."[50]

The message was clear. The Lakotas of Pine Ridge were technically free to make their own decision. But did they really want to find out what would happen if their course of action differed substantially from the federal government's agenda?

3

"Any Reasonable Request..."

Office of Indian Affairs Political Power During the Early Oglala Sioux Tribal Council Era

TOWARD THE END OF 1940, Nancy Crazy Horse was residing in the Sioux Sanatorium in Rapid City, South Dakota. She still owned property on the Pine Ridge Reservation, including a team of two horses (a colt and a yearling), a wagon, and a harness. She had placed these items under the care of Joseph Short Bear, and by December she wished to sell the team. Although the horses were her property, purchased with her own money (dividends from a turn-of-the-century Lakota land cession), Crazy Horse still had to get the Office of Indian Affairs' (OIA) permission to sell them. And the OIA was generally not shy about intervening in such matters in the name of protecting the interests of Native Americans.[1]

She contacted the Office, and OIA Field Aide Francis F. Fielder went out to Short Bear's residence to inspect the animals and equipment. He decided that the animals would in fact not be sold on the grounds that the current market for such horses was soft. Nonetheless, this did not preclude Fielder from contacting Short Bear on December 30 and admonishing him about the care with which he tended to the animals. Fielder informed Short Bear that he was concerned the horses were not being provided with a sufficient amount of hay. The field aide warned him that he would be stopping by on or around the eighth of January to inspect the stores. Fielder let him know in no uncertain terms that as far as the OIA was concerned, Short Bear was now "being held responsible for the proper care for those animals until released therefrom."[2]

As July 1941 rolled around, the horses were still in Short Bear's care, and the field aide was still meddling. By now, Crazy Horse had changed her mind and no longer wanted the animals sold, but that would not stop OIA officials from interfering. At the request of Agricultural Extension Agent Rex D. Kildow, Fielder investigated Short Bear again so that Kildow could make a judgment in the matter. In August, Fielder apprized Pine Ridge Reservation Superintendent W. O. Roberts of the situation. Fielder had also changed his mind about disposing of the horses. If Short Bear's care of them was not deemed proper, then he would have them sold, "not withstanding the desire of Miss Crazy Horse."[3]

Crazy Horse had asked Short Bear to mind her horses, and Short Bear had agreed. But this was not enough to satisfy the OIA. There was not much Crazy Horse could do from the sanatorium in Rapid City other than to be adamant in her correspondence that she had selected Joseph Short Bear to look after her two animals and that was how she wanted the matter handled. Nonetheless, by October, the field aide and extension agent were in agreement. They were not satisfied with Short Bear's treatment of the horses and decided that the animals should be sold: it would be in Crazy Horse's "best interest."[4]

THE OGLALA SIOUX TRIBAL COUNCIL (OSTC) emerged in 1936. As laid out by the Indian Reorganization Act, the federally sanctioned Council was the new official governing body on Pine Ridge Reservation. In theory, it was the sovereign power on the reservation. The primary concern in this chapter, however, regards the real limitations of that power. To what extent was the new council a legitimate, authoritative governing body, and to what extent was it merely a phantom institution, operating in the shadow of the much more well-established Office of Indian Affairs? As the case of Nancy Crazy Horse suggests, even by the dawn of America's involvement in World War II, more than five years after the establishment of the OSTC, the OIA's presence was still a powerful influence on Pine Ridge and its Native denizens.

There has been much commentary on this topic, both by scholars and people working in Indian affairs. As early as 1942, Nez Perce tribal member and OIA employee Archie Phinney, who was, for the most part, a staunch supporter of the IRA, openly criticized the tribal council system. Despite his admiration of the IRA, he admitted that the councils largely functioned as instruments of the OIA instead of representing Indian peoples, observing that community participation in the new political scheme on most reservations was minimal. In 1948, anthropologist Henry F. Dobyns lauded the IRA, but not because it returned sovereignty to Native nations. Rather, he praised the bill's capacity to foster the assimilation of Indians into the mainstream of American society, something that in one light is completely irrelevant, and actually detrimental to the notion of Native sovereignty in another. By 1969, the legal scholar Vine Deloria, Jr., would paint a picture of tribal council chairmen who were not the equals of their federal and state counterparts and in fact, had their success measured by their "ability to gain concessions from governmental agencies." In more recent times, Indigenous scholar Taiaiake Alfred has in essence agreed with Dobyns's assessment, but with a highly critical slant instead of a laudatory one, asserting that the IRA uses "the cooperation of national [Indian] leaders . . . to legitimize the state's longstanding assimilationist goals."[5]

With regard to Pine Ridge specifically, there has also been healthy debate as to the effectiveness of the IRA government. In 1966, anthropologist Robert K. Thomas stated flatly that the Pine Ridge "tribal government is, in effect, without power. Most of the day to day decisions about Sioux life, about roads, schools, relief, are made by Bureau [of Indian Affairs] personnel." In 1980, scholar Karl Schlesier declared the OSTC to be little more than a puppet government, staffed largely with Indigenous turncoats who shilled for the BIA, contrary to the best interests of their own people.[6]

More recently, anthropologists Thomas Biolsi and Paul M. Robertson have considered the matter, especially with regard to the early years of the Pine Ridge IRA government, which is also the focus of this chapter. In 1992, Biolsi came to the conclusion that the federal government's dominance on Pine Ridge Reservation "did not disappear" with the emergence of the OSTC. Rather, he makes the case that the OIA retained its authority, maintained its position, and in the process routinely frustrated the new council in its attempts to assert power. In 1995, Robertson first countered that the OSTC had in fact mustered some very real political currency, albeit misspent in an effort to benefit a small group of self-interested, mixed-blood elites with an agenda contrary to the wishes and detrimental to the welfare of the larger Oglala populace. Still, viewed even in this light, Robertson did admit that during its early years the Council was largely "ineffective" on many matters.[7]

Although Robertson has set himself at odds with Biolsi over this issue, it would nonetheless seem that there is common ground for the broaching. On the one hand, the early Oglala Sioux Tribal Council was in fact very weak in relation to the established bureaucracy of the Office of Indian Affairs. The OIA continued to wield a great deal of authority; in theory it was receding in power, but in practice it maintained its ability to administer American colonial policy on the reservation. On the other hand, while the OSTC was largely impotent on most matters, it did occasionally attempt to test the boundaries of its limited sovereignty by pursuing its own agenda and challenging the strictures of federal authority.

In assessing the nature of Pine Ridge politics from the founding of the IRA-sponsored OSTC in 1936 through the end of World War II, this chapter will examine several important areas. First will be a series of factors that defined OIA control of Pine Ridge, particularly the reservation's economy, land base, legal institutions, and educational institutions. In addition, and perhaps most compelling, evidence will show that the residents of Pine Ridge themselves were quite aware of the political realities on their reservation. They understood that the new Oglala Sioux Tribal Council was, despite the self-governing rhetoric of the IRA, still subordinate to the Office of Indian Affairs.

MONEY

In December 1940, James Janis of the Pine Ridge Reservation town of Porcupine approached OIA Field Aide Francis Fielder with an innovative idea. Janis wished to apply for a $1,000 loan from the federal government in order to set up a gas station to service the automobiles that were appearing in increasing numbers on the reservation. The idea contained foresight and the possibility of achieving the loan program's ostensible intention: offering Indians the means to become financially independent. However, Fielder was a government bureaucrat who appears to have placed more importance on the specificity of rules and regulations than on the ends they were designed to attain. The letter of the law carried more weight for him than its spirit. Fielder tentatively filled out an application for planned productive loans, the initial step in procuring the federal funds needed to finance Janis's vision, but he did not immediately file the form. Instead, he wrote a letter to Rex D. Kildow, the reservation's agricultural extension agent. In it, Fielder voiced his concerns about the agricultural orientation of the federal loan program and how this project might not be appropriate.[8]

More than a month later, fellow OIA bureaucrat Kildow finally responded, confirming Fielder's pessimism. The loan money in question, he stated, should not be used for any purpose not "involving the purchase of livestock." In his brief missive, dated January 22, 1941, Kildow offered no alternative suggestions for acquiring the money. The loan request was denied, allowing the rather promising idea to fizzle. And Janis was not alone. At roughly the same time, Charlotte Huebner had the same idea for opening a gas station, but she also needed financial help to get started. She too faced OIA rejection. There is no record of either Huebner or Janis soliciting the Oglala Sioux Tribal Council for aid in developing their projects.[9]

The above story, and many others like it, point to a hard political fact during the early IRA era: the OIA continued to wield the majority of power despite the presence of the new Oglala Sioux Tribal Council. The first, and perhaps most important, weapon in the OIA's arsenal was money. Janis's and Huebner's plans were foiled for lack of it. The OIA, on the other hand, had quite a lot of it, especially by the standards of a place as impoverished as Pine Ridge, where the average per capita income for an Indian in 1939 was a staggeringly meager $166.18. As a result, the OIA was able to use its vast financial resources not just to fund various programs and ventures under its charge, and to squelch projects it did not favor, but also to create leverage in exercising political authority on the reservation. This point is also backed up by hard statistics. In-depth figures on the reservation for the fiscal year ending June 30, 1939, lend insight.[10]

During that fiscal year, OIA officials on Pine Ridge administered $1,209,918 in federal funds. Sub-dividing this total, the OIA's regular operating budget of $761,663 was augmented by $448,255 in emergency funds that covered Indian New Deal programs, the largest of which was the $255,000 that funded the Indian Division of the Civilian Conservation Corps (ID-CCC). Of the nearly three-quarters of a million dollars in its regular operating budget, almost one-third ($222,090) went to cover OIA salaries, administrative expenditures, the construction and maintenance of OIA buildings, and other miscellaneous costs.[11]

One of the results of this massive outlay of capital was for the OIA to maintain and entrench its dominant position on Pine Ridge. Another was to subsidize Indian wages, thereby keeping Lakotas dependent on federal sources of income. Thomas Biolsi has done substantial work in examining the details of what he refers to as the "artificial economy" that federal programs created on the reservation during this era. His term refers to the notion that these programs further reenforced Lakota reliance on the federal government by expanding a labor force that was dependent on Washington subsidies for its wages. Furthermore, he contends that these programs did nothing in the way of developing a self-sustaining economy for the reservation, despite the modest improvements they made to reservation life. Broader statistics bear out his earlier work.[12]

Enabled by its sprawling budget, the OIA was by far the largest single employer on Pine Ridge. Through this function, it was able to exert a tremendous amount of influence. The OIA boasted 267 authorized employees with annual salaries totaling $368,780, plus another 143 temporary and part-time employees. Of these 410 workers, 149 were Indians, including 115 Sioux. Incredibly, the OIA's payroll to its Indian employees accounted for *over 40 percent of all wages earned by Pine Ridge Indians.* And to make matters worse, this was a very large piece from a very small pie. Only one of the employees cited made over $2,500 during the fiscal year in question. The rest made less than $2,000. One-hundred and thirty-nine of them made less than $1,438, and more than 45 percent of them made between $600 and $1,079. About two-thirds of these workers were male. And just as the positions were weighted in favor of low salaries and male employees, so too were they weighted against full-blood Indians: only twenty-eight in all. The bulk of them were one-quarter or more Indian lineage, but less than full.[13]

In addition to regular OIA employees, there were temporary federal jobs through the Indian New Deal. The Indian Division of the Civilian Conservation Corps hired 276 men over the course of the twelve months analyzed. The ID-CCC was a New Deal program aimed at providing financial assistance to Native Americans in the midst of the Great Depression. It was a subsidiary of the larger Civilian Conservation Corps and administered through the OIA.[14]

At any given time during that year, the ID-CCC employed an average of twenty-one workers on a variety of projects on Pine Ridge, including digging wells, building truck trails, stringing telephone lines, constructing a bridge suitable for vehicles, and fire suppression and prevention activities. The primary service ID-CCC workers brought to the reservation was the building and mending of fences. However, despite the ID-CCC's dedication to easing unemployment among Native people, typically only nine of those twenty-one workers were Indian. The other twelve were white. But for those nine Indian laborers, the impact was enormous. For the average Indian who found work with the ID-CCC, it accounted for almost one-sixth of his annual wages. And ID-CCC wages, combined with other forms of federal relief such as social security and direct relief, added up to nearly one-third of the annual income for the average Pine Ridge Lakota involved with the program. The above is succinctly illustrated by the following statistic: during the calendar year of 1938, the United States federal government supplied 82.55 percent of the total income (in cash, goods, and services) for the entire Indian population of Pine Ridge Reservation. By contrast, private sources of income, such as agriculture and livestock, hunting, fishing, gathering, and the sale of crafts, generated less than 9 percent of Indian income (see Table 3.1).[15]

TABLE 3.1

Sources of Indian Income on Pine Ridge Reservation: 1938

Sources of Indian Incomes	Income	Percent of Total
Work Relief	249,015.87	15.85
Direct Relief	422,972.23	26.94
Government Employment*	146,577.64	09.34
Other Govt. Sources	477,783.52	30.42
Private Sources	273,922.38	17.45
Total	1,570,271.64	100.00

* Includes revenues from pro rata share payments on the principal from tribal trust funds, Works Project Authority, and the Agricultural Administration Act.

Source: "Resident Pine Ridge Indian Income for Calendar Year of 1938," File 052 General Statistical Records and Reports, 1 of 2, Box 172, Main Decimal Files, General Records of the Pine Ridge Agency, Pine Ridge, South Dakota, Records of the Bureau of Indian Affairs Record Group 75, NARA-AR.

As a whole, the nearly 8,500 Pine Ridge Lakotas of wage-earning age were clearly dependent on the federal government. Furthermore, this dependence went beyond mere wages. The OIA was not only the reservation's biggest employer, but also distributed other kinds of subsidies. In addition to wages and direct relief, the OIA made available self-betterment projects such as the Reimbursable Loan Program, which provided low-interest loans that served as investment capital for Indians who wanted to get involved in cattle raising. However, such programs were enmeshed in the arbitrary nature of the OIA's authority, as Hudson Bird Head found out in 1939.

The year was drawing to a close and Bird Head was in need of help. On December 2, he scrawled a handwritten note explaining his urgent need for a team of horses and sent it to Pine Ridge Superintendent W. O. Roberts. Bird Head needed to take a loan out immediately, and he inquired if there were any program available that might be able to help. A notation at the bottom of the letter indicates that he needed about thirty-eight dollars. His plea was forwarded to Agricultural Extension Agent R. F. Coulter, who in turn mailed a reply toward the end of the year. Coulter suggested that Bird Head contact his local farm agent for details about a reimbursable loan, but the agent sounded dubious, noting that Bird Head's revenue from land leases was small, that he had not garnered much income from outside work during the last several years, and that his past loan record was not in very good standing. In addition, Coulter informed Bird Head that while there was loan money available, OIA policy was designed to "help a man get on his feet, rather than giving small amounts which do not assist a man in making a better livelihood." This may very well have seemed like cruel hair-splitting to Hudson Bird Head.[16]

The Office of Indian Affair's economic presence on the reservation was nearly omnipresent and at times arbitrary, but it went even deeper. As Thomas Biolsi has pointed out, the Office used its position to exert political authority and keep Oglalas dependent. For example, Individual Indian Money (IIM) accounts were government-controlled bank accounts into which Native people were required to place any money that the government defined as "unearned." This might include payments received from the leasing or sale of land or dividends and pro rata shares from tribal trust funds. Native people wishing to access money from their IIM accounts first had to suffer the indignity of having the superintendent declare them "competent." They then had to receive further approval from the OIA chief clerk and reservation superintendent for each individual withdrawal. Even then, OIA policy only allowed for limited withdrawals for unsupervised spending and discouraged such withdrawals for subsistence.[17]

The face of local OIA authority in this scenario was the boss farmer. There was one boss farmer for each of the reservation's seven districts. Renamed extension agents in 1931, they were usually locals in good favor with the reservation agent (later superintendent) who appointed them. An example is White Cow Killer, an Oglala who was the Wounded Knee District boss farmer until Benjamin Reifel took over the position in the early 1930s. The boss farmer wielded tremendous power, doing everything from running the local trading post to overseeing the police and even approving requests for all purchases to be made with "unearned" money. He also determined how much of a monthly stipend from their IIM accounts each eligible Lakota in their district should get, based in theory on their given situations. In a regular and semi-ritualized display of authority, Oglalas would gather at his office after he received their monthly checks; as the assistant farmer publicly called out their names, Indians would each step up and personally receive their check from the boss farmer.[18]

Thus, when Margaret Blue Bird Conroy wanted to buy $300-plus worth of cattle with money from her IIM account in 1941, she had to be deemed competent, get permission for the transaction, and then fill out a two-page IIM purchase order in triplicate, which included a warning to potential vendors that the sale of anything to Blue Bird Conroy not listed on the form could result in a $10,000 fine and/or up to ten years imprisonment. The fact that Blue Bird Conroy was the wife of Oglala Sioux Tribal Council member Harry Conroy garnered her no exception in the matter. And when Enoch Kills On Horse Back received $300 for the sale of four cows shortly before entering the military to serve in World War II, the OIA deposited the money into his IIM and budgeted it back to him as follows: $200 for the purchase of government bonds, $15 to pay expenses for Kills On Horse's induction into the army, $50 for a relative's debt accrued at a store, and $35 "for his personal use during his sojourn in the army." The paternalism of the situation might be comical if it were not so pervasive, officious, and serious.[19]

The colonial legacy and depth of authoritarian leverage in these measures is illustrated by the following fact. Among the "unearned" income that

Pine Ridge Lakotas had to deposit into their tightly monitored IIM accounts was what the OIA called Sioux Benefit money: government payments that Indians continued to receive from the federal government in return for millions of acres previously ceded to the United States. Thus, when Jerome Brown Bull wanted to have his mother sell his cattle while he served in the Army Air Corp's 11th Tow Target Squadron at Ontario Air Field in California, he had to provide a written document to grant her permission to do so. Moreover, the money had to be funneled through his IIM account since the cattle had been originally purchased with Sioux Benefit money. It speaks volumes that the government would not even let Lakotas control capital that they derived from the proceeds of land sales pried out of them in the aftermath of their defeat to the United States. In other words, not only had the colonial conquest of Lakotas contributed to their current state of poverty, but subsequent U.S. colonial policy mitigated Indians' ability to access the undervalued cash payments that the U.S. had given them to help justify forced land cessions.[20]

The OIA's control over Pine Ridge Reservation through economic means can also be expressed in matters beyond its overwhelming and restrictive monetary presence. Indeed, it frequently used that presence as leverage to micromanage and otherwise interfere in the lives of Pine Ridge Lakotas. Government money came with strong strings attached, even money in the form of loans and other programs ostensibly designed to move Lakotas toward self-sufficiency.

The OIA tightly monitored cattle purchased with government help. For example, when residents of Red Shirt Table, located at the northern end of the reservation, butchered some livestock without OIA approval in 1942, Agricultural Extension Agent Rex D. Kildow referred the matter to a representative of the OIA's Law and Order Division. Kildow ordered an investigation into the matter and, with an air of flippancy and maliciousness, concluded, "The horse trade between Thomas Fly and Isadore Poor Thunder is thrown in for good measure." In fact, Kildow kept close tabs on cattle all over the reservation, and in May of that same year he compiled a list of offenders. In all, he counted thirty-five individuals who, he asserted, had disposed of 128 head of cattle without the OIA's permission. "We are authorized by the Washington Office to hold any and all funds that may accrue to their accounts until settlement in regard to the . . . [cattle] is made," he declared in a memorandum to the IIM Division, as he prepared to flex federal muscle. "We request that you withhold half of any money that may accrue to their accounts until further notice."[21]

Unauthorized dispossession of cattle was not the only transgression that could summon the OIA's wrath. When word got back to Field Aide Peter Cummings that five cows and calves belonging to the Kills In Water family had been seen wandering off their designated range area in 1942, he contacted the family and applied pressure. He wrote them a letter, reminding them of their responsibility for the cattle. He also ordered them to have the entire herd assembled in a corral so he could tally the livestock and inspect their hay. Rather than employing the legalistic threats that marked Kildow's memorandum, Cummings warned the Kills In Waters that their behavior might "result in your inability to find them later, as it is possible for them to drift out of your reach." Nonetheless, whether the tone of such comments was tyrannical or paternalistic, it underscored the power that the Office of Indian Affairs wielded.[22]

Furthermore, federal control was not restricted to cattle, but applied to any and all property obtained through federal programs. In 1942, George Young Bear was preparing for his induction into the armed forces, ready to fight in World War II. Quite logically, he wished to sell a wagon, plow, and harness that he would no longer need. However, OIA officials told him in no uncertain terms that this would not be possible. Young Bear had bought the items with Sioux Benefit money. He would therefore have to delay the sale until his official military induction papers arrived and he filed a proper sales permit. Even then, the proceeds would have to return to his IIM account and be rebudgeted by the Office of Indian Affairs. So it was that a soldier prepared to fight for the United States could not get an exemption from bureaucratic restrictions on paltry sums his forebears had received after resisting the United States.[23]

LAND

Clearly, the Oglala Sioux Tribal Council, let alone any individual Native American, was in no position to compete with the kind of 300-pound political gorilla that was the Office of Indian Affairs. Compounding the situation was the reality that the OSTC controlled very little of its own land base. One reason for this was that during the pre-IRA years, the OIA had done next to nothing to safeguard the Indian lands of Pine Ridge (or those of most any other reservation, for that matter) or to promote its use by Lakotas. To the contrary, some scholars have made compelling assertions that the Office actively contributed to the diminution of Indian land holdings on the reservation. Regardless, on Pine Ridge, Lakota land tenure was tenuous.[24]

On the national level, the federal government had asserted its authority over Native lands through a piece of congressional legislation entitled the General Allotment Act (a.k.a. the Dawes Severalty Act) of 1887. This bill had outlined the practice of forcibly fracturing Indian reservations into individually owned allotments, reservations that, until then, had often been held in common by their Indigenous residents. The effects nationwide would prove to be disastrous. After reshaping patterns of Native landownership, the federal government defined as "excess" land the plots left over after allotments were divided among the Indians. It then auctioned off the "excess" to white settlers, thereby transferring vast acreages of reservation property to non-Indians. Further Indian alienation from their land followed as more than half of the Native people affected by the Dawes Act lost their individual allotments and were living in a state of poverty by 1921. The loss of these allotments was due to a variety of reasons, including tax default, sale in the face of poverty, and even outright fraud. Collectively, the results were catastrophic. In less than fifty years (1887–1934), land holdings by Native nations fell by more than two-thirds, from 138 to 48 million acres. One scholar has attributed this process of dispossession to a combination of "misguided idealism, crippling legislation, destructive Indian policy and BIA regulations, hostile or indifferent courts, and white greed." Pine Ridge was hardly immune to these developments.[25]

The Great Sioux Reservation, as it was once known, was the far ranging area of land that the various Lakota and Nakota peoples of the Great Plains, including the Oglalas, had secured for themselves in the 1868 Second Treaty of Fort Laramie. It included a massive reservation proper that consisted of half of the modern state of South Dakota: everything west of the Missouri River. It also explicitly acknowledged Lakota and Nakota rights to parts of what are now Nebraska, Montana, Wyoming, Colorado, North Dakota, and even a smidgen of northwestern Kansas. However, in the aftermath of conquering the Northern Great Plains, the federal government unilaterally pared down these lands on several occasions. A February 28, 1877, federal bill, which was inspired retribution for the spectacularly failed invasion of Lieutenant Colonel George Custer's Seventh Cavalry less than a year earlier, seized all of the Lakota lands beyond what the United States would later recognize as the western portions of North and South Dakota. More than a century later, the U.S. Supreme Court would eventually deem this to have been an illegal land seizure. Next came a congressional act on March 2, 1889, that broke up what was left of the Great Sioux Reservation into six smaller pieces: the Cheyenne River, Crow Creek, Lower Brule, Pine Ridge, and Rosebud Reservations in South Dakota, and the Standing Rock Reservation, which straddles the North Dakota-South Dakota border (see map 1). Amid this process of parceling, the federal government confiscated an additional nine million acres. In return for the lost land, the Lakotas received meager payments ranging from fifty cents to three dollars per acre, plus 1,000 bulls and 2,500 cows.[26]

Like many Native nations, the Lakotas were caught in the gears of the process. In 1890, the Lakota and Nakota Indians of South Dakota collectively still held title to over 11.6 million acres of land. By 1933, after forty-plus years of forced cessions, the Dawes Act's ravages, and the OIA's degenerate stewardship, those land holdings in South Dakota had been cut by more than half, to just over 5.5 million acres. The Pine Ridge Reservation was now an atomized entity, a mere 2,047,602 acres in the southwest corner of the state.[27]

To Commissioner of Indian Affairs John Collier's credit, his administration under President Roosevelt did seek to reverse this trend of Native dispossession, but it was able to do little. Section 3 of the Wheeler-Howard Act did place previously unassigned reservation acreage under the authority of the new tribal councils. By this provision, the Oglala Sioux Tribe received more than 9,500 acres. The federal government also purchased another 3,513 acres on behalf of the OST under the provisions of section 5 in the bill, which had set aside money for that purpose. Despite these efforts, however, barely 10 percent of the reservation, less than 250,000 acres, was under the control of the new tribal council as late as 1939, five years after its passage. In his original draft of the IRA, Collier had wanted to force all Indian landowners to forfeit their allotments to the new tribal councils. But this, along with several other provisions, had been struck from the bill before final congressional approval in 1934. As a result, by 1939 individual allottees held the lion's share of the Pine Ridge land base: 1,758,273 acres. The federal government itself controlled another 47,362 acres directly.[28]

Despite Collier's efforts, the new tribal councils had little land with which to work. Instead, they remained in the private ownership of Indians and non-Indians alike. And to make matters worse, the many individual Indian allotments scattered throughout the reservation were often not under the control of their Oglala owners. Indeed, there were historical factors beyond the misguided allotment policy and the IRA's shortcomings that contributed to the alienation of Oglalas from their land, not the least of which were OIA negligence and malfeasance. The OIA had done very little over the years to ensure that Oglala landowners had sufficient opportunities to use their land productively. Instead, various OIA officials on Pine Ridge (and on countless other reservations) had actively encouraged them to lease their lands to local white settlers and outside corporations for well below market values. Given the abject poverty of the reservation and the paucity of available opportunities, such urging was often heeded. These long-term rental leases contributed to many Oglalas losing control of their land and created a class of impoverished landlords. Compounding this were allotments partitioned by heirship; South Dakota law mandated the partible inheritance of land when its owner died intestate. As Oglalas often died without written wills, by the 1930s many allotments, once large in size, were now too fractioned to be used effectively, further encouraging their leasing to outside interests.[29]

The consequences would have been startling had they not played out so similarly on so many other reservations. By the end of 1938, Indians used less than one-quarter of Pine Ridge for their own ends, a scant 446,354 acres. Meanwhile, nearly half of the reservation (1,021,543 acres) was being used by non-Indians, and another 12,000-plus acres were home to OIA administrative sites. The final 567,008 acres were left idle, the OIA deeming nearly half of this to be barren or wasteland. Put another way, in 1938, non-Indians controlled about half of the productive land on the Pine Ridge Reservation, while Indians utilized less than one-third of the open grazing land, less than one-third of the timber land, less than 15 percent of the farm land, and less than 10 percent of the land the OIA classified as "other."[30]

Many allottees, particularly those with one-half Indian lineage or less, had lost their land base in the aftermath of the Dawes Allotment Act for reasons previously cited. Those Indians who had held on to their land had been encouraged by the OIA to lease it to local white interests. Those who had leased their land often realized very little in return. The average Indian landlord received less than ten dollars per year in lease money, royalties, and permits. And as far as using its ample sums to help those Indians who had held on to their lands, the OIA did not offer much. Only 3.8 percent of its regular operating budget for 1938 was allocated to *combined* expenditures on land management ($1,400), forestry ($4,600), and extension services and industry ($23,188), leaving little doubt that the organization was, at best, inefficient. Perhaps the most telling statistic with regard to OIA spending patterns on Pine Ridge is the following. During the fiscal year ending June 30, 1939, the OIA spent no money for the construction of hospitals, schools, or heating or power plants. However, it did spend $12,000 building residential quarters for its own employees.[31]

One might reasonably presume that because the OIA did not allocate large amounts of money for the development of Indian lands, it did not exercise much control over those lands. However, such a presumption would be gravely mistaken. The OIA exercised a tremendous amount of control over much of the Pine Ridge land owned by the Oglala people in addition to the land directly under its own control. For example, even though it was owned by the Oglala Sioux Tribe, timber land was nonetheless subject to OIA restrictions. The Office had an agenda of maintaining such resources on a sustained yield basis. This may sound noble, but the upshot was OIA control in lieu of Oglala control. In a 1940 memorandum to numerous other OIA personnel on Pine Ridge, Range Supervisor George V. Hedden reminded them of this policy and that the secretary of the interior had limited the cutting of timber to only those people, Indian or otherwise, who had acquired proper OIA permits. And only members of the Forestry and Grazing Division (Hedden's division) or the Extension Division could issue such permits. In addition, all green timber had to be marked by a Forestry and Grazing representative before a permit could be obtained. Even the gathering of large quantities of dead wood required a Forestry and Grazing permit. Hedden went on to implore fellow OIA employees that if they were to purchase "timber or forest products from an Indian, please see that the seller has a proper permit to cover the same." As restrictive as this was, OIA control over Indian land went far beyond the management of timber reserves.[32]

Federal authorities also monitored and tightly regulated individual landownership. Thus, when John Little Elk wished to lease 480 acres of land to a Mrs. MacLacey in 1941 in return for a team of horses, he needed the approval of the OIA. In fact, Superintendent W. O. Roberts hesitated, deciding he needed specific information on the value, age, and weight of the horses in question before he could sign off on the transaction. "[T]he team offered might have a cash value of eight or eighty dollars," he noted. "The interest of John Little Elk should be protected. In such cases the office is not in favor of such transactions unless the Indian receives a cash value equal to the cash rental of such lands." While the ostensible purpose of protecting Native people from being swindled by the unscrupulous may, at first glance, seem commendable, issues of overbearing paternalism also come to mind. Moreover, distasteful observations about the infantilizing of Native people are not the sum total of relevant concerns. Indeed, paternalism often lends itself to authoritarianism, as the cases of Benjamin Chief and Calvin Clincher demonstrate.[33]

In 1941, Benjamin Chief had to apply to the OIA for "competent authority" to rent from his *own wife.* Worse yet, he was denied. The reason? He had incurred a debt to the U.S. government for cattle he had purchased with federal money. "It is not the policy of this office," declared Roberts, "to grant authority for leasing of such land when the individual is indebted to the United States Government."[34]

In 1945, Calvin Clincher wished to lease some of his own recently inherited land for $100 per year to a Kansan bent on raising wheat. He too failed to gain approval for the transaction. The land in question had never been broken by a plough, and the OIA's (and Department of Agriculture's) New Deal policy since 1935 had been to retire from agriculture unbroken Native land, such as Clincher's, which they deemed unsuitable for farming. Only grazing projects would be approved. The ecologically wrong- or right-mindedness of such Dust Bowl–era policies is beside the point. Benjamin Chief's wife and Calvin Clincher may have possessed land on Pine Ridge, but they did not possess control over it. The OIA did.[35]

Furthermore, the extent to which the OIA controlled Pine Ridge land went beyond simple issues of leases and allotments., It concerned the very nature of human spatial relations. When Mr. and Mrs. Robert Fast Horse purchased livestock, presumably with federal money, it in effect bound them to the reservation by the discretion of the superintendent. Thus, when they wished to leave the reservation in 1945 to find work, Roberts addressed a letter to Agricultural Extension Agent R. B. McKee, advising him that the Fast Horses "have permission to leave the reservation to secure work elsewhere, for approximately a three month period, at which time they are to return to the reservation to care for their livestock."[36]

That such a letter could be written in the middle of the twentieth century, by a federal official concerning the whereabouts of American citizens who had committed no crime, is nearly incomprehensible. Nevertheless, in concert with the details cited above, it speaks volumes about the degree to which the Office of Indian Affairs, as opposed to the Oglala Sioux Tribal Council, held sway over the land on Pine Ridge.

LEGAL INSTITUTIONS

Another important indicant of a people's sovereignty concerns legal institutions. The extent to which a people are at the mercy of others to make and enforce their laws is a reflection upon the erosion of their sovereignty. During the era of direct colonial rule prior to John Collier's assumption of the OIA commissionership, the federal government brandished de facto absolute legal authority on all Indian reservations. However, while the federal government designed and implemented the legal institutions used on reservations, it was also willing to employ reservation Indians in certain roles for enforcement. In 1883, the U.S. government instituted the Court of Indian Offenses to preside over crimes committed by Indians against Indians on reservations. Reservation agents appointed Indian policemen who were endowed with significant legal powers. Beyond law enforcement, OIA police were assigned to serve as prosecutors, judges, juries, and jailers of those they arrested. The real authority in this configuration, however, was the reservation agent. He hired and fired Indian policemen/judges according to his whims. He even had the discretion to alter their verdicts if they were not to his liking. In this autocratic environment, the agents frequently used the institution to attack Native cultures and religions. And if controlling on-reservation legal institutions were not enough, the federal government soon concocted justifications for hauling Indians off their reservations under certain circumstances.[37]

The same year that the Court of Indian Offenses first appeared, the U.S. Supreme Court issued its decision in *Ex Parte Crow Dog* (1883). On the surface, it seemed a victory for Native legal culture, as the court recognized the validity of aboriginal legal institutions. But this was never the court's intention, and with a wink and a nod, Congress picked up where the case left off by passing the Major Crimes Act in 1885. It listed seven felony charges (murder, manslaughter, rape, arson, assault with intent to kill, burglary, and larceny) for which federal law enforcement authorities could enter reservations without permission and apprehend Indians accused of committing these crimes against other Indians. Once arrested, Indians would then stand trial in federal court.[38]

The Major Crimes Act was federal legislation and thus beyond Commissioner John Collier's ability to tamper with. However, the Court of Indian Offenses was another matter. In 1935, he used his executive powers to mitigate some of the abuses inherent in the system. First, he gave Indians on reservations a say in the appointment and removal of Indian Court judges (who were by now separate from the reservation police). Second, he ordered reservation superintendents to consult with the new reservation governments in drawing up new legal codes to replace the old Code of Indian Offenses. The Code had been little more than a legal codification of colonial rule and the hammer of attempted cultural genocide. Instead, the Oglala Sioux Tribe would now have its own judiciary. Collier's moves were definite improvements over the previous situation, but there were still two problems.[39]

First, the reservation legal system that Collier had modified was still foreign in nature to the people with whose care it was charged, and it was therefore acting as a force to repress Indigenous legal institutions. As Sidney Harring has observed, the courts represented the imposition of a foreign legal culture and its institutions upon the pre-existing Indigenous legal cultures. Collier's modifications did not address this issue.[40] An example of this can be seen in the case of Vincent Fast Horse.

In 1940, Vincent Fast Horse was convicted of bastardy in the recently established Pine Ridge Junior Court, Judge Rose Ecoffey presiding. After his conviction, Fast Horse asked the judge if he might be able to make amends to the plaintiff, Louise Running Shield, in a manner in accordance with traditional Lakota legal culture. He offered to pay Running Shield one bay mare and one colt. Restitution was a firmly established Lakota legal principle. Precedence can be seen in the case of Spotted Tail and Crow Dog. On August 5, 1881, Crow Dog shot Spotted Tail to death during a tense confrontation. The U.S. government had recognized Spotted Tail as the "supreme chief" of the Sichanghu (Brule) band of Lakotas (who now mostly reside on the Rosebud Reservation), and his own people recognized him as a man of eminence and one of several important Sichanghu leaders. In the immediate aftermath of the killing, a Sichanghu council ordered Crow Dog's family to pay Spotted Tail's family six-hundred dollars, eight horses, and one blanket as just compensation. Crow Dog's family complied, and according to Lakota legal culture the matter was now considered closed.[41]

Fast Horse attempted to offer Louise Running Shield restitution for his transgression, and indeed, Judge Ecoffey was inclined to allow him to settle the matter in this fashion. However, the federal government had not accepted the validity of Indigenous legal institutions in Crow Dog's time; in fact, it was Crow Dog's shooting of Spotted Tail that had led to the *Ex Parte Crow Dog* case and the subsequent passage of the Major Crimes Act. Fifty-five years later, the federal government still refused to recognize their validity, and now stepped in to curb this latest attempt to breathe life into Lakota legal culture. Since Fast Horse had purchased the animals with financial help from the federal government, federal authorities had immediate leverage over the situation. OIA Field Aide Francis F. Fielder felt that the solution as suggested would be a misusage of the horses. Consequently, he recommended that Fast Horse not be allowed to use them as compensation, noting in a letter to Agricultural Extension Agent Rex Kildow that the government could step in and sell Fast Horse's entire herd if he attempted to use any of the animals for unapproved purposes. Kildow concurred and denied the transaction. A Pine Ridge court judge had just been trumped by an agricultural extension agent. Clearly, the new legal system, as introduced and modified by the IRA, was still in conflict with traditional Lakota legal culture, and the latter would yield to the former when clashes occurred.[42]

The second mitigation of Collier's executive orders of 1935 was the Major Crimes Act itself. As a piece of congressional legislation, it was immune to any attacks that the executively appointed commissioner might wish to make upon it. In fact, the scope of the act has been greatly enhanced since its original inception, now encompassing more than twice the original seven crimes, and it continues to exist today as a severe impediment to the legal foundations of Native sovereignty.[43]

By examining statistics from a sample year, we can illustrate this picture further. The numbers from 1938 indicate that Native Americans in general, and specifically the Oglalas of Pine Ridge, had not witnessed a substantial restoration of their legal culture. Nationwide, superintendents reported that in 1938 almost 9,000 Native people were arrested on reservations and brought before various state, federal, and reservation courts for 39 different crimes, including contempt of court (288), traffic violations (101), delinquency (102), vagrancy (33), and murder (15). As a group, these Indians faced a conviction rate of more than 90 percent. For eleven select crimes[44] reported in-depth by the Department of the Interior, more detailed statistics are available. A total of 1,484 Indians had been arrested, and 1,331 of them were convicted, a rate of 89.6 percent. This number may seem incredibly high by today's standards, but it must be kept in the perspective of the times. Non-Indians arrested on reservations for crimes against or relating to Indians were convicted at a comparable rate of just over 81 percent. However, more relevant to this discussion is the fact that nationally, only 38 percent of all crimes committed on reservations were settled in reservation courts. Almost half of all such cases were heard in federal courts, and about one-eighth in various state courts.[45]

Perhaps the most amazing figure is that of the nearly 9,000 Indians around the country who were tried in various courts during 1938, more than 10 percent of them (909) came from Pine Ridge Reservation, while less than 2 percent of the non-Indians who stood trial for crimes against or relating to Indians were from Pine Ridge. Of those Pine Ridge Indians (presumably most of them were Oglalas and other Lakotas), we find that 770 of them were male, more than half of them were twenty-five or older, and 10 of them were under the age of fifteen. As a group, 90 percent of their cases were heard in reservation courts, but that offered them little consolation. Their conviction rate there was nearly 95 percent.[46]

Finally, let the case of Vincent LaPoint serve to dispel any lingering notions that the Pine Ridge Tribal Court system, despite its foreign legal culture and mitigation by the Major Crimes Act, may have actually reflected some vestige of Lakota sovereignty as a legal institution of the Oglala Sioux Tribe. When the Tribal Court sentenced LaPoint to serve sixty days in the Pine Ridge jail in 1939, he had been working for the Indian Division of the Civilian Conservation Corps. Agricultural Extension Agent R. F. Coulter felt that LaPoint's job of copying maps for the Extension Department and National Resources Board was too important a matter to be interrupted by the trifling of the OST's legal system. Consequently, on July 27, Coulter contacted the court clerk to "request the services of Mr. LaPoint, as prisoner, to continue with map work that he was doing under the direction of CCC-ID draftsmen." There is no surviving record of the court clerk's response. One can only imagine.[47]

EDUCATION

Beyond economy, land tenure, and legal institutions, subtler social factors are also indicative of sovereignty. One important measure is a nation's capacity to educate its own children. Once again, in Oglala society this was a sphere dominated by outside forces, particularly the federal government. And as with other issues examined in this chapter, the new Oglala Sioux Tribal Council had virtually no influence over education on Pine Ridge.

Federal control over the education/indoctrination of Indian children had been a central tenet of the government's assimilation policy of the preceding half-century. During these years, America's goal was nothing short of the eradication of Native cultures, and assimilationists saw schools as a perfect vehicle for bleaching Indigenous traditions from Native children. The U.S. government conscripted Indian children and shipped them off to boarding schools hundreds, sometimes thousands of miles from their homes. Most Indian parents were loath to give up their children, but they were living in the shadow of conquest and in a state of utter dependence upon the federal government for their very survival. Threats to withhold rations (supposedly guaranteed in treaties) were oftentimes sufficiently dire as to coerce a parent into sacrificing a child to the great American experiment in cultural genocide.[48]

After having been wrested from their families, Native children from around the country landed in places like the Haskell Institute in Lawrence, Kansas, and the Carlisle Indian School in Carlisle, Pennsylvania. Once there, school officials subjected boys and girls alike to a program of education and manual labor in an attempt to reshape Indigenous children as Euro-Americans. Educators attacked every outward sign of Native cultures, cutting children's hair, throwing out their Indian clothes, and replacing their religions with Christianity. Children even faced corporal punishment for speaking their Native tongues.[49]

John Collier's new policies were an improvement, discouraging the previous draconian endeavors to forcibly remove Indigenous children from their homes and ship them off to distant boarding schools. Nonetheless, these institutions were maintained. OIA budgetary allocations in 1939 for the Pipestone School in Minnesota were over $220,000. The Chilocco Indian School in northern Oklahoma likewise received almost a quarter of a million dollars. The Haskell Institute in Kansas got more than $260,000. And for those children who did not leave, the OIA continued to exercise control over educational programs on reservations through reservation day schools and boarding schools, both of which were federally funded and operated. The federal government did not yield this vital institution to the authority of the new tribal councils, and Pine Ridge is a case in point.[50]

During the 1938–1939 school year, more than two years after the establishment of the Oglala Sioux Tribal Council and almost five years after Collier's ascension to the position of commissioner of Indian affairs, the OIA allocated a regular operating budget of $761,663 for the Pine Ridge Reservation. Of this, more than half ($335,750) went toward education. For its part, the OSTC had no education budget. That year, there were nearly 3,000 children of school age (6–18) on the reservation. The large majority of them were enrolled in schools (89.4 percent). More than half attended government schools, mostly on the reservation itself (see table 3.2). Among the more than 1,100 students who did not attend federal schools, about half had been sent to institutions located off the reservation: parochial mission schools, private schools, and some state institutions. Only eight of those children were able to live at home. Most of the other students not enrolled in federal schools attended public schools located off-reservation. Another nineteen children were admitted to the Sioux Sanatorium, which received over $126,000 in OIA funds that year. Six attended special schools for children with handicaps or colleges and universities; perhaps tellingly, OIA statistics made no distinction between post-secondary education and facilities for young children with disabilities (see table 3.3).[51]

It is also worth noting that statistics for 1938–1939 are emblematic of the entire early OSTC era. In fact, from the school years 1938–1939 to 1941–1942, the percentage of Pine Ridge school children, ages six to eighteen, who attended federal schools actually increased every year, from 57.3 percent in 1938 to 63.7 percent in 1942. During each of these years, the remainder of school children was split, more or less evenly, between local public schools and a category the OIA labeled "Mission, Private, State and Special."[52]

By the 1941–1942 school year, then, the number of Pine Ridge children

TABLE 3.2

School Enrollment of Pine Ridge Reservation Indian Children
Ages 6 to 18: 1938–1939

Schools by Category	Pine Ridge School Children, Ages 6 to 18 (Percentage)
Federal	1,500 (57.47)
Mission, Private, and State Day Schools	8 (00.03)
Mission, Private, and State Boarding Schools	506 (19.38)
Schools for Handicapped Students	6 (00.02)
Public Schools	590 (22.60)
Total	2,610 (99.50)

Source: United States Department of the Interior. United States Indian Service, *Statistical Supplement to the Annual Report of the Commissioner of Indian Affairs* (Washington, D.C.: Government Printing Office, 1939), 20.

TABLE 3.3

Distribution of Pine Ridge Reservation Indian Children Enrolled in
Federal Schools: 1938–1939

Federal Schools	Pine Ridge School Children, Ages 6 to 18 (Percentage)
Day Schools (on-reservation)	1,106 (73.73)
Boarding Schools (on-reservation)	361 (24.06)
Boarding Schools (off-reservation)	14 (00.90)
The Sioux Sanitorium (Rapid City, S.D.)	19 (01.26)
Total	1,500 (99.95)

Source: United States Department of the Interior. United States Indian Service, *Statistical Supplement to the Annual Report of the Commissioner of Indian Affairs* (Washington, D.C.: Government Printing Office, 1939), 20.

scattered to distant, federal boarding schools such as Haskell and Carlisle was quite small, thanks in part to Collier's new policies. However, more than half of the reservation's school children were still attending schools that the federal government funded, owned, and operated. Only now, they were on Pine Ridge, where the government ran no less than nineteen schools with a daily average attendance of 1,492 children. For that year, a total of nearly 64 percent of the reservation's school children attended federal schools, (though only 1 percent went to off-reservation federal boarding schools), and 19 percent attended local public schools, and 17 percent went to private mission schools (either on or off the reservation) that were affiliated with various Christian denominations.[53]

In short, the education of Pine Ridge's children was still dominated by the federal government and other outside forces. The Oglala Sioux Tribe played no role in the education of the reservation's children, serving as a clear indicator that the Lakota people did not possess real sovereignty despite the fanfare of John Collier and the Indian Reorganization Act.

The abuses of distant boarding schools are well documented. But within the halls of the reservation schools, similar conditions also prevailed. Pressure to assimilate into mainstream American culture was stiff, living conditions were wanting, and discipline was harsh. As a boy, future Oglala medicine man Pete Catches of the Wakpamani District attended a federal government school on Pine Ridge. Punishments he endured included spankings, soap in his mouth, having his hair cut, having sticks put into his ears, being whipped with rubber hoses, being subjected to solitary confinement, being forced to stand for hours on end, being restricted to a bread and water diet, and being forced to wear girls' clothing in public as a form of public humiliation.[54]

Mildred McGaa Stinson also attended a federal school on Pine Ridge in the years leading up to the IRA. Later in life she recalled the debased living conditions, such as being served oatmeal with worms in it. The sadistic cruelty of individual white teachers and personnel was compounded by institutional autocracy. For example, the students' letters home were censored by the administration in an effort to prevent families from discovering the abusive conditions at the school. Such censorship even included erasing revelations of illness. On more than one occasion, McGaa remembered children dying at the school and the children's parents knowing nothing of the illness until they received news of the death. Such was the case with her own cousin, who died at the Holy Rosary Mission School. Tuberculosis in particular frequently claimed young lives. Despite such hardships, McGaa graduated as her high school's valedictorian in 1935. She then received a loan for tuition to further her education in Ames, Iowa, but could not afford to go, so she instead went to work.[55]

With adult retrospection, Mildred McGaa felt the prevailing attitude within the institution was racist, and she believed that this had encouraged the abusive treatment and rampant corruption. But instead of being bitter over her experiences, she expressed admiration for the one school principal who treated the students well. "I know there is one man, one white person that I can really trust and this is Mr. Newport," she professed more than thirty years later. "And as I look back over it now, I realize how that man jeopardized his job just to love us and to take our part." Some might celebrate Mildred McGaa's remarkable ability to find the silver lining in an otherwise very dark cloud. Some might mourn that, during her twelve years of schooling, there was only one. Both the celebration of exceptional people like McGaa and the mourning of their experiences are part of these children's stories.[56]

Given such stories, it should come as no surprise that a number of Pine Ridge families who valued their culture and heritage, loved their children, and historically distrusted the imperialistic motives and whitewashing effects of government- and religiously funded schools, managed to keep their children out of educational institutions altogether. Exact numbers are unknown. But during the 1938–1939 school year, there were approximately 300 Pine Ridge children of school age who were not enrolled in any school at all. By 1941–1942, the number may have been as high as 391 (see table 3.4). This act of cultural survival by some Lakota families continued throughout the 1940s. For example, even as late as the 1950s, Lakota Henry Crow Dog, grandson of the man who shot Spotted Tail to death in 1881, kept his son Leonard from attending school altogether. Instead, the family lived on his rural allotment on the neighboring Rosebud Reservation, where Leonard was reared with a traditional Lakota education.[57]

TABLE 3.4

School Enrollment and Nonenrollment of Pine Ridge Reservation Indian
Children, Ages 6 to 18: 1938–1939 and 1941–1942

Enrollment Status	1938–1939	1941–1942
Enrolled	2,610 (89.41)	2513 (86.53)
Not Enrolled	244 (08.35)	391* (13.46)
Information Not Available	65 (02.23)	N/A*
Total	2,919 (99.99)	2904 (99.99)

*The 1939 figures include separate categories for "Indian children not enrolled 6 to 18 years" and "Definite information not available (6 to 18 years only)." However, the 1942 figures offer neither category, only "Number Children Enumerated (6 to 18) Years" and "Number Enrolled in School: Children 6 to 18," leaving the reader to do the math for himself or herself. It would seem that the sixty-five children with no information available in 1939 were definitely not in the federal system (since the federal government collected the data), and either did not attend non-federal schools (likely) for which records were kept, or did, but were somehow uncounted (less likely). The same must be said for the 391 children of 1942 who were not indicated as enrolled in any school. For that reason, I have chosen to list them as "Not Enrolled." The reader should note that some of them may have attended non-federal schools, but with no records of their attendance available.

Source: United States Department of the Interior. United States Indian Service. *Statistical Supplement to the Annual Report of the Commissioner of Indian Affairs* (Washington, D.C.: Government Printing Office, 1939), 20, and "Statistical Report of the Superintendent of Indian Education," 3, in Superintendent of Indian Education George C. Wells to Roberts, October 12, 1942, Box 172, File 052.5 Day School Inspectors, NARA-AR.

PEOPLE BYPASSING THE TRIBAL COUNCIL IN FAVOR OF THE OFFICE OF INDIAN AFFAIRS

Statistics are a hard, skeletal limner. People's stories are the flesh and blood that give it life. Combined, they offer the portrait of a reservation where the Office of Indian Affairs retained a phenomenal amount of political, economic, and social control over the lives of the people who lived there. And Oglalas were not oblivious to this fact. It had been a part of their reality since their confinement to the reservation over the course of the 1870s. While the Lakota nation had won many battles against the United States, in the end they lost the war, and officers of the federal government were now setting many of the rules. This had been true for more than a half-century.

The coming of the IRA certainly rounded some of the edges of colonial rule and blunted some of the sharper weapons of cultural genocide. For example, certain religious ceremonies were no longer forbidden, and the Lakota language was now encouraged instead of persecuted. But the Oglalas of Pine Ridge had no delusions that the OIA was no longer an authoritative figure in their midst.[58]

Anthropologist Thomas Biolsi has advanced the argument that the people of Pine Ridge were largely unable to discern this reality. He has shown that the buildup to establishing the Oglala Sioux Tribal Council on the reservation was accompanied by massive amounts of OIA propaganda that centered around promises of Indian sovereignty. The OIA proclaimed that the IRA would grant a substantial degree of self-government to reservations that chose to reorganize and establish tribal councils. Biolsi claims that the Lakotas of Pine Ridge bought into these promises and wrongly presumed after 1936 that their new council did in fact possess substantial power. He believes that most Lakotas were blind to the reality that the OIA had maintained most of its authority, that they did not see that the new OSTC's political power was in many ways stillborn.[59]

The first half of Biolsi's argument, the maintenance of the OIA's power in the post-IRA scenario is accepted and reinforced in this book. However, the second half, that Oglalas were unaware of the relatively unchanged political dynamics on their reservation, is more problematic. As discussed in the previous chapter, there was indeed substantial OIA propaganda about reorganization and the governing powers of the new Oglala Sioux Tribe. But the notion that Oglalas bought into these false promises and continued to believe them even after they began to ring hollow, seems to rest on two propositions. One is the willingness of the people on Pine Ridge to quickly cast aside more than fifty years of precedent. More than two generations of Lakotas had endured the heavy hand of the conqueror. The OIA had been the official and present arbiter of U.S. colonial policies. For people to believe that the United States would suddenly and effectively relinquish this power was not impossible, but it would certainly require a leap of faith that contradicted their recent experiences.

However, it is the second proposition that is more troubling. It supposes that Lakotas on Pine Ridge, particularly the many full-blood critics of the IRA, were too politically naive and unaware to realize that the OIA had in fact maintained its position and continued effectively to rule the reservation in many important ways—that Lakotas, in essence, failed to tabulate the real power equations on their reservation.

Biolsi of course never says this. In fact, he does not even believe it. To the contrary, he thinks the Lakota critics of the IRA were actually quite "politically astute."[60] But in asserting that the people of Pine Ridge misunderstood the new reservation political landscape because they unquestioningly accepted federal promises about the OSTC, the seemingly unavoidable subtext is that Lakotas were dupes.

In his analysis of the referenda that accepted reorganization, Biolsi dismisses former Rosebud Reservation President Robert Burnette's claim that many full bloods on Pine Ridge and Rosebud had boycotted the vote as a traditional way of expressing their dissatisfaction with the IRA; that they had in effect voted with their feet, refusing to confer legitimacy on a process they disapproved of by not participating; and that in so doing, they miscalculated the effects of their abstention on the outcome. Biolsi counters that Lakotas had been voting in general elections since 1924 and that some of them had in-depth experience with other aspects of the American political process. He believes they were too savvy not to realize the consequences of such a boycott. If he is correct, then could Lakotas really be simultaneously unwitting about the reality of the ensuing political situation on their own reservation? That is to say, could they be "politically astute" enough to grasp the vital importance of voting in lieu of traditional abstentious behavior, but be politically oblivious enough to believe that the OSTC effectively usurped the OIA to become the new power on the reservation simply because of OIA promises to that effect?[61]

Biolsi's *Organizing the Lakota* is well established in the literature, and rightly so. In fact, this book proudly leans on some of the outstanding research contained therein. However, his interpretation of this issue is not acceptable. There is ample evidence that the people of Pine Ridge were cognizant of the political realities on their reservation. They turned to the representatives of the OIA on innumerable occasions for advice and redress on countless matters. They did this not merely from force of habit, but because they understood that the Oglala Sioux Tribal Council usually could not offer them the help they needed, and that the OIA was clearly still the most important political institution on Pine Ridge. Such was the case with Lucille LeClair, who had squatters on her land in 1941 and appealed directly to Superintendent W. O. Roberts for aid. Likewise, in the aftermath of Sampson Bear Killer's death, when his family tried to retrieve his horse and cultivator that were in the possession of Gilbert Cottier, they called on the OIA for help. That the OIA assigned Cottier's brother Henry to look into the matter may reflect poorly on the Office for ignoring an obvious conflict of interest (predictably, Henry declared Gilbert's possession of the items legitimate), but it does not diminish the fact that the Bear Killer family approached the OIA to begin with, not the OSTC.[62]

The reason people continued to turn to the OIA is simple. The OIA had retained most of its power despite the recent creation of the OSTC, and the people knew it. They understood that it would often be futile to petition the newly established Council for redress. Instead, Oglalas did what made sense. They continued to solicit the OIA for help when they required political intervention. This is not to imply that they completely ignored the OSTC in lieu of the OIA. As we shall see in the next chapter, Oglalas did approach the early Tribal Council government with certain issues. But for the most part, when seeking help for many of the large issues that confronted them, as well as many of the smaller affairs in their daily lives, the Oglala Lakota people of Pine Ridge Reservation continued to turn to OIA officials in the years through World War II.

After all, even Pine Ridge Lakota Benjamin Reifel, himself an OIA employee, a staunch supporter of the IRA, and a future South Dakota congressman and commissioner of Indian affairs, had to admit that early on, "there was this feeling that the tribal councils did not get enough authority to really do the things they wanted to do in behalf of the people they represented."[63] There are numerous examples to illustrate this reality.

Noah Bear Robe had a large family. During the summer of 1940, they were living in a tent. The tent was hardly large enough to accommodate them and it was also in poor condition. Bear Robe's long-term plan was to build a house in the fall, and he had already made provisions for procuring lumber. However, in the interim he felt the need to acquire a new tent. He turned to Max C. Jensen, the OIA farm agent in Kyle. Temporary housing is hardly the kind of subject matter generally associated with the responsibilities of an agricultural advisor. Nonetheless, Bear Robe chose to solicit assistance from this OIA representative. Likewise, Jensen did not direct Bear Robe to the Oglala Sioux Tribal Council. Rather, he contacted a social worker in the village of Pine Ridge, explained the circumstances, vouched for Bear

Robe's clean credit, and implored the social worker to get him the tent.[64]

Noah Bear Robe was not alone in consulting OIA representatives on matters of housing, though usually it hardly fit their job descriptions. In 1939, Thomas Black Bear of Porcupine was elderly and had a house in need of repair. He contacted a teacher at a government-run school. The request was forwarded to an educational field agent, and it then progressed further up the OIA ladder. Eventually, a plan was devised to replace the house altogether: the OIA supplied the building materials and ten local men volunteered their services. There was no OSTC involvement.[65]

Philip Good Shield was also from Porcupine, and he too approached a teacher on a matter that was, at best, only nominally related to teaching. Good Shield needed money to obtain winter feed for his horses. In addition to his own purposes, he also used the team to bring his children to the Brave Heart Day School when weather rendered the two-mile walk impractical. John Powless was a teacher at the school. At Good Shield's request, Powless wrote a letter to Superintendent W. O. Roberts on the man's behalf, and even championed his cause. "He deserves some consideration, don't you think?" the teacher prodded Roberts.[66]

So profound was the OIA's influence over the reservation, and so keen was the Lakotas' comprehension of this reality, that they bypassed the OSTC and consulted the OIA even in the most finite of circumstances. In August of 1940, Sarah No Belt had recently returned to Pine Ridge from the Sioux Sanatorium in Rapid City, South Dakota. She suffered from tuberculosis, which had been diagnosed as terminal. In addition, she had no immediate family. Yet even in light of this dire reality, she still contacted the OIA for permission to sell her property, including a mower, a rake, and a team of draft animals, so that she could use the proceeds to purchase some clothing and food in her final days. The reservation superintendent, in a particularly callous missive, assigned a farm agent to see "if the facts are as stated," before assisting the girl. In his reply, the farm agent informed the superintendent that No Belt had died two days before he received his letter.[67]

If imminent death did not diminish the authority of the OIA in the minds of many Lakotas, then it should come as no surprise that neither did the event for which many Americans were prepared to die: the Second World War. After Pine Ridge resident Raymond Hernandez became U.S. Army Private Raymond Hernandez, he still wrote the OIA's extension office in June, 1944, seeking permission for the sale of his two head of cattle that were being tended to by his brother. Unable to look after them himself, Hernandez wished "to get them off my mind." In addition, his brother needed the money to buy hay for his own livestock. Nearly a month after Hernandez made his request, his brother Joseph was finally issued a sales permit.[68]

The reality that the OIA, as opposed to the OSTC, was still the real authority on the reservation was clear not just to the residents of Pine Ridge Reservation, but to nearby whites as well. When the Midwest Collection Service of Rapid City, South Dakota wanted help collecting money from a Porcupine man, they too turned to the Office of Indian Affairs. In May 1945, Midwest got a Pennington County Circuit Court judgment against Gene T. Bush of Porcupine, verifying that he owed them $82.37. Having received only twenty dollars by the beginning of 1946, they sought help enforcing the judgment since jurisdiction for this local misdemeanor offense could not penetrate the boundaries of the federally recognized reservation. Yet, instead of asking the OSTC to get involved, they turned to the OIA, hoping that the Office would be of assistance in this matter. In fact, the OIA had no authority to force Indians to pay outside debts unless the transactions had received prior sanction from the reservation's superintendent (which was rare). Nonetheless, it is telling that outsiders would occasionally make such presumptions about the OIA but never, as far as can be ascertained, about the Oglala Sioux Tribal Council.[69]

Likewise, when Indians from Pine Ridge needed help with outsiders, they turned to the OIA. When a number of Indians were concerned that a man named Paul Schriner was trespassing on their land, they contacted the superintendent. Then there was the case of a Lakota named Joseph Harvey, who had trouble collecting six dollars owed to him by a local school principal. Harvey was looking to collect after having sold a used tire to the principal when the latter needed to replace a flat on his trailer while poisoning grasshoppers. Harvey notified the extension agent, who demanded an explanation from the principal.[70]

The OIA was often sought out for settling disputes among Lakotas within the reservation. In April of 1944, Lizzie Eagle Hawk, Lucy Dreaming Bear, Pugh and Taylor Soldier Hawk, and Katie Short Bull contended that their land was being trespassed by cattle from the He Crow, Loneman, and Cottier families. After failed attempts among the parties to settle the discrepancy, the aggrieved looked to the OIA extension agent for redress. He in turn assigned a field aide to mediate the affair. And when, later that year, Orlando Clifford, Edna Johnson, Vina Lessert, and George Ruff from the Allen District had a complaint over their land inheritance from the late Mary Ruff, they appealed to Superintendent Roberts. It seems that Johnson, who owned the largest part of the estate, had commenced leasing her shares without the consent of the other three, who wanted to consolidate their interests in Clifford's hands. Rhiner Johnson, Edna's husband, had also begun cutting hay on the land, and the three challenged his authority to do so. Roberts took the matter seriously and assigned Agricultural Extension Agent R. B. McKee to sort out the affair.[71]

No problem, it seems, was too pedestrian. Even the matter of bedbugs was not too mundane an issue for Pine Ridge residents to seek help from federal authorities. In the summer of 1940, Home Extension Agent Mamie Searles responded to a request from the residents of Porcupine regarding the fumigation of the troublesome critters. She indicated that her office did in fact have pyrethrum powder needed to make fly spray. The powder itself could be obtained free of charge, but there would be a service fee of thirty-two cents per 1,000 cubic feet for those people who wanted their houses fumigated for them. For the average Indian home on Pine Ridge, she observed, this would come to about $1.00 to upwards of $1.50.[72]

From these examples, one may draw the conclusion that the Lakotas of Pine Ridge simply approached and respected the OIA out of habit. After all, the OIA had ruled their reservation, and many aspects of their lives, for more than a half-century. It would seem logical for them to have developed the habit of turning to the OIA for matters like those mentioned above. Perhaps, one might presume, the people of Pine Ridge did not turn to the new Oglala Sioux Tribal Council because they were not used to doing so. To the contrary, however, there is evidence to show that they clearly understood the OSTC was at the bottom of the federal pecking order: when people did not find suitable redress with the OIA, they did not turn to the OSTC as their second source of help and wisely so, for this probably would have been rather fruitless. Instead, recognizing the federal chain of command, Lakotas often moved *up* the ladder instead of down and solicited help from their congressional representatives and even their U.S. senators in an attempt to go over the OIA's head. The record indicates that Lakotas understood it was these men, not the OSTC, who could exert some pressure on the OIA on their behalf when the Office had failed to render decisions to their liking.

Joseph Rooks of Kyle applied to the OIA in 1939 for a federal loan to purchase livestock. The program to which he applied offered monies to Indians for such purposes, but there was not enough for everybody who desired it, and the current policy was to give larger loans to a select few who could muster larger enterprises. Rooks was turned down. Unhappy with the OIA's decision, he made his feelings known to U.S. Representative Francis Case from South Dakota, who was not only Rooks's congressional representative, but also a member of the very important and very relevant House Appropriations Committee. Case took up the matter, writing to Superintendent Roberts on Rooks's behalf. In response, Roberts sent a letter to Rooks, clarifying the reasons for the rejection and justifying the decision in writing. Rooks forwarded this response from Roberts to Case, who again beseeched the superintendent. Case observed that Rooks already had land and machinery in place, requiring only a team to get started, but he was currently unable to work without one. "[I]f there is a chance of this man getting started for himself," Case wrote, "it would seem possibly advisable to try and furnish him with a team." The Congressman was diplomatic, but partisan. "You may have known all of these things when the application was considered, but if not, I am passing them along to you for whatever possible effect they might have on the case." Roberts responded directly to Case in July. He again justified his decision to decline Rooks based on the policy's design, but this time he left the door open, stating, "so far we have found it necessary to decline Rook's application. We hope, however, to be able to take up his case out of further allocations."[73]

Indeed, it would seem that Case's intervention had its desired effect. The OIA staff on the reservation took care to help Mr. Rooks re-apply for the loan, making sure the forms were properly filled out (all six copies of them) and filed. Finally, an undated, handwritten memo implies that Case's involvement had not been in vain, suggesting that Rooks received $140 for a team of mares and $100 for two milk cows.[74]

The evidence that Representative Case's involvement was the reason for the apparent reversal is circumstantial. However, it is virtually inconceivable that the OSTC could have fomented a similar outcome. Furthermore, the case of Joseph Rooks was not an isolated one. Other Lakotas appealed to Congress, not the OSTC, when attempting to go over the head of the OIA.

In 1940, Paul War Bonnet of Porcupine also approached Congressman Case for help in acquiring a federal loan to develop his land, which was located on the Rosebud and Cheyenne River Reservations, as well as Pine Ridge. Case again contacted Roberts on his constituent's behalf. Roberts responded by explaining the loan program to War Bonnet and directing him to an OIA representative who could help him apply. And when Frank A. Eccofey's request for a loan was rejected in 1942, he went all the way to the U.S. Senate to seek redress. Invoking passionate, patriotic rhetoric shortly after America's entry into World War II, he reminded South Dakota Senator Chan Gurney that all Indians had been made U.S. citizens by federal legislation in 1924 and that Pine Ridge had, "250 Indians boys fighting for democracy." Furthermore, Ecoffey felt he was very qualified to acquire livestock and offered references. How was it, he demanded to know, that white men could get loans from the Farm Security Administration but he could not? "I want to be put on equal basis as my white friends," he demanded. Gurney forwarded Ecoffey's complaint to the commissioner of Indian affairs. The assistant to the commissioner responded by demanding a report from the superintendent of Pine Ridge explaining why Ecoffey's loan had been rejected.[75]

In 1934, John Collier had assured full-blood Oglala chiefs Frank Fools Crow and Charles Red Cloud in no uncertain terms that reorganization would drastically change the politics of Pine Ridge. "You cannot make requests to the agency," he insisted. "This will be handled by an organized government of your own called the tribal council."[76]

Collier's public statements aside, during the first decade of the IRA-sponsored Oglala Sioux Tribal Council's existence, the Office of Indian Affairs did in fact maintain its position of authority on Pine Ridge. Controlling and influencing institutions as widespread as finance, education, land tenure, and the law, the OIA's presence was necessarily and actively one of penultimate political power, subject only to the superior government authority further up the federal ladder. It is no wonder then that as early as 1937 Senator Lynn J. Frazier of neighboring North Dakota was vociferously criticizing the IRA. Frazier claimed that despite Collier's promises of limited self-government for Indians, the OIA was now actually curtailing home rule instead of promoting it. The senator was so disillusioned that he even introduced legislation to repeal the IRA altogether, though the bill quickly foundered.[77]

Furthermore, although the OIA had promised the people of Pine Ridge that the new tribal council would return to them a substantial degree of sovereignty, Lakotas on the reservation saw through the tatters of this threadbare pledge. From the beginning of the Tribal Council era in 1936 through World War II, Pine Ridge Oglalas continued to appeal to the OIA on any number of issues, including the OIA itself.

In the summer of 1944, Noah Tall of Manderson was displeased with the work of Field Aide Peter Cummings. Specifically, Tall felt that Cummings played favorites, was overbearing, arbitrary in his decision making, and generally abused the powers of his OIA office. Cummings had also rebuffed Tall's efforts to spend money in his IIM account, which had been generated from selling his own land. Why? Tall wanted to pay for his son's return home from the war, but this was not a pre-approved expenditure in his IIM budget, and Cummings had dogmatically rejected this discretionary spending request. In an angry, handwritten letter to Superintendent Roberts, Tall rhetorically demanded to know who had "given almighty power" to Cummings? The superintendent responded, defending Cummings' record and assuring Tall of the aide's fairness. "Any reasonable request for funds which will be helpful to you in carrying on your operations will, I am sure, be recommended by Mr. Cummings and approved by me," Roberts concluded.[78]

Of course, as Noah Tall was no doubt well aware, it was entirely up to Roberts and his OIA staff to determine the meaning of "any reasonable request."

4

"Detrimental For the Best Interests of the Sioux People"

The First Ten Years of the Oglala Sioux Tribal Council

DESPITE THE PASSAGE of the Indian Reorganization Act (IRA) in 1934 and the subsequent formation of the Oglala Sioux Tribal Council (OSTC), the Office of Indian Affairs (OIA) had retained most of its authority on Pine Ridge Reservation. In so doing, the OIA effectively mitigated the OSTC's political presence. Furthermore, this was not a case of imperceptibly veiled federal power, shrouded behind a curtain in the shape of the OSTC; to the contrary, the people of Pine Ridge were quite aware of the political realities that framed the reservation and their lives.

However, it is important to note that the OSTC was not completely devoid of power. Rather, it was able to advance its own agenda at times, which from the outset frequently represented the interests of a small elite. The Council was almost completely subordinate to the OIA, but could move forward on its programs when the OIA did not prevent it from doing so. In other words, the OSTC was able to govern up to a point: as much as the OIA allowed. An investigation of local politics on Pine Ridge Reservation during the first decade of the OSTC's existence (1936–1946) verifies this observation.

The early IRA era on Pine Ridge featured a political landscape in which there were a multitude of interested parties and a complexity of agendas, almost to the point of convolution. The only consistent factor was the welfare of the Oglala people and how it was alternately advanced and deterred in this political landscape.

The goal of this chapter is to elucidate the political scenario on Pine Ridge during the period in question. The method for accomplishing this will be to examine the politics of the reservation itself. Rather than looking at the reservation as a place where Washington, D.C., simply manifested its Indian policy, Pine Ridge will be accepted as a political entity in its own right, with internal political dynamics and a variety of political influences that spring from within as well as without. So doing will not only provide a fuller understanding of the political situation on the reservation through those early IRA years, but it will also provide the context for interpreting the reservation's politics twenty-five years later, on the eve of the Wounded Knee occupation.

Two formal political institutions on Pine Ridge will be studied in detail: the new Oglala Sioux Tribal Council and the federal government's Office of Indian Affairs acting through its resident superior official, the superintendent. The OSTC had any number of different members during this time frame and three different chairmen, most notably its initial chief executive, Frank G. Wilson. There was but one superintendent during this period, William O. ("W. O.") Roberts.

These were (and still are) two very important political institutions on the reservation. However, they are not the only ones. Three other factors in particular will come into play. First are the Oglala Lakota people themselves, unhappy with the OSTC either because the council did not always act in their interests (or worse, acted against their interests), or because they did not accept the institution's legitimacy, seeing it as a foreign imposition from Washington, or some combination of those two factors. Oglala people were also often dissatisfied with the superintendency. While the superintendent is charged with operating in the interests of the Lakota people, he in fact does not *represent* their interests. This is an important difference. The superintendent, in short, is the federal government's colonial administrator on the reservation, the immediate representative in the pyramid of federal suzerainty. In reaction to this political situation, Lakota people have acted, either individually or through a variety of grass roots political organizations, to effectuate positive changes during the last sixty-five years.

Second are non-Natives. Often motivated by economic interests and frequently employing racism to justify their exploitation of Native lands, resources, and people, they may be individuals living on the reservation itself or within close proximity to it, or they may even be large, distant corporations.

Finally, there are American political institutions other than the federal government's executive branch. Just as the federal government has supremacy over the states in dictating Indian policy, the Supreme Court and Congress may also directly affect a reservation through their actions. And to the extent that the federal government allows it, state governments too may affect reservations within their boundaries. In this case, that is South Dakota.

The OSTC and the superintendency, as noted, shall be given the most consideration. But these other political players are also important, particularly the Oglala people, for whose benefit these political institutions supposedly exist. Consequently, all will receive proper and appropriate attention.

PINE RIDGE SUPERINTENDENT WILLIAM O. ROBERTS

W. O. Roberts was not new to the job of reservation superintendent when the OIA appointed him to that position on Pine Ridge in 1936. In fact, he was not even new to working with Lakota people or Pine Ridge itself. Immediately before coming to Pine Ridge, he had served as superintendent at the neighboring Rosebud Reservation which is also in South Dakota, was once part of the Great Sioux Reservation and is largely home to Sichanghu (Brule) Lakota people. Before that, he had been the OIA's chief clerk on Pine Ridge during the mid-1920s, the tail end of the assimilation era.[1]

Roberts' immediate predecessors in the Pine Ridge superintendency were E. W. Jermack and James H. McGregor. Jermack had been highly dictatorial, going so far as to forbid the annual Sun Dance, a central component of Lakota religion. Jermack had made the decision out of sympathy for local whites who feared that Sun Dancing would encourage Indians to go "on the warpath again." To his autocratic ways the agent added micromanagement. During his tenure, he required Oglalas to obtain passes personally signed by him before they could physically leave the reservation.[2]

McGregor was a kinder man, with a strong streak of paternalism, and he also opposed the idea of Pine Ridge adopting the IRA. But Collier's administration considered it to be an important reservation because of its large size and population. Roberts was more sympathetic to the IRA, and he also had a strong professional rivalry with McGregor. Roberts won out and replaced McGregor as superintendent in 1936, shortly after the reservation voted to reorganize. He had snagged the leadership of a reservation that was considered a prize plum within the Indian office because of its size.[3]

Indeed, Roberts had been the agent of Rosebud when that reservation had also voted to accept reorganization. The OIA had judged his tenure on Rosebud to be successful, and not merely for his efforts in securing passage of the IRA. He had also been active in community development, looking for ways to incorporate the traditional Lakota tiospaye in social and economic development projects.[4]

In the traditionally decentralized sociopolitical structure of Lakota life, the *tiospaye* is the basic form of organization. Commonly thought of by Euro-Americans as an extended family group, a tiospaye was originally comprised of one or more *wico tipi*, or groups, that camped together. A wico tipi itself could be as small as two tipis, but was usually larger. Theoretically then, a tiospaye could range in size from a scant two tipis of a single wico tipi (unusual), to a dozen or more tipis among several wico tipi, with all of the members related either by blood, marriage, or adoption.[5]

Roberts' approach as agent of Rosebud, exemplified by his attempt to incorporate tiospayes into federal development projects, was in line with Collier's ideas. The commissioner generally advocated a program of Indigenous cultural revival and the rejuvenation of traditional social forms. OIA bureaucrats noticed Roberts' efforts on Rosebud and gave him high marks. His reward was a coveted transfer to the adjacent Pine Ridge Reservation where the transition to reorganization had not gone as smoothly.[6]

Roberts mirrored the commissioner in one other important aspect. He believed that in order for Native people to improve their economic situation, they had to recapture control of their land. Collier's Indian New Deal had finally ended further allotments, the policy that had divided reservations into individually owned parcels. The commissioner had also hoped to bring about a stringent land reform policy that would result in the consolidation of most reservations' acreage in the hands of the new tribal councils. As discussed previously, Collier had been largely thwarted in this attempt when Congress omitted certain relevant provisions in the Wheeler-Howard Act's original draft. Nonetheless, he still used his executive power to make up for the legislation's shortcomings wherever he could.[7]

Collier became aware of the specific problems of Indian land tenure and fractioning on the five Lakota reservations located wholly within the bounds of South Dakota when he attended the Glacier Park Land-Tenure Adjustment Conference in August of 1938. As a result, he organized a conference in 1941 for all of the OIA field personnel and Washington officials associated with those five reservations. The "primary purpose" of the conference, according to Collier, was to make these federal employees aware of "the importance of the speedy correction of the land-tenure maladjustments on these Sioux reservations" and the need to simplify and consolidate the highly fractioned pattern of land ownership. "I cannot emphasize too strongly the urgent necessity of producing results in the field of land-tenure and land-use adjustments," Collier told those at the conference. Producing such results, he declared, would "in large part be the measure of the reservation administration's success or failure."[8]

W. O. Roberts concurred with the commissioner. He too believed that the control and use of reservation resources by Native people was the key to improving their social and economic situation. "The policy of the Pine Ridge Office," he stated, "is to put the land back into the use of the Indian people as rapidly as the Indian people are ready and anxious to use their land."[9]

Thus, after coming to Pine Ridge, Roberts used his position as superintendent to develop a model project that combined these two ideals: to rejuvenate traditional Lakota social forms, particularly the tiospaye, and return control of reservation resources to Native people. His flagship project to these ends was known as the Red Shirt Table Cooperative.

The Red Shirt Table community is an area of roughly 300 square miles in the northwestern part of Pine Ridge. It was settled in the early days of the reservation by two tiospayes led by Red Shirt and Two Bulls. Later on, the Tubuas tiospaye also became prominent. By the early twentieth century, the community had developed a fairly successful ranching enterprise. However, it was economically ravaged by the end of World War I. The downfall of Red Shirt Table community ranching occurred from a combination of corrupt OIA officials and land-hungry white settlers who gained access to the land and began to farm the area. After initial profiteering, the outside interests eventually faltered in the face of a postwar drop in agricul-tural prices, a deterioration of environmental conditions, and the onset of the Great Depression. By 1936, the Red Shirt Table community had regained access to some of its land, but retained only a smattering of live-stock and little in the way of infrastructure; even the houses were in disre-pair.[10]

When Roberts decided to develop a model for social and economic rehabilitation on Pine Ridge, he selected Red Shirt Table specifically because it was in a severe state of economic disarray when he arrived and because the tiospaye system there was still strong. Even before Collier's appearance on the scene, Roberts had spent a year studying the tiospaye system with OIA anthropologist H. Scudder McKeel. Now, as Pine Ridge superintendent, he worked with a committee comprised of Native people and representatives from such federal agencies as the Agricultural Exten-sion Service and the Soil Conservation Service to set about organizing the Red Shirt Table Cooperative.[11]

Anticipating friction between local full bloods and mixed bloods, Roberts divided Red Shirt Table into two components: a cattle-raising cooperative operated by nine full-blood families, and a gardening and housing construction venture for eighteen mixed-bloods families. In addi-tion to the cooperatives, there would be a nearby federal day school on the Cheyenne River. While membership in either group was strictly voluntary, the full-blood organization would be designed with an informal structure that left room for elements of traditional Lakota governance to emerge. The mixed-blood organization was organized with a tighter, formalized struc-ture that would be more appealing to people interested in modeling their efforts on America's mainstream corporate and political cultures.[12]

By keeping the operation small in scale, Roberts was able to maintain real authority: he could plan, coordinate, and supervise the project in a hands-on manner. This meant, in part, that Red Shirt Table would serve not only as a model for community development on Pine Ridge, but it would also be a project that was designed, developed, and maintained by the Office of Indian Affairs, not the new Oglala Sioux Tribal Council. Although the superintendent had encouraged the people of the Red Shirt Table community to participate in the planning of the cooperatives, he had hardly abdicated the role of the OIA. And once the project was underway, he made sure that the Office, particularly through its educational institutions, continued to shape and even directly participate in the venture.[13]

For example, before placing the cooperative's goat herd on its own land, the animals were originally maintained at the new federal day school. This was also the case with the turkey flock, which was initially funded by the extension division and tended to by the school's teacher. While Roberts's goal was to see the people of Pine Ridge become economically self-sufficient and socially cohesive, he nonetheless felt that Lakota people lacked more than just adequate capital and control of their land. The superintendent shared not only Collier's ideas on social and economic rejuvenation, but also a large measure of the commissioner's infamous paternalism. Roberts believed Lakotas were largely ignorant of the possibilities and means necessary for their betterment. With regard to achieving that betterment, he proclaimed, "We feel that it is entirely an educational procedure." To that end, he continually tried to tie his development programs directly to the federal education system.[14]

To help get the project off the ground, the federal government bought land by the Cheyenne River and built a small dam and irrigation system that watered 130 acres. In 1942, Roberts declared the project a success, and it seems that there was some merit to his claim. One year later, the thirty-five participating families at Red Shirt Table owned 130 acres of irrigated gardens that supplied produce, a community canning kitchen where the surplus was preserved, livestock worth $60,000, and a poultry operation that brought in $2,000 per year. In addition, the cooperative, along with the OIA, had participated in the erection of seventeen new buildings and the rehabilitation of numerous others. Included was a brand-new school house, which also functioned as a community center.[15]

The success of Red Shirt Table was not permanent, however. Sharing and generosity are an important part of Lakota culture and a central component of the tiospaye system. For the full-blood families, feeding less prosperous relatives generally took precedence over decisions to grow and maintain their herds. Meanwhile, mixed-blood families were very successful at acquiring more land for their operations, but a more individualistic outlook encouraged them to divide the cooperatives' capital among themselves. Under these circumstances, it was not long before the Red Shirt Table Cooperatives were defunct.[16]

The historian Graham D. Taylor sees Superintendent W. O. Roberts as an energetic and creative government official, someone who was genuinely interested in using his office to benefit Native people, rather than simply seeing it as another mundane administrative task. To bolster this view, Taylor cites praise that Roberts received from two prominent OIA employees, Ben Reifel and H. S. Mekeel.[17]

On the other hand, anthropologist Thomas Biolsi views Roberts as an entrenched federal bureaucrat with no commitment to the concept of Indigenous sovereignty, a man who was "clearly hostile in principal to tribal self-government." Biolsi also cites another OIA employee, Flathead tribal member D'Arcy McNickel, whose assessment of Roberts contrasted with those of Reifel and Mekeel. For his part, McNickel felt that Roberts had neither a good grasp on, nor a firm conviction in, the notion of Lakota self-government.[18]

The main reason for the divergent opinions between these two scholars is that they are interpreting Roberts through different lenses. Taylor examined the superintendent in light of his efforts to bring about economic reform. Biolsi saw him as an OIA administrator who was frequently at loggerheads with the new Oglala Sioux Tribal Council, and who occasionally used his position to trump the council.

Lakota Benjamin Reifel, who was just beginning his life-long OIA career at the beginning of the Collier regime, worked with Roberts on many occasions. On the one hand, he respected Roberts as a "very brilliant fellow" and an efficient administrator. For example, when Roberts came over from Rosebud Reservation, he astutely brought with him his unofficial lieutenant, Charlie Brooks, a fluent, bilingual, full-blood Oglala. Brooks frequently spread Roberts's messages more effectively than he ever could have himself. However, Reifel also felt that the superintendent was aloof and "autocratic" and did not have any real confidence in Indian self-government; according to Reifel, Roberts believed that Native people needed him more than he needed them. W. O. Roberts was, in short, an effective administrator who delegated very well, but who had no strong connection to Native people and preferred to keep them at arm's length, to the point of not even wanting them to come to his office. As for his true motives, those remain unknown, though it is worth noting that toward the end of Reifel's own illustrious career, he observed that every superintendent "had one eye on the tribal council and one eye on where he was going to land next." These were career men.[19]

THE OGLALA SIOUX TRIBAL COUNCIL

"WHEREAS; The Oglala Sioux Tribe of the Pine Ridge Reservation in South Dakota is [a] recognized Indian tribe organized under the constitution and by-laws ratified by the tribe on December 14, 1936, pursuant to section 16 of the Act of June 18, 1934 (48 Stat 378) as amended by the act of June 15th 1936 (49 stat 378) now, be it therefore resolved by the Oglala Sioux Tribal Council."[20]

The above legal jargon is typical of the language incorporated into the ordinances and resolutions of Oglala Sioux Tribal Council during its first decade (and, indeed, even to this day). It is clearly modeled on American legalese rather than any aspect of traditional Lakota legal culture, much less the Lakota language. This particular phrase was the opening clause to the fourth resolution the council passed on February 20, 1937. The resolution itself empowered the Oglala Sioux Tribe to create a law and order code for Pine Ridge Reservation. The quoted section refers specifically to the OST's establishment under the auspices of the 1934 Indian Reorganization Act, federal recognition of Pine Ridge's acceptance of the IRA by the binding referendum, and the OST's subsequent federally approved constitution and bylaws.[21]

The OSTC was first seated in 1936, shortly before Superintendent Roberts' transfer to Pine Ridge. The council was composed of nineteen members from seven districts and chaired by a non-voting ex officio chairman (or president). In addition to the general council, which met quarterly, there was an executive council that met weekly. The executive council was comprised of the chairman and vice chairman (or vice president) who were elected in a reservation-wide election, and a secretary, treasurer, and fifth member who were drawn from the tribal council and elected to their positions by their fellow council members. In addition to chairing the tribal council, the president also chaired the executive council. The chairman, like the rest of the board, served a two-year term. The first tribal chairman of the Oglala Sioux Tribe was Frank G. Wilson.

In 1937 and early 1938, much of the Oglala Sioux Tribal Council's efforts was channeled into establishing itself as a governing body, and the Oglala Sioux Tribe as a sovereign political entity. These efforts can be divided into two categories: the establishment of bureaucracy and the raising of funds. Other than instituting a law-and-order code, the OSTC tackled such issues as establishing a hierarchical relationship with the reservation districts and their local councils, nominating junior tribal judges, appointing tribal police, retaining a tribal attorney, assuming control of land the OIA purchased on its behalf, and authorizing the treasurer to collect money on behalf of the OST.[22]

The OSTC set out to establish itself as a governing body and create the OST as a political entity more or less from scratch. It was a mountainous task. The new government had to overcome a severe shortage of resources as well as the apathy that much of the reservation felt toward their initial endeavors. Councilmen like Thomas Conroy had not even bothered to actively campaign when running for office during the early years. The Wounded Knee District, a stronghold of resistance of the IRA, flatly refused to even participate for the first few years. Once the body began to meet, most members traveled to meetings as Henry Standing Bear did, by horseback or wagon. They would pack their bedrolls and sleep on the floor for the duration of the session.[23]

Perhaps not surprisingly, more than half of OSTC's legislative actions during this period were designed to either raise money or outline how its members would be paid. In fact, the first resolution the council ever passed, on May 1, 1936, fixed the per diem and mileage reimbursements for its executive members: five dollars per day and five cents per mile for the chairman, vice chairman, secretary, and treasurer when engaged in official business, in addition to the monthly paycheck that all council members brought home (the aforementioned executive members receiving substantially higher pay than the rest of the council).[24]

The council also passed a variety of measures to raise funds, twenty-three in all. They included a land tax of $10–20 on all commercial interests; a 1 percent gross tax on business by insurance salesmen and motor vehicle dealers; a $1 fee on every lease approved by the superintendent; a $15 annual fee on all salesmen, livestock dealers, and well-diggers; an "amusement tax" of 5 percent on rodeos and fairs; $10 on all district celebrations; and the mandating of annual hunting and fishing licenses ($1 for Pine Ridge residents, $2 for non-residents). There was also a $5 fee, "for each machine electrically equipped," and used for commercial purposes, and even a $1 licensing fee to any "circus or other firm taking Indians from the reservation."[25]

What did the council do with this revenue? The vast majority of its expenditures were for the salaries, per diems, and mileage reimbursements of the council's various members, particularly the executive committee. For example, in the 1942–1943 fiscal year, the OST generated $5,189 of income (exclusive of federal sources). All of it was earmarked to be paid out in per diems to tribal council members, particularly the executive committee. Any nominal funds that might be left over in a given year generally went toward covering the basic costs of setting up the government: no more than $100 to furnish tribal junior judges and police officers with books, files, furniture, and the like; $15.36 for the purchase of sixteen tribal police badges; and $26.40 for a like amount of billy clubs.[26]

With few sources of income in its early years, the OST was always on the verge of bankruptcy. For example, in January of 1943 the tribe did not have enough money to pay its judges, and operations temporarily shut down. After huddling with Superintendent Roberts, the council shuffled its finances and worked out a new payment system designed to reduce costs. Some judges would now be paid on a piecemeal basis instead of a regular salary. For example, a judge might receive two dollars per case depending on the nature of the case. The judges resumed work under the new system in February, and the tribal police were soon being paid in a similar manner.[27]

With the Oglala Sioux Tribe up and running, even if barely, the major question yet to be answered was the following: how would the new council fit into Pine Ridge's political landscape? The new OSTC had very little power in relation to the Office of Indian Affairs. But this does not mean it had no power whatsoever. To the extent that the superintendent was interested in nurturing Commissioner John Collier's vision of limited Indian self-government, the council would be able to employ its authority. New superintendent W. O. Roberts, as noted above, did share Collier's ideology to a large degree, though careerism seems to have tempered his philosophy. Therefore, a moderate ideological predisposition could have led him to encourage the council to act as a sovereign entity. However, Roberts also seems to have been genuinely concerned at some level about the welfare of Native people, regardless of what one may think of his actual job. Thus, to the extent that the new council might act with disregard for the welfare of the Lakota people, Roberts would be more hesitant to let the council indulge its limited prerogative. In fact, it would be this very dichotomy that was destined to shape much of the reservation's politics during the period from the council's inception through the end of World War II, the years that roughly coincide with Roberts' superintendency.

As a series of complex cultural conflicts on the reservation subsequently mushroomed into political conflicts, Roberts found himself increasingly pitted against the council as time went by. Guided by his desire to guard the welfare of the Lakota people, albeit paternally so, he was increasingly concerned that the new Oglala Sioux Tribal Council did not act on those same priorities. Thus, the superintendent's commitment to Indian self-government would come to be tested in ways that he perhaps did not anticipate.

FULL BLOOD / MIXED BLOOD DYNAMICS

In the aftermath of the OSTC's establishment, a pre-existing rift on the reservation worsened. The post-1936 era witnessed a political conflict between full bloods and mixed bloods (see chapter 2 for a discussion of these terms and their complexities). Many mixed bloods generally disparaged traditional Lakota culture, advocated assimilation into the mainstream of American culture, and immediately dominated the new tribal council. Many full bloods, also known as "old dealers," (as opposed to those who embraced the tribal council system introduced by the New Deal) frequently cast aspersions on the OSTC's legitimacy, advocated a more traditional form of government, and pointed to the 1868 second Treaty of Fort Laramie for legal sanction.[28]

The decision over whether to reorganize under the IRA had exacerbated this cultural rift on Pine Ridge. As previously noted, many of the landed, full-blood advocates of traditional Lakota government had opposed reorganization, while many landless, mixed-blood advocates of assimilation into American society had supported it. Once reorganization was under way, this division continued to rend the reservation. From the outset, many full bloods were concerned that landless mixed bloods might usurp the new system of government, using it as a vehicle to advance their own agendas. It was not long before antagonisms between the two groups infected the tribal council system.[29]

The assimilationist mixed-blood class generally had more social and economic clout on the reservation. As early as 1937, Leon Clements compiled a statistical study of the disparity between full bloods and mixed bloods in terms of housing, health conditions, and economic status. His findings reveal that there was a scale to the overwhelming poverty of the reservation. Specifically, full bloods were at a significant disadvantage in comparison to mixed bloods in all three categories (see tables 4.1–4.3).[30]

Full bloods, looking to incorporate elements of traditional Lakota government into the new system, were foiled from the start. When the debate arose over how to organize the new Oglala Sioux Tribe, full bloods called for a system based on tiospayes. OIA anthropologist H. Scudder Mekeel had championed this approach in 1936, and new superintendent W. O. Roberts was somewhat sympathetic to the idea. His positive views of community organizations led him to promote tiospayes' socio/economic self-sufficiency, as at Red Shirt Table. And while superintendent of Rosebud, he had personally pushed to have that reservation's IRA tribal council successfully divided among its tiospayes. However, in the end Roberts felt the tiospaye system on Pine Ridge had dilapidated to the point that it was now too weak to use as a model for organizing the OST. Instead, he advocated a Euro-American form of organization: districts based on geographical boundaries. His about-face may have been based in a sober analysis of the situation, but it also lends credence to the contention that his earlier support for tiospayes may have been driven more by a desire to curry favor with Collier than by his personal philosophy. The idea of district-based sys-

TABLE 4.1

Housing Quality on Pine Ridge Reservation, Distribution by Ethnicity: 1937

	Good Homes Number (Percent)	*Fair Homes* Number (Percent)	*Poor Homes* Number (Percent)
Full Blood	8 (2.0)	108 (28.0)	249 (70.0)
Three-Quarters	4 (3.6)	36 (33.0)	67 (63.4)
One-Half	9 (5.5)	76 (47.0)	77 (47.5)
One-Quarter	24 (10.2)	104 (54.4)	63 (35.4)
Less than One-Quarter	24 (28.0)	51 (57.0)	13 (15.0)
All	69 (7.5)	375 (41.2)	469 (51.5)

Source: L. E. Clements, "Possibilities of Rehabilitating the Oglala Sioux" (M.A. thesis, Colorado State College of Education, 1938), 17.

TABLE 4.2

Economic Status of 913 Lakotas on Pine Ridge Reservation, Distribution by Ethnicity: 1937

	Owning 160 Acres Number (Percent)	Using Their Land Number (Percent)	Over $250 Accumulated Number (Percent)	Earn >$90 at least 1 month Number (Percent)	Rec. Sioux Benefit Number (Percent)	Rec. Pro Rata Share Number (Percent)
Full Blood	201 (55.0)	69 (18.9)	92 (25.2)	18 (4.9)	209 (57.0)	274 (75.0)
Three-Quarters	63 (58.8)	19 (17.6)	26 (25.0)	13 (12.0)	71 (66.0)	107(100.0)
One-Half	80 (49.4)	24 (14.8)	43 (33.4)	24 (14.8)	88 (54.3)	137 (90.7)
One-Quarter	116 (60.7)	29 (15.0)	51 (26.7)	57 (29.8)	140 (73.3)	180 (94.2)
< One-Quarter	61 (69.3)	8 (9.0)	30 (34.0)	43 (48.0)	46 (52.0)	88 (100.0)
All	520 (56.9)	149 (16.3)	242 (26.5)	155 (17.0)	274 (62.8)	786 (86.0)

Source: L. E. Clements, "Possibilities of Rehabilitating the Oglala Sioux" (M.A. thesis, Colorado State College of Education, 1938), 37.

TABLE 4.3

Health Status of 913 Lakotas on Pine Ridge Reservation Expressed in

Percentages, Distribution by Ethnicity: 1937

	Suffered from *Acute Illness*	*Living in Poor* *Health Conditions*
Full Blood	29.0	70.0
Three-Quarters	38.0	63.0
One-Half	20.0	48.0
One-Quarter	16.0	35.0
< One-Quarter	15.0	15.0
All	24.0	46.0

Source of Information: L. E. Clements, "Possibilities of Rehabilitating the Oglala Sioux" (M.A. thesis, Colorado State College of Education, 1938), 48.

tem was also supported by government lawyer Benjamin Reifel, who was himself Lakota. "I just don't think the tiospaye business as a government unit . . . had very much viability by this time," he observed a number of years later. Though Reifel's father was German, he had been raised by his mother in the Hollow Horn Bear tiospaye on Cut Meat Creak. Mekeel acquiesced, albeit unenthusiastically.[31]

Instead of a sociopolitical delineation based on the tiospaye, the reservation was divided into seven voting districts[32] based on the federal government's old boss farmer (farm agent) stations. Ironically, these sites had originally been established for the distribution of rations and other treaty proceeds. As the distribution sites were converted into farm stations, their boundaries followed the watersheds that ran from north to south, cutting Pine Ridge into vertical swaths. With an organization based on colonial geographic borders instead of Indigenous political culture, it was not long before both Lakotas and federal OIA personnel began to speculate that subsequent problems with the OSTC resulted from the fact that it did not reflect the Oglala political organization.[33]

With the new system in place, the worst fears of many Lakota full bloods began to take shape. The council was dominated by its chairman, Frank G. Wilson, a man whose motives were not necessarily in the best interests of the Pine Ridge citizenry. Wilson was a mixed blood who had obtained an allotment in 1906 while living in Lawrence, Kansas, hundreds of miles from Pine Ridge. Although his maternal grandmother had an allotment in the reservation community of Porcupine, he chose to settle in the southeastern part of the reservation, which was soon opened to homesteaders, re-organized as Bennett County, and placed under the jurisdiction of South Dakota during the 1911 land cession (discussed in chapter 2). His election in 1936 set a precedent of mixed bloods dominating the new presidency, interspersed with the occasional full blood who was highly articulate in English. Wilson's rise to power was helped immeasurably by his political expediency. Though he had few connections to the full-blood community of Pine Ridge, he was bilingual (English/Lakota) and had showered full-blood voters with promises of how he would "turn the Indian agency inside-out." While Wilson would certainly create a series of firestorms, they were not what most people had had in mind.[34]

Chairman Wilson's conduct in tribal council meetings was in line with neither the ethos and protocol associated with traditional Lakota government that many full bloods would have preferred, nor with the rules of parliament and corporate decorum that the OIA would have preferred. More fluent in English than most of the council, he used this to his advantage to run roughshod over them. He routinely exceeded the boundaries of his office, going so far as to have the council occasionally pass resolutions despite not having enough members present for a quorum. He acted without proper sanction from the council, ignored the council's decisions, interfered with the judicial process, and even threatened the treasurer and other council members with physical violence. In short, he was loud, boorish, and autocratic.[35]

Mixed-blood domination of the new system threatened the impoverished full-blood community in a variety of ways. At times, Wilson's council (as well as subsequent ones) persecuted traditional Lakota culture. At other times, it worked to the economic detriment of the full blood community as Wilson sought to profit from his position.

A symbolic gesture came on February 18, 1937, when the council decided that all of its meetings would be held in the town of Pine Ridge. Pine Ridge village was, and is, the largest town on the reservation of the same name. But it was also fairly inaccessible to many people living in more rural areas as it is located in the southwest corner of the reservation. More importantly, as described by anthropologist and Pine Ridge resident Paul Robertson, the town was "a largely mixed blood settlement that grew up around the Bureau of Indian Affairs." Thus, selecting it as the permanent site of all tribal council meetings set a certain tone.[36]

Another symbolic gesture concerned the fate of bison on the reservation. The buffalo is an integral part of traditional Lakota culture. Having once been the most important natural resource to Lakota people living on the Great Plains, it is also a central component to Lakota religion. So when the council made several efforts to rid the reservation of bison, it was at the very least an indication of how far removed the new government was from the values of many of its constituents. On October 28, 1942, the council voted to remove all bison from tribal land. The following year it voted 11–7 to turn the Pass Creek buffalo pasture over to cattle. And a unanimous vote championed the same fate of the buffalo pasture north of the town of Allen. "Whereas, it is believed that the operations of the buffalo herd does not contribute materially to the best economic development of the tribe," the council stated in 1944, "[T]he tribal council hereby authorizes and instructs the Superintendent of the Pine Ridge Indian Agency to take such steps as necessary to terminate the activities of the buffalo herd."[37]

When the council passed a vague ordinance in the summer of 1938 that required a two-dollar licensing fee to be collected from people who offered, among other things, "extracts, [and] remedies," it had the potential to regulate traditional Lakota medical practitioners. And a resolution of the same year declared that the council would "protest, object and demand prohibition of pre-inca, stone age, or other North American *uncivilized* [emphasis added] practices of Oglala Sioux now exhibited for show and amusement purposes off the Pine Ridge Indian Reservation." For this council, the showcasing of traditional Lakota culture off-reservation was clearly less an issue of labor and cultural exploitation, and more a concern of embarrassment. Many mixed bloods did in fact consider traditional ways to be "uncivilized." Wilson dismissed the traditionalists as "unlettered tribesmen" and claimed that tiospayes were based on communism, a notion that is even more bizarre than the "pre-inca" reference in the 1938 resolution.[38]

Wilson often called full bloods "ration Indians," a derisive reference to their reverence for the second Fort Laramie Treaty of 1868, their eligibility for Sioux Benefit money, and an accusation of laziness. The irony of this attempted belittlement and stereotyping is that mixed bloods were generally just as likely as full bloods to receive Sioux Benefit money (see table 4.2). The chairman's animosity was so pronounced that he tried to deny the validity of full-blood participation in the reservation's governance. "We also object to ration Indians [who] take the liberty of representing non ration, progressive, intelligent members of the Oglala Sioux Tribe in matters of vital tribal importance," he declared. He went on to characterize them as "peyote users, those who receive pensions and those who receive rations. They are afoot, do not own stock and are not earning their own living."[39]

As might be expected, many full bloods reciprocated the antipathy. In 1938, Amos Red Owl wrote a letter to CIA John Collier in which he objected to mixed-blood domination of the tribal council system and questioned the validity of *their* participation in the tribal government. "They are white people, essentially, they are no more Indian than you . . . [There] should be some separate provision excluding [them] from the benefits of the [Indian Reorganization] Act. They make too much trouble on the reservation."[40]

Such mutual antagonism had the potential for serious political and economic repercussions. The case of the Corn Creek Cattle Association is exemplary. The association was a cooperative ranching venture located in the community of Corn Creek in the northeastern end of Pine Ridge. Made up of mostly full bloods, the Association ran a herd of 760 cattle over their own land, which they had pooled together, helping to fund the operation with a reimbursable loan from the OIA. The association was doing well, and Superintendent Roberts had approved their expansion through a lease of adjacent, unalloted land. Members of the Association then approached Wilson's council in November 1939, to get OSTC approval of the lease. Wilson stalled them on a technicality. He also hid from them, and the rest of the council, the fact that he had entered into secret negotiations with a mixed-blood rancher named Emery Amiotte. Wilson had already offered the land in question to Amiotte, despite the fact that the man lived forty miles away.[41]

When Roberts had federal workers fence off the land for use by the Corn Creek Cattle Association, Wilson personally intervened, directing the foreman to stop work. Roberts then pulled rank on Wilson, ordering the workers to resume. When Wilson sent a self-righteous letter to Congressman Francis Case, he framed the dispute as an instance of unnecessary government regulation and demanded the firing of a Roberts lieutenant, OIA Extension Department Manager Russell Coulter. In his letter, Wilson mentioned neither Amiotte nor Corn Creek.[42]

One can only speculate as to Wilson's real motivation for favoring Amiotte: kickbacks, bribery, cronyism, racism, or perhaps a combination thereof. Regardless, the tribal chairman was clearly at odds with the full-blood residents of Pine Ridge, and used manipulation, threats, intimidations, legal technicalities, and patronage, not to mention the inherent power of his office, to control the new IRA government and further his own ends. Moreover, Wilson was also increasingly at odds with Superintendent Roberts, whose own agenda to foster the economic and social rejuvenation of the reservation's full-blood communities clearly contrasted with the tribal chairman's agenda.

After Corn Creek, another battle between the two men erupted over the Blue Lands Plan, a sweeping proposal made by the superintendent. Using a blue pen to outline demarcations on a map of Pine Ridge, Roberts identified the land around almost 1,600 Oglala Lakota homes on the reservation, which he sought to exclude from leasing to outside interests. Roberts' intention was to return control of the land and its attendant resources to the Oglala people. While many Indians still owned land (see table 4.2), full bloods were more likely to lease it out for a pittance of its value. In contrast, mixed bloods or non-Indians more often had enough capital to undertake a commercial venture. The Blue Lands Plan had the potential to affect about 75 percent of the families on Pine Ridge. Understandably, it was a very popular proposal among the Oglala people. By Roberts' own count (biased though it may be), only some twenty families among all those potentially affected were opposed.[43]

The Blue Lands Plan may have received the overwhelming support of the Oglala Lakota people, but it was obviously anathema to the ranchers who leased these lands from Indians, usually for a fraction of its real value. It would seem that if the OSTC were interested in helping the people they represented, they would have favored the plan. And in fact, most of the members of the council did support it. Chairman Wilson and Vice Chairman Harry Conroy, however, did not. Once again, they sided against the interests of the full bloods, and indeed, many mixed bloods as well, and stood with a small minority of Pine Ridge mixed bloods and a number of outside interests who were profiting from the status quo at the expense of most of the Oglala people. In fact, Wilson generally refused to entertain motions in council that sought to so much as recognize the very existence of tiospaye communities.[44]

THE CONFLICT WIDENS

It had not taken long for Chairman Wilson and Superintendent Roberts to develop a mutual antipathy. When Wilson had first won election as the inaugural chairman of OST, previous Superintendent James McGregor was preparing to step down. Wilson had presumed that as the new chairman, he would simply run the tribal operations out of McGregor's old office. So he moved in. When Roberts arrived on the reservation and walked into his office to find Wilson's proverbial boots on his desk, he made no attempt at diplomacy. He angrily ordered Wilson to pack up and get out *post haste*. Roberts had been affronted. Wilson was humiliated. It was not a good start to the relationship.[45]

One of the first tasks Wilson and the new Oglala Sioux Tribe had faced was the issue of whether the OST should incorporate. Incorporation was the third step of the IRA process, following reorganization and adoption of a constitution and bylaws. If Pine Ridge voted in favor of incorporation after yet another reservation-wide referendum, the OST would receive a non-profit corporate charter from the federal government and qualify for certain federal loans. By now, however, resentment was building among many Oglalas, and their resolve against having more government policy pushed on them grew. Collier was not there to harangue them personally this time. Instead of a looming authoritarian figure, the OIA representative in charge of promoting incorporation among Northern Plains tribes was one of their own: Benjamin Reifel. Though born on Pine Ridge, Reifel's credibility on the reservation was by now compromised. Many Oglalas viewed him as an OIA Indian, and his influence was minimal. The real job of pushing for incorporation therefore fell to Roberts and Wilson, both of whom supported the idea.[46]

Living in the shadow of allotment's failures, many full bloods now worried that the new loan programs offered through incorporation would lead to land forfeiture. Although the loans were guaranteed by the federal government, one could hardly blame Oglalas for their skepticism given their experiences of land loss during the preceding decades. Opposition to the charter was led by Ben American Horse, son and namesake of the famous Oglala leader. Momentum against the charter built as the process dragged on. In the end, it went down to defeat as Oglalas rejected the third part of the IRA in yet another referendum.[47]

Thomas Conroy, a mixed-blood councilman who had supported the charter, attributed its failure to the unfounded worries of full bloods over potential law suits, land loss, taxation, and debt. He felt the OIA needed more time to make its case. Roberts, on the other hand, blamed Wilson for the charter's failure. He believed that the chairman's alienation of full bloods had led to its demise; most full bloods did not trust Wilson and instinctively opposed any cause he championed. The already-shaky relationship between the superintendent and tribal chairman worsened, and it never recovered. It would not be long before they were locking horns in episodes such as Corn Creek and Blue Lands.[48]

With minimal full-blood participation in the new tribal council system, Wilson was re-elected to a second consecutive term as chairman in 1938. An OIA audit later that year revealed that the chairman had embezzled more than $200 dollars of OSTC funds. This may seem like a trivial amount by modern standards, but one must remember that this represented a tremendous sum of money when considering both the dire financial situation on Pine Ridge (described in chapter 3) and the fact that the figure represented approximately 5 percent of the OSTC's entire annual budget, virtually all of which was already directed toward compensating the council's members.[49]

Superintendent Roberts used this situation as ammunition in his widening political imbroglio with Wilson. He disclosed the details of this transgression to the old dealers, the full bloods who were at odds with Wilson's council. They in turn used the information to bolster their argument that the entire OSTC should be abolished and the IRA constitution scrapped altogether. They organized a petition drive to that end and garnered more than 1,000 signatures. They even organized a delegation, which visited John Collier to make its case. OIA representatives on the reservation feared that if a referendum were held on the matter, the constitution would be abolished. Predictably, the OIA never sanctioned such a move. However, the affair did contribute to Wilson's eventual impeachment.[50]

As the new political situation on Pine Ridge continued to unfold, there was fear in Washington, D.C., that the Oglala Sioux Tribal Council would, if left to its own devices, persecute indigenous religious institutions and leaders, exceed the boundaries of its new constitution, mismanage its finances, indiscriminately remove and appoint the reservation's OIA personnel, and even proscribe political opposition. The first of these fears was realized in 1942.[51]

In February 1942, the OSTC passed an ordinance making peyote contraband. Possession or sale of the plant would warrant a penalty of up to six months in jail. Another resolution in April added a fine of up to $360. This was a blatant attack on the Native American Church, which employs peyote as a religious sacrament. The church is an intertribal religion chartered and recognized by the U.S. government. Superintendent Roberts was concerned that the proposed ordinance amounted to an unconstitutional attack on the freedom of religion guaranteed by the First Amendment. However, he simultaneously speculated that the OSTC might not be subject to the authority of the United States Constitution since it was a sovereign government. Nonetheless, he invoked his authority under the Indian Reorganization Act to veto the measure.[52]

The veto meant that, after a ninety-day waiting period (ending July 16), the council could petition the commissioner of Indian affairs to review the case. This they did, and CIA John Collier received the Oglala Sioux Tribal Council's request for secretarial review on August 5. However, Collier did not act, implementing something akin to a pocket veto; he did not forward the matter to the secretary of the interior for consideration. The council's attempt to override Roberts' veto thereby foundered, and the resolution died. The possession of peyote on Pine Ridge Reservation would not be a crime.[53]

The council was nonetheless adamant, and they continued to pass new versions of the resolution. As they repeatedly faced rejection from federal authorities, mixed-blood efforts to persecute an Indigenous religion became entangled with issues of tribal sovereignty. Undoubtedly egged on by at least some of the many Christian churches on Pine Ridge Reservation whose leaders viewed the Native American Church as competition, the OSTC unanimously passed a similar ordinance the following year. It became the fourth anti-peyote bill that Roberts vetoed. As the council predictably overrode his veto, debate within the OIA and the department of the interior concluded that while the ordinance was within the discretionary power of the OSTC, it challenged the first amendment to the U.S. Constitution and contradicted Commissioner Collier's wider policy concerning religious freedom for Indigenous people. Consequently, when Collier finally passed the resolution forward, the secretary of the interior upheld Roberts' veto. In a letter to the council, the secretary advised the council that the department would consider a revised ordinance that made allowances for the use of peyote in religious services.[54]

This case offers a perfect example of the dichotomies and ironies inherent in the new system. On one hand, the tribal council system, which had been founded to benefit Native Americans, was being turning against them. On the other hand, despite all of the previous ballyhoo about the IRA restoring Native sovereignty, the Oglala Sioux Tribal Council's authority was mitigated by the superintendent, the commissioner of Indian affairs, and the secretary of the interior. The Indian Reorganization Act had not returned any real measure of sovereignty to Indigenous nations. Rather, it simply incorporated them into the pyramid of the federal government's executive branch, which flowed downward from the president to the interior department to the Office of Indian Affairs. And as the OSTC was frequently run by men whose own agendas differed from that of the OIA, tension increased between the council, local Oglalas, and the superintendent.

During his first nine years as superintendent of Pine Ridge Reservation, which were also the first nine years of the Oglala Sioux Tribe, W. O. Roberts had tangled with the tribal council on numerous issues that had the potential to affect substantial numbers of people. It is perhaps ironic then, that his downfall came over a dispute about one person, a wrangle over a government employee. The request for Roberts' removal resulted from a power struggle over reservation personnel. ˙

As 1945 began, some council members were unhappy with OIA employee Hilda Livermont. They felt she was slow in attending to her duties, particularly in disbursing leasing revenues and that she spent too much time volunteering for the Red Cross. Worse yet, she was allegedly, "discourteous to members of the Oglala Sioux Tribe." So stated the resolution they passed asking that she be replaced.[55]

Despite his battles with the council, over the years Roberts had often withheld his veto power and signed off on numerous ordinances and resolutions he disagreed with. When he had exercised his veto on the peyote issue, it was after much deliberation and with the encouragement of the OIA. Now the council was asking him to fire one of his own employees. This is where he drew a line. Roberts vetoed the resolution.

At the April 10–13 session of the OSTC, the council voted 19–1 to override the veto (two-thirds being required). At the same session, they passed Resolution 259. It read in part:[56]

> Whereas: to retain Mr. Roberts here as Superintendent would not only be detrimental to his best interests, but also detrimental for the best interests of the Sioux people, and, the Re-Organization Act. That to retain him would only cause disunity and friction among the council members, the sioux people and the Indian office in Washington, D.C. and the Chicago office. The council and people feel that Mr. Roberts, has not fulfilled the obligations of his office for the best interests of the Interior Dept. controlling the Indian Service. That the council has a right to judge the Indian Service on how well it meets its tasks of readjusting itself in its relation with our tribe. That the citations discussed will be followed by affidavits, statements, etc. or furnished to the proper authorities upon investigation for the immedieate [*sic*] removal of Mr. Roberts.[57]

The resolution was followed up on April 30, 1945, when OSTC Secretary Matthew High Pine wrote a letter to new Commissioner of Indian Affairs William H. Brophy (Collier had recently resigned after the death of President Franklin Roosevelt). In it, he requested that the CIA investigate Roberts for possible removal.[58]

One historian has attributed it to increasing bitterness over his experiences with the council and despondency over his wife's ongoing illness. Perhaps it was political astuteness. Either way, Superintendent W. O. Roberts chose not to veto the resolution that asked for his removal, though it would have been within his discretion to do so. The OIA transferred Roberts from Pine Ridge shortly thereafter, and he had a promotion and a pay raise to show for it. He became the Office of Indian Affairs area director for Eastern Oklahoma and later for the Northern Plains area before retiring in the mid-1950s[59]

CONCLUSION

Anthropologist Paul Robertson casts Superintendent Roberts heroically as someone who attempted to fight off the vested interests of racist white ranchers who leased Indian lands for their own ranching enterprises while offering Lakota people little in the way of compensation. In contrast, anthropologist Thomas Biolsi judges Roberts as a man who was "clearly hostile in principal to tribal self-government." The truth is perhaps somewhere in the middle. It seems that Roberts was committed to the ideal of *limited* sovereignty, but found himself in a situation where the new government was not always acting in the interests of the people, and he was torn by the dichotomy. A perfect example of Roberts' efforts to moderate his own control over the council can be seen in the issue of alcohol.[60]

Though alcohol had been banned on all reservations by federal decree, the new IRA tribal councils now had the opportunity to formulate alcohol policy for themselves. Consequently, in 1946 the Oglala Sioux Tribal Council voted to repeal the ban, calling it "a discrimination against the Indian citizen of the United States." On the surface, the resolution seems like a simple case of the Oglala Sioux Tribe asserting its sovereignty. After all, the United States' constitutional prohibition of alcohol had been repealed some thirteen years earlier. However, alcoholism was a serious problem on the reservation, even with the ban in place. Indeed, it would continue to be a problem in the years and decades that followed. Many feared that a repeal would lead to a degeneration of social and economic conditions. And given the OSTC's history of ulterior motivations during its first decade, one can only wonder who stood to gain by the new reservation business. Knowing all of this, Roberts still did not veto the resolution. Rather, he signed it but attached a letter stating why he believed it was in the best interests of the reservation to maintain the ban.[61]

Thomas Biolsi has interpreted the Red Shirt Table cooperative and other ventures like it as signs of an expanding federal presence and influence during the New Deal. This is not inaccurate. As discussed previously, the government's presence on Pine Ridge did increase during this era, as it did on most reservations. Indeed, the New Deal witnessed an expansion of the federal government's presence throughout most of the country. It is also vitally important to note, as Biolsi does, that W. O. Roberts was still functioning in the capacity of an ambitious colonial administrator. However, there is more to the story surrounding the political situation on Pine Ridge. Projects like the Red Shirt Table Cooperative, the Corn Creek Cattle Association, and the Blue Lands Plan also represent the efforts of a superintendent who was more interested in, attuned to, and sympathetic toward the needs of the traditional Lakota people than many of the mixed-blood men who ran the OSTC. This may mean that Robertson was only the champion of Oglala full bloods by default, but it was nonetheless the case.[62]

Part of the reason why Biolsi has misinterpreted some of the political disputes of the early IRA era can be found in his use of blood quantum figures. As he points out, the majority of the early councils' members were "full bloods" if one uses the term strictly to describe genetic descent. He therefore presumes that the council spoke for the interests of the full-blood people. But the issue is not one of blood quantum per se. Rather, it is a question of representing constituencies. Lineage, of course, is not a binding factor in someone's outlook. People are, after all, human beings. Thus, a person like Matthew High Pine, an OSTC executive committee member with no European descent, could vote for the elimination of the bison reserve and act as an instigator in the removal of Superintendent Roberts, while a mixed-blood council member like Peter Dillon could deride Chairman Wilson for being dictatorial.[63]

Paul Robertson has assessed the complexities of the situation differently. He notes that while it is true that the early councils were composed mostly of full bloods, they were dominated by a mixed-blood chairman and vice chairman, Frank G. Wilson and Harry Conroy, respectively. Robertson does an effective job of employing an interpretive model of a culturally cross-bred colonized elite. He asserts that this colonized elite acted as intermediaries between the colonizer and the colonized while competing with the colonizer for local control so that they could profit at the expense of the colonized. In this context, he paints an in-depth portrait of the OSTC's initial chairman as someone who not only worked to line his own and his friends' pockets at the expense of full-blood, traditional Lakotas but also went so far as to actually resent, patronize, and despise the traditional Lakotas, deeming this large portion of his constituency to be stubborn, backward-thinking, and dangerously ignorant. Given the council's general impotence in the shadow of the OIA and its questionable motives and activities when it did employ its limited governing powers, is it any wonder that many Oglalas resented and bypassed the OSTC? Even Biolsi notes the instance of one Lakota who was given to appealing directly to the superintendent for assistance in his affairs, and who was intransigent toward suggestions that he might find redress with the OSTC.[64]

However, one should not take this as an apologia for Superintendent Roberts or the Office of Indian Affairs. From the above narrative, it would be possible to conclude that the OSTC was composed entirely of self-interested mixed bloods who worked to the detriment of the reservation's Lakota people, while the federal government was a beneficent entity that, on behalf of the full bloods and through Roberts, valiantly battled the Frankenstein political monster of its creation. This, of course, would be a grossly inaccurate portrayal. In 1984, Benjamin Reifel offered Biolsi the following anecdote about Roberts. "Joe Jennings and I stopped in to see him about something and was he going to consult the tribal leaders on something, and he said why should I? We were disappointed." Reifel went on to describe Roberts as cold. "He had no feeling that way for Indian people."[65]

On the one hand, there were, at any given time, a number of honest, well-meaning members of the Oglala Sioux Tribal Council who worked diligently and fairly on behalf of the people, members like Guy Dull Knife, Sr., who represented the Medicine Root District over the course of four different decades and worked hard to combat the mixed-blood cultural influence and to benefit the traditional people of the reservation.[66]

On the other hand, the federal government was not always a benevolent force in the lives of Native people. Somewhat typical of the Progressive Era heritage of John Collier and his administration, Roberts had a fairly condescending view of the people he was trying to help, and this was frequently reflected in his actions. Moreover, the ambiguous gestures of an individual OIA representative such as Roberts were never as important as the overarching policies crafted in Washington, D.C. The federal government had created and more or less foisted the entire IRA system of government upon the Lakota people. Beyond that, the colonial officials in Washington continued to make decisions that directly affected the lives of Pine Ridge residents, and not always for the better.

One feature of the relationship between tribal councils and the federal government clearly demarcates the flow of power: the structural hierarchy. Tribal councils grew out of federal legislation. Congressional legislation and executive enactment is the source of their legitimacy, and the provisions of that legislation subordinate the councils to higher federal officials: the reservation superintendent, the commissioner of Indian affairs (now known as the assistant secretary of the interior for Indian affairs), the secretary of the interior and, at the top of the pyramid, Congress, the U.S. Supreme Court, and the president. Tribal council decisions are not only subject to potential veto by the reservation's superintendent, but also require the approval of the Interior Department's assistant secretary for Indian affairs (CIA) and secretary, all of whom are themselves executive appointees. Furthermore, in 1903 the Supreme Court established Congress's plenary power over Indian nations with its rather spurious decision in *Lonewolf v. Hitchcock*. It states that Congress has the power to unilaterally legislate on behalf of Native people, regardless of the objections of Native people, or even the mandates of treaties that might otherwise explicitly forbid Congress from passing such legislation. In other words, Congress can do whatever it wants, Indians be damned.[67]

And in the end, the IRA itself is nothing more than a piece of federal legislation. In theory, Congress could abolish the entire system tomorrow with a countering piece of legislation. In fact, this nearly came to pass less than three years after the IRA's passage. In March 1937, two senators, Lynn J. Frazier of North Dakota and one of the bill's own sponsors, Burton K. Wheeler of Montana, put forth legislation that would have overturned the Indian Reorganization Act altogether. The senators had diametrically opposite criticisms of the IRA but could unite in their displeasure with it. Frazier believed that the IRA's promises of Indian self-government had been hollowed by OIA interference. Burton, on the other hand, complained that the IRA was interfering with the assimilation of Native peoples into the American mainstream. He claimed to have been mislead about the bill's actual purpose, which he believed would be limited only to administrative and economic concerns. That two powerful critics, one claiming the IRA did too much and the other that it did too little, could be equally outraged is perhaps a testament to Collier's centrist goals. While the IRA did beat back the cultural tenets of assimilation to some extent, it in no way represented an end to colonialism, but rather a modification of colonial policies.[68]

Thus, as we discern the nuances of Pine Ridge's political landscape during the early IRA-era, we find a pyramid of power. At the top was still the federal government, operating through the Office of Indian Affairs, most immediately its superintendent, William O. Roberts. Beneath this we find the Oglala Sioux Tribe, governed by the Oglala Sioux Tribal Council, a political entity created by the federal government and whose very existence was contentious; many Oglala Lakotas did not want it in the first place, and its agenda was often set in favor of the interests of a local, mixed-blood elite and non-Indians from within and even without the reservation. Beneath this, at the very bottom of the structure, we see the traditional, full-blood

Lakota people who, despite having some representation on the OSTC, found their real political power severely curtailed within the new tribal council. And as the council continually did little for them, or at times even acted in a manner that was deleterious to their interests, full blood Oglalas sought redress time and again from the colonizing authority, the OIA; the Office had retained most of its power and, ironically enough, was often more sympathetic to their situations than their own elected officials.

By the early 1970s, however, the scale would tip. The federal government would still be the strongest political participant in the equation. But the government would eventually come to side with the OSTC, openly supporting the OST in its ongoing dispute with the full-blood people of Pine Ridge Reservation.

Pine Ridge children milling around a federal reservation day school, 1940.
Courtesy National Archives, photo no. RG 75-N PR-42.

An Oglala woman applies mud plaster insulation to the creases in her
log cabin, 1940. The cabin is typical of Indian housing on
Pine Ridge during this era.
Courtesy National Archives, photo no. RG 75-N PR.

Lakota men gather on Pine Ridge for the distribution of surplus federal food, 1940. Food from the federal government is commonly known as "commodity."
Courtesy National Archives, photo no. RG 75-N PR-71.

The Oglala Sioux Tribal Court in session, 1940.
Courtesy National Archives, photo no. RG 75-N PR-70.

Commissioner of Indian Affairs John Collier posing for a portrait, ca. 1940. The impact of Collier's long tenure (1933–1945) was profound. His devotion to indirect colonialism led him to design the Indian Reorganization Act.
Courtesy National Archives, photo no. 75-N-WO-36.

James H. Red Cloud, 1940s. He was named for his grandfather, the famous nineteenth-century Oglala leader who signed the second Treaty of Fort Laramie (1968) and led his Lakota followers to settle on the part of the Great Sioux Reservation that would eventually become Pine Ridge. James Red Cloud was an advocate of traditional Oglala politics and religion.
Courtesy National Archives, photo no. RG 75-N PR-21.

Pine Ridge Oglalas Jake Herman (r.) and Ben Chief at a Sun Dance, 1956. Herman served on the Oglala Sioux Tribal Council from 1952 to 1956, 1960 to 1962, and 1964 to 1970, and he was twice a member of its executive committee. Chief was the son of American Horse, an Oglala leader and outspoken opponent of accepting the IRA on Pine Ridge.
Courtesy National Archives, photo no. PS-B-56-4572.

Benjamin Reifel, 1962. As a young man. Reifel became enamored with the IRA and worked on Collier's behalf to promote it among his fellow Lakotas. He went on to serve as the first Indigenous Superintendent of Pine Ridge Reservation (1954) and a Republican Congressman from South Dakota (1961–1971). Shortly thereafter he became the last commissioner of Indian affairs before a BIA restructuring caused the position to be renamed assistant secretary of the Interior for Indian affairs.
Courtesy National Archives, photo no. PSD-62-4154.

Part II

1 9 7 0 – 1 9 7 3

5

The Next Wilson

The Transition from Gerald One Feather to Dick Wilson

THE FEDERAL LANDSCAPE

INDIAN REORGANIZATION ACT-sponsored governments, like the Oglala Sioux Tribal Council (OSTC), had been formed on reservations throughout the country during the mid-1930s. And while the Wheeler-Howard Act remains a binding piece of federal legislation to this day, the ascendancy of the Truman and Eisenhower administrations during the post–World War II era witnessed a shift in federal Indian policy that sent shock waves through much of Native America. The policy, known as termination, raged from the late 1940s until the mid-1960s.

The basic thrust of termination was the federal government's attempt to divest itself of treaty obligations to and trust responsibilities for Native Americans. To achieve this, federal politicians targeted a number of reservations for "termination." Tantamount to a fatal attack on tribal sovereignty, their proposal would have incorporated reservations into the American body politic by transforming them, for example, into national parks or counties within states. The result would have eliminated any especial tribal rights or positions, regardless of previous treaties, laws, and/or court rulings. Political supporters of termination tried to frame it as a move toward

Indian self-determination; they declared that removing the meddlesome Office of Indian Affairs (OIA) from Indians' lives would free them to do as they wished. While the OIA may have been very broken, the honorable thing to do would have been to fix it, not throw it out altogether. Given the treaty status of Native nations, they should have a federal liaison. The real motivation of termination's advocates was not the welfare of Indian peoples but merely cost-cutting and a desire to go backward; termination was the mid-twentieth century's version of assimilation. By dissolving reservations and severing the federal government's obligations to American Indians, terminationists hoped that Native peoples would simply melt into the mainstream. The policy is generally acknowledged today as an unmitigated disaster. Fortunately for the residents of Pine Ridge, their reservation was not terminated.[1]

By the mid-1960s, the tide of federal Indian policy was turning away from termination. On October 13, 1966, South Dakota Senator George McGovern, a member of the Senate Indian Affairs Subcommittee, addressed his colleagues. From the floor of the Senate he lauded the Indian Reorganization Act (IRA) and urged Congress to adopt a new policy statement on Indian affairs. While he was clearly opposed to termination, and he bandied about phrases like "self-determination," "self-help," and "grass roots," McGovern was not really pushing for true Native sovereignty. Rather, he was espousing an updated approach to the Indian New Deal. He was not interested in dismantling the colonial framework. He merely voiced a need for "greater participation and cooperation of the Indians themselves in the government's efforts to improve their well-being." In light of termination's spectacular failures, he could posit a return to Collieresque concepts as a step forward. But in fact, McGovern was not even completely opposed to the termination of the tribes' trust status, just the "arbitrary" nature with which it had been handled. When tribes were ready to be terminated, he said, "orderly plans should be developed to relieve the Federal Government of further responsibility for their welfare."[2]

After concluding his speech, McGovern offered a resolution that encapsulated many of his neo-Collierist ideas. While the resolution itself died in committee, his effort had helped set the tone for a shift in federal policy away from termination and back toward embracing IRA ideals.[3]

Less than seventeen months later, on March 6, 1968, Lyndon Johnson became the first president in the twentieth century to send an address to Congress that dealt specifically with American Indian issues. Entitled "The

Forgotten American," the speech offered a new policy direction that the president referred to as self-determination. He announced a forthcoming executive order to create the National Council on Indian Opportunity, a collection of various Native leaders and presidential cabinet secretaries who would review federal programs and make recommendations. He also proposed reforms in Indian education, health care, economic development, civil rights, and reservation infrastructures. The address was reminiscent of the general tone permeating Johnson's Great Society programs. However, only twenty-five days later he announced that he would not seek re-election. His lame duck status precluded any real changes for the remainder of his term in office.[4]

For most Americans, the legacy of Johnson's successor, Richard M. Nixon, has been seriously tarnished by his handling of the war in Southeast Asia, his involvement in the Watergate scandal, and his subsequent resignation from office, not to mention his easily targeted personality traits, such as a noticeable lack of charisma and a deep grain of paranoia. Thus, given his general lack of posthumous esteem, it may strike some as being ironic that, when compared to the presidents who preceded and followed him, Nixon may have done more than any of them to mitigate the U.S. government's colonial authority over American Indian nations and restore a small modicum of their sovereignty in a manner not entirely dissimilar to the efforts of former Commissioner of Indian Affairs John Collier.

Nixon's policies and actions should not be confused with a movement to *eliminate* American colonial authority over Indians. In the larger picture, Nixon made no such move. No president ever has. Rather, within the context of maintaining colonial authority, he sought to reduce certain elements of direct control in favor of more indirect administration. As Philip S. Deloria has stated, the move from termination to self-determination, which Nixon oversaw, "reflects only a tactical shift in the fundamental commitment to bring Indians into the mainstream, not a movement toward a true recognition of a permanent tribal right to exist."[5] Moreover, as will be shown later, Nixon's administration severely hampered Native rights in other important ways. Nonetheless, within the context of this study, the Nixonian shift to self-determination is worth observing to the extent that it affected the local politics of the Pine Ridge Reservation.

After his victory in November 1968, President-elect Nixon followed Johnson's lead by making a speech of his own concerning Indian affairs. He railed against "unwise and vacillating federal policies" and outlined a new program that would repudiate termination and foster economic development with input from Indian people. Upon taking office, Nixon kept the policy moniker of self-determination intact and expanded its vision. In so doing, he offered the first constructive policy shift on how the federal government should relate to tribal governments since the passage of the IRA some thirty-five years prior. On July 8, 1970, Nixon sent a special message to Congress insisting that the legislative body issue an official renunciation of termination. Furthermore, he stated that tribal governments, not the Bureau of Indian Affairs (BIA), should have control of Indian education, federal credit, and other federally funded programs. He also pushed for the restoration of tribal lands where possible and for the establishment of an independent source of legal council that would have no conflict of interest in representing Indian claims against the government.[6]

Nixon's message to Congress had been written in part by Louis R. Bruce, the president's new commissioner of Indian affairs. Bruce was born in 1906 to Ganiengehaga (Mohawk) and Oglala Lakota parents on the Onondaga Indian Reservation near Syracuse, New York. He had taken office on August 8, 1969, after an extensive search for a candidate who was politically palatable to the new administration. He expanded Nixon's vision by announcing his own goals in November 1970. He wanted to replace the BIA's management-oriented agenda with one that was more geared toward serving Indian people. He sought to make Bureau offices more cooperative, extend aid to off-reservation Indians by using Native organizations as intermediaries, and reaffirm the trust status of Native lands instead of "terminating" them. Perhaps most threatening to many of the BIA's careerist bureaucrats, Commissioner Bruce wanted to offer Native nations the opportunity to bypass the Bureau altogether in some instances; instead of exclusively relying on BIA administration, tribes would now have the opportunity to contract directly with the federal government for certain services.[7]

To assist him in his planning, Bruce chose a group of advisers that came to be known as the "Young Turks." They were mostly young Native Americans and BIA outsiders who favored radical policy shifts designed to restore Native sovereignty to a degree beyond anything Nixon had outlined in his speech. The forward thinking iconoclasm of the Young Turks, combined with the nature of Bruce's reforms, which seemingly threatened the authority and security of many BIA bureaucrats, created a fair amount of resentment against the new commissioner within his own Bureau and from some members of the Nixon administration.[8]

In April 1971, Bruce involved himself further in issues of tribal sovereignty by starting to work closely with a new intertribal organization, the National Tribal Chairman's Association (NTCA). He worked with the group to establish the new system of direct contracting between tribes and the federal government. Resentment over Bruce's new policies bubbled within the Bureau. Some bureaucrats, who were disgruntled at watching part of their own duties syphoned off to the tribes, justified their recalcitrance with racist paternalism. They maintained that Indians were simply incapable of handling their new responsibilities.[9]

The emerging political backlash to Bruce's ideas was soon compounded by changes within the Department of Interior hierarchy. Secretary Walter G. Hickel, who had supported Bruce's innovations, was forced to resign toward the end of that year over matters unrelated to Indian affairs. His replacement, Rogers C. B. Morton, was a politician who proved to be less flexible, less open, and less innovative than his predecessor. He was also antagonistic toward Bruce. One of Morton's first attacks was to appoint as Deputy Commissioner of Indian Affairs John O. Crow, who himself had thirty years of experience in the Bureau. Crow mimicked Morton's own conservative views and had the bureaucratic credibility and political support to effectively undercut Bruce. As will be shown in the next chapter, Bruce was about to be caught between a political rock and a public hard place.[10]

THE PINE RIDGE LANDSCAPE

"The Indian doesn't like to go back to the farm," Pine Ridge Oglala Jake Herman said of his fellow reservation denizens in the summer of 1967. The effort to acculturate Lakotas into the American agricultural economy had wrought few, if any, benefits for most full bloods. Herman himself had gained regional notoriety during the first half of the century as a rodeo clown. But he had seen increasing numbers of Oglalas leave the reservation in search of jobs in far away cities. Economic salvation, as he and many others reckoned, would be found in creating those same jobs on the reservation. "What they [Oglalas] need is factories . . . we need employment here."[11]

However, by 1968, the economic condition of Pine Ridge Reservation had not substantially changed for the better. The internal economy of the reservation had not developed much during the intervening quarter-century. It still lacked the infrastructure and capital needed to generate substantial revenue or to create jobs. A federal report noted that industrial development was hampered by the reservation's distance from potential markets, a detriment compounded by a deficient transportation system.[12] The report described housing on the reservation as a "critical problem." It also noted that while 92 percent of Indian-owned land was used for cattle raising, the business was dominated by outsiders because most Pine Ridge Lakotas did not own enough land or contiguous land to partake in this enterprise; leasing was still predominant. During the 1960s, using a sustainable ratio of sixteen acres of reservation grazing land per head of cattle, ranchers could expect an income of about seventy-five cents per acre. Thus, about 250 head of cattle roaming over 4,000 acres were necessary to provide sufficient income for one family. However, among Pine Ridge Indians that still owned land, about 60 percent of them owned less than 180 acres, enough for only about eleven head of cattle. As a result, many who had held onto their land continued to lease it at undervalued rates to outside interests.[13]

Other sources of income were not readily forthcoming. Unemployment rates on the reservation were still consistently over 50 percent. In 1970, the people of Pine Ridge collected over $600,000 from the federal government's General Assistance program (welfare), or nearly $50 for every man, woman, and child. In 1971, Pine Ridge Superintendent Brice Lay called unemployment "the greatest single obstacle to real social progress" on the reservation. And the following year, one tribal official had no compunction about telling the BIA that "the Tribe is in critical financial condition at the present time." The problem was bad enough that many Oglalas were forced to take their entire families off the reservation to work seasonally as migrant farm laborers. Lay decried the typical situation of "a large family traveling around the country, working for low wages, and usually living in undesirable housing, and returning to the reservation—sometimes after school has begun—with no money and sometimes without a home to move into."[14]

The federal government still supplied more than half of the jobs and most of the capital on the reservation. The annual federal budgets for Pine

Ridge during the late 1960s and early 1970s generally approached $10 million, about half of which supported Bureau of Indian Affairs operations. The BIA employed more than 200 people, the Office of Economic Opportunity nearly as many, and the Public Health Service close to a hundred. In addition to these federal mainstays were a myriad of grants, loans, and programs designed to study conditions, develop infrastructure, and achieve any number of ends.[15]

In 1972 alone, the Economic Development Administration (EDA), an office within the Department of Commerce, poured close to a half million dollars into Pine Ridge's economy by funding three public works projects, two technical assistance projects, and three planning grants. Most of the money went into building an industrial park, developing an airport, and constructing a sewage treatment plant. Of the three, only the park had any positive economic impact: a moccasin factory had created 180 new jobs. One hundred seventy-five of the employees were Indian, though perhaps predictably, the plant supervisor was not. One hundred seventy of the employees worked on a piece-rate basis, generally earning between $1.80 and $2.40 per hour and generating about $708,000 of overall income (less than $4,000 per person on average). And even at that, as the EDA itself noted, the building of the industrial park had failed to improve "the ability of the tribe to secure financing for development projects." Since 1969, the factory had been owned by a company from New Mexico, and before that by a company from Wisconsin. This of course meant that it largely provided low-paying wage labor, while the profits left the reservation. And the industrial park as a whole attracted no other outside businesses.[16]

The airport and sewage plant were even less successful. The EDA had spent nearly $200,000 on improvements to the reservation's airfield by the end of the 1960s. Though the Oglala Sioux Tribe (OST) owned the small airport, which boasted two runways (one lighted, one not), the BIA performed all maintenance, and the tribe had not created a formal organization to run the airport. It was used mostly by BIA personnel and private citizens with private planes (needless to say, this excluded the overwhelming majority of Pine Ridge Oglalas). By 1972, the airport had failed to produce any of the 200 jobs for which the tribe and the EDA had originally hoped. The new sewer lagoon and outfall line was completed by 1969. The federal government had contributed $142,500, and the Oglala Sioux Tribe had put forth $800 and land. It had no direct economic impact, but it had improved living conditions and allowed for the construction of 100 new homes in the mostly mixed-blood town of Pine Ridge.[17]

As one would expect given the severely depressed reservation economy, commercial services were minimal. The village of Pine Ridge had two grocery stores and two service stations. Other villages, such as Porcupine and Manderson, might have nothing more than a single grocery store, if that. There were five cafes scattered about the reservation's 4,350 square miles. Non-reservation border towns, particularly across the Nebraska state line just to the south, supplied most of the goods and services required by reservation residents, despite the fact that hardly any of those towns had a population nearly as large as Pine Ridge's 13,000 people. Lakotas were also largely excluded from the few successes there were in Pine Ridge's commercial sector. Of 124 total businesses on the reservation in 1972, only twenty-one of them were Indian-owned, with another six co-owned by Indians. The other ninety-six, or nearly 80 percent, were owned by non-Indians.[18]

The Oglala Sioux Tribe's economic development plan was typical of a third world nation, focusing on attracting outside capital to develop natural resources (specifically land). The BIA actively encouraged the OST to pursue economic development along those lines. The moccasin factory was the most successful of numerous efforts to lure outside businesses. Representatives of the Omni Corporation, a Minneapolis-based electronics company, visited Pine Ridge in August 1968 and decided to build a plant there. However, this was atypical. It was more common for the few companies that visited Pine Ridge to tender no offer to move there. Over all, unemployment was still high, and Pine Ridge residents usually had to leave the reservation for semi-permanent and seasonal positions, rather than working on the reservation.[19]

For example, in September of 1968, the same month that Omni announced it would set up in Pine Ridge, sixty-six Pine Ridge men took mostly seasonal jobs cleaning, canning, packing, stacking, and loading tomatoes for the H. J. Heinz Company in Muscatine, Iowa. Another twenty-five took three- to four-week positions harvesting and processing corn at two plants in Minnesota. The latter group had to pay their own transportation to and from Minnesota (reimbursable only if they worked the whole season) while earning $1.60 per hour. Another thirty men spent two months at the end of the year harvesting 225,000 Scotch Pine Christmas trees in Cadillac, Michigan. Most ironic was the situation of five Pine Ridge Oglalas (along with fifty-four Lakotas from Rosebud Reservation) who left for Mexico in October to work on the set of the motion picture *A Man Called Horse*, where they portrayed Lakotas, supposedly on the northern Great Plains during the nineteenth century.[20]

PINE RIDGE POLITICS

Politics on Pine Ridge remained contentious. Friction was ongoing both between the Oglala Sioux Tribal Council and the Bureau of Indian Affairs, and between the council and the people. For example, when the biennial election was initially scheduled for January 23, 1968, the council tried to cancel it by challenging the validity of primary elections held the previous December. BIA Superintendent Brice Lay stepped in and declared the primaries valid and ordered the general election to go on as scheduled. The council appealed to the secretary of the interior, who upheld Lay's position, and the election was rescheduled for March 5. After all was said and done, Enos Poor Bear had been elected chairman for the 1968–1970 term of office, succeeding Johnson Holy Rock.[21]

Tribal Council elections were not only frequent (every two years), but also given to resulting in great administrative upheaval because of their unstaggered cycles. Election cycles for the federal government of the United States, in contrast, are strategically staggered to avoid such problems. For example, the United States constitution mandates that congressmen be elected every two years, the president every four years, and senators every six years. And within the Senate, there are never more than approximately one-third of the seats up for election at one time. Such staggering serves to foster the kind of personnel overlap and institutional memory that are needed to maintain a certain level of order and continuity. The Oglala Sioux Tribal Council on the other hand is plagued by an all-encompassing election cycle. Every two years, every member of the council, including the president, vice president, and members of the executive committee, is up for election. This is a tremendous hindrance to continuity, especially when one considers that IRA governments do not have an executive branch that is separate from the legislature. Nearly forty years after foisting the tribal council system on Pine Ridge, the federal government admitted that such dramatic administrative turnover was "extremely disruptive of any planning or development process on the Reservation."[22]

As was usually the case with OST chairmen, Enos Poor Bear proved to be a one-term president. In 1970, thirty-one-year-old Gerald One Feather unseated him to become the youngest-ever chairman of the Oglala Sioux Tribe. His vice chairman was David Long.

During the years since the scandals and self-interest politics of the Frank G. Wilson administrations of the late 1930s and early 1940s, full-blood Lakotas had become somewhat more inclined to participate in the IRA-sponsored political process, although that did not necessarily mean they were any more enamored of it. A strong tradition of partisan politics had developed on the reservation, and after Wilson's victories in the first three elections, it was rare for an incumbent chairman to win reelection. The One Feather–Long administration was one of the periodic political cycles that some observers might interpret as a sideways victory for full bloods. That is, while the full bloods were not strong advocates of the system as a whole, many of them might feel that they had men in One Feather and Long who would support their policies, or at least not overtly damage their interests. However, this did not mean that the administration would be immune from the general contentiousness and occasional controversy that tended to swirl around the Oglala Sioux Tribal Council.[23]

One Feather had most recently worked on the reservation for the federal government's Office of Economic Opportunity. Not long after he took office, trouble arose over the OSTC's handling of the reservation's Head Start program, a federally funded preschool designed to close the usual education gap between poor children and their more well-to-do counterparts. When Head Start came to Pine Ridge at the beginning of the Poor Bear administration in 1968, the OST's Civil Service Board had appointed Leland Bear Heels from the nearby Crow Creek Indian Reservation to run the program, thereby making him the first Native person in the nation to direct a Head Start operation on a reservation. In August 1970, the selection committee of the outgoing OSTC renewed Bear Heels's appointment. Less than a month later, the new council took office. A selection committee with an almost entirely new membership rescinded the reappointment and named a new, hand-picked person to the position.[24]

The committee's action elicited an outcry from a number of community members and Office of Economic Development employees, the federal branch that funded and administered Head Start. Bear Heels appealed to the tribal council for an injunction barring his removal. The council moved swiftly to repudiate the cronyism of the Selection Committee. Meanwhile, all of this had taken place while the chairman and vice chairman were away from the reservation on business. One Feather promptly used the largest newspaper in western South Dakota, the *Rapid City Journal,* as his bully pulpit. He called the Selection Committee's action a violation of the OST's constitution and bylaws, and claimed that the committee only had an advisory role and no powers to hire or fire.[25]

The federal government accepted as almost routine such political tribulations on Pine Ridge. Its own analysis found that "voting within the Council is usually based on power alignments rather than on the merits of the proposal under consideration, and a change in administration has invariably coincided with a change in personnel throughout the executive branch." If this were not bad enough, the same federal report confessed that "relations between the tribe and the BIA have been historically strained." In other words, the federal government was all but admitting that nearly forty years after reorganization, the Oglala Sioux Tribe was dysfunctional and had poor relations with both its federal suzerain (the BIA) and its own constituency. The One Feather administration was not immune to these endemic problems.[26]

While the Bear Heels controversy was still percolating, unnamed members of the OSTC were accused of taking bribes over the still contentious issue of alcohol on the reservation. Whereas the council had unsuccessfully moved to legalize the possession and sale of alcohol on Pine Ridge a quarter-century earlier, the new accusations were inverted. The *Oglala War Cry,* a reservation newspaper, alleged that members of the council were receiving money in return for voting to keep the reservation's alcohol ban in place. The source of the alleged bribes? The owners of lucrative off-reservation bars who stood to lose substantial profits if Pine Ridge residents no longer had to leave the reservation to procure and consume alcohol. The charges were not confirmed, but they are indicative of the mistrust of OSTC politicians that permeated the reservation, as well as the volatility of Pine Ridge politics.[27]

In general, One Feather worked to decentralize the tribal council system and empower the districts and local communities, something that could be seen as a positive development for those who favored traditional, tiospaye-based governance. As early as 1964, One Feather had been voicing the idea that reservation programs should be initiated at the grassroots level instead of from above. He also sought to minimize the turmoil caused by the rapid and pervasive turnover in the two-year election cycle. His solution was to more clearly delineate the executive functions from the legislative functions in a government that had no separate executive branch. To accomplish this, he set up a merit personnel system for appointed tribal employees who filled many of the de facto executive positions. Through this, the new chairman hoped to create continuity in the administration of tribal government.[28]

After his tenure as chairman, One Feather continued to pursue these goals. During the 1980s he served as police commissioner on Pine Ridge. In that capacity, he worked to increase community involvement in policing whereby local boards set policing priorities, approved all local expenditures, and even hired and fired their own police. However, One Feather was not impervious to controversy and accusations of corruption during his administration; there were claims that he injudiciously juggled various sources of tribal revenue without consulting interested parties.[29]

Furthermore, in January 1971, Oglala Sioux Tribal Court Chief Judge C. Hobart Keith found Gerald One Feather, Vice President David Long, Treasurer Zona Pourier, and Secretary Esther DeSersa all to be in contempt of court during a wrangle over tax assessments. An OSTC ordinance of the previous year asserted that the OST held primacy in collecting taxes from Indian-owned businesses on Pine Ridge, thereby eliminating South Dakota's authority to do so. But with no sales tax system in place, One Feather had agreed to have South Dakota start collecting the 4 percent tax from Indian-owned businesses on January 1, 1971, in the name of the OST. In exchange for the service, the state would keep half of the revenues. The OST would relieve the state of South Dakota and keep the entire 4 percent once a tax collection system was in place. Keith ruled that the executive committee's participation in this plan was beyond its authority. He viewed the deal with South Dakota as negating the ordinance that had given the OSTC the exclusive right to collect said taxes in the first place, and only the secretary of the interior could negate an OSTC ordinance.[30]

One Feather weathered a more highly charged political attack the following month. Matthew High Pine, an OSTC representative from the

Wounded Knee district who had led the charge to remove Superintendent Roberts twenty-five years earlier, now submitted a resolution to suspend One Feather and Long for thirty days each. Among his charges were subverting the will of the council and slandering and libeling certain members of the council and the tribe as a whole. High Pine also maintained that "Gerald One Feather and David Long have demonstrated [a] total lack of respect for the Oglala Sioux Tribal Council and are in complete disregard of the basic concepts of their oath of office." Ironically, this was nearly identical to a charge he had levied against Roberts in 1945. Despite the acrimony of the charges, they were not accompanied by written evidence, which would have been necessary for an impeachment. The OST's constitution and bylaws make no provision for an actual suspension of its members outside of impeachment proceedings. Furthermore, the council did not show the inclination to pursue the matter, and One Feather and Long successfully survived the attack.[31]

However, neither financial matters nor accusations of corruption would emerge as the most powerful political issue during the One Feather administration. In fact, it would not even stem from an event on Pine Ridge. Instead, it would erupt from without, the result of an unprovoked act of

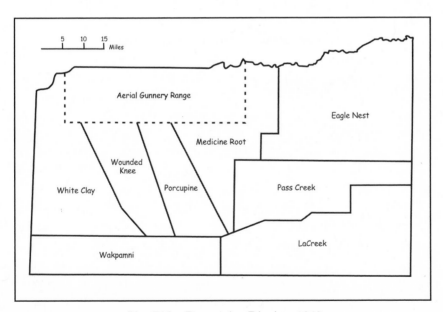

Pine Ridge Reservation Districts, 1969

violence against an Oglala man in a Nebraska border town. His name was Raymond Yellow Thunder.

YELLOW THUNDER

Pine Ridge Reservation is located in the southwestern corner of South Dakota. A string of border towns, all within less than twenty miles of the reservation, runs across the south side of the Nebraska state line. Among them are Rushville, Gordon, Hay Springs, and White Clay. The Native people of Pine Ridge have always had an uneasy relationship with these towns, and vice versa. There has been a parasitic relationship between the towns and the reservation. These towns generally range in size from a few hundred to a couple thousand people. Their economies are mostly driven by the reservation dollars that pour into them. The towns provide the goods, services, and infrastructure that the reservation has never developed. Native people have historically gone to the towns to purchase items unavailable on Pine Ridge, not the least of which is alcohol. They also go for jobs.

Compounding matters is the fact that Native people have encountered a tremendous amount of racism during their time in the border towns. To this day, an interested listener will find no shortage of stories from Native people about the indignities, wrongdoings, and occasional brutalities they have encountered in the Nebraska panhandle. The problem is pervasive enough that it almost always finds its way into the published memoirs and autobiographies of Native people from the region. Local whites perpetrated misdealings in commercial transactions, unleashed acts of violence with impunity, and hung signs in store windows that said things like, "No Indians or Dogs Allowed!" The extreme brutality one man suffered at a Nebraska border town in 1972 led to political mobilization on Pine Ridge.[32]

On the afternoon of February 20, 1972, two boys were playing in a used car lot in the border town of Gordon, Nebraska. There they came across the body of fifty-one-year-old Oglala Raymond Yellow Thunder, splayed across the front seat of a truck. Eight days earlier, while walking down the street, Yellow Thunder had been kidnapped by a group of whites. They were a combination of current Gordon residents and former Gordon residents who had since moved to Longmont, Colorado, and were back in Nebraska for a visit. The group included brothers Leslie D. and Melvin P.

Hare, Robert Bayliss, Bernard Ludder, and Jeannette Thompson. Having decided to assault a random Indian for fun, they crossed paths with the hapless Yellow Thunder. They beat him, stripped him naked from the waist down, locked him in the trunk of Bayliss' car, and drove around. They then threw him, still nude, into the Gordon American Legion Club. The dazed victim got out of the club and was walking down the street when he was accosted and beaten again by the same group. After finally being let go, he made his way to the local jail where he asked to spend the night. His supplication was granted, and at about seven o'clock the following morning, he staggered off to the car lot. He lay down inside the truck and died sometime within the next couple of days.[33]

Raymond Yellow Thunder was a grandson of American Horse, the famous nineteenth-century Oglala resistance leader who had lived long enough into the twentieth century to protest the coming of the IRA. One of seven children, Yellow Thunder was born near the reservation town of Kyle. He had shown artistic promise as a youth, but spent most of his life as a ranch hand near Gordon, breaking horses for extra money. Divorced with no children, he had returned to the reservation to visit his family on most weekends. Friends and family remembered him as humble, sober, and hard-working, a quiet man who was fond of children, well liked by those who knew him, and a person who had no enemies.[34]

Yellow Thunder was not the first Indian to turn up dead in a border town for unexplained reasons. This time, however, the situation would turn political. His relatives had expected him on the reservation the night he was attacked. Fearing the worst from the start, they made numerous trips to Gordon to look for him during the ensuing eight days. When Yellow Thunder's body was finally discovered, his family was devastated. They had suspected foul play from the start. They were then confronted with an act by Nebraska authorities that they correctly interpreted as attempts to gloss over the issue. The state of Nebraska refused to allow Yellow Thunder's relatives to view his body until after it was prepared for burial. When finally allowed to see him, their worst fears were confirmed: the mortician's cosmetics had not been able to fully conceal a beaten face.[35]

Unsubstantiated rumors began to fly around the reservation: Yellow Thunder had been forced to dance "Indian style" in the American legion hall; he had been tortured with lit cigarettes; he had been physically mutilated, perhaps even his genitalia. The Pine Ridge Tribal Court posted a twenty-four-hour guard around his grave to prevent vandalism and defilements. The family was not willing to stand by and let Yellow Thunder's attackers go unpunished. They appealed to Nebraska state authorities, to the BIA, to Pine Ridge legal services, and to the Oglala Sioux Tribal Council. All of this, they felt, was to no avail. In the mean time, five arrests had been made, but all of the suspects were free on bond and most had left the state.[36]

Raymond Yellow Thunder's sisters, who lived in the reservation town of Porcupine, continued to agitate for justice. They turned to their one political connection. Theyir nephew Severt Young Bear was chairman of the Porcupine District Council. He was also a member of the American Indian Movement (AIM). They told him, "We want a full investigation."[37]

Young Bear contacted members of AIM, who were quick to respond. They arrived on the reservation within the week, heightening an already tense situation, and along with the Oglala people, they began organizing protests, marches, and boycotts in Gordon. The case soon gained national attention. After the *Omaha World-Herald* picked up the story, national media began to descend on the sleepy Nebraska town. Pawnee attorney John Echo Hawk, a founder of the Native American Rights Fund, began representing the family. In his presence, a second autopsy was performed. The rumors of mutilation turned out to be false. However, the victim did have bruises and lacerations about the head, right side, and right leg. The coroner concluded that Raymond Yellow Thunder had died from a cerebral hematoma. It covered the entire right side of his brain and was caused by a blunt instrument other than a fist. It may have been the result of bouncing around in the trunk of Bayliss's car, or he may have been beaten to death. Either way, the bond of $6,250 that had released the suspects seemed negligible, and the charges of involuntary manslaughter and false imprisonment seemed tame. As far as the family was concerned, it was kidnaping and murder. To their chagrin, the charges were not upgraded, perhaps because the Hare brothers were the sons of Dean Hare, a wealthy local rodeo stock breeder, rancher, and businessman.[38]

The case had not been terribly hard to solve after all. By Friday, March 24, Bernard Ludder was in the Sheridan County Courthouse testifying against his cohorts. "They tromped him pretty good," he said. Ludder also claimed that Bayliss and the Hare brothers had urged him to join in the pummeling: "Go ahead and hit him—it was fun." Of course, Ludder denied having taken part. The defendants were convicted.[39]

The incident led to increased tension on the reservation. For many full bloods, the murder of Raymond Yellow Thunder was emblematic of the abuse and mistreatment they had suffered in border towns like Gordon for as long as anyone could remember. Some people, however, including a number of mixed bloods, were put off by the protests and boycotts, as well as by AIM's presence on the reservation and in Gordon. Chairman One Feather responded favorably to the boycott. He removed nearly $1,000,000 of tribal money from Gordon banks. Possibly in response, on Monday, March 13, an unknown assailant fired a bullet through a window of One Feather's home. No one was harmed.[40]

Things were so bad that on March 20 concerned members of the tribe founded The Committee for Oglala Sioux Unity. The committee sponsored their own newspaper, the *Oglala Nation News,* which premiered a week later. The initial issue featured an editorial entitled "Indian vs. Indian." "Few people are not affected by feelings of anxiety, fear, anger, and pride," it noted. "But there are also feelings of hate." And those feelings had manifestations. "Threatening telephone calls have been received by government officials, tribal leaders, and school teachers."[41]

In the midst of this brewing storm, there was another tribal election. This time it was Gerald One Feather's turn to be unseated. He lost his chairmanship to a man named Richard "Dick" Wilson.

THE NEW REGIME

The mid-1930s had seen the arrival on Pine Ridge of a new superintendent, W. O. Roberts, and the new tribal council system with Frank G. Wilson assuming the position of chairman. These developments had created great stress on the political landscape of Pine Ridge. Many of those tensions, stemming from rivalries between mixed-blood and full-blood Lakotas and growing out of the implementation of reorganization, were still present in the early 1970s and were compounded by the demonstrations that sprung from the Raymond Yellow Thunder affair. In the midst of these persistent and growing tensions, a new superintendent and tribal chairman again appeared on Pine Ridge Reservation in 1972: Superintendent Stanley David Lyman and Chairman Dick Wilson.

Lyman was a lifetime federal employee. A tall man who wore glasses and smoked a pipe, he was born in South Dakota and raised on a ranch at the edge of the Black Hills. He began his government career during World

War II with the Farmers' Home Administration (a.k.a. the War Food Administration). He recruited Mexicans to work in the United States as temporary farm laborers. In the early 1950s, he joined the Bureau of Indian Affairs on Pine Ridge, running the ill-conceived relocation policy (discussed in chapter 6) that encouraged Indians to leave the reservations for cities, while his wife worked at the Oglala Community School in Pine Ridge village. He left in 1953, climbing his way up the BIA ladder and establishing a name for himself as a capable administrator. He served as superintendent of the Fort Peck (Montana) and Uintah-Ouray (Utah) Indian reservations. In December 1971, he returned to Pine Ridge as BIA superintendent.[42]

Much like William O. Roberts some three and a half decades earlier, the federal government viewed Lyman as the kind of person who could come into Pine Ridge and improve the situation. And just as Roberts had been a supporter of the then newly introduced Indian New Deal, Lyman was an ardent believer in the new Nixonian policy of self-determination: supporting the integrity of tribal governments and serving primarily in an advisory capacity. "To me sovereignty means the tribal government being equal to the State of South Dakota and having jurisdiction over all land and individuals within the exterior boundaries of the reservation," he said shortly after his appointment to Pine Ridge. "As time goes on, the Oglala Sioux Tribe should grow stronger and more powerful."[43]

Unfortunately, however, as time went by Lyman proved himself to be far less politically astute than Roberts. Rather, he was first and foremost a bureaucrat working to execute the Bureau's policy of supporting the Oglala Sioux Tribal Council. And as the council came to be dominated by mixed bloods who were openly hostile toward full-blood interests, much as it had during the 1930s and 1940s, instead of reading the political landscape Lyman would show himself to be a man who blindly followed the dictates of policy, supporting and openly aligning himself with the OSTC regardless of how detrimental it was to the interests of many Lakota people.

The 1972 chairman's election has sometimes been painted as a showdown between a traditional full blood (One Feather) and a progressive mixed blood (Wilson).[44] This interpretation makes perfect sense in hindsight, given what was about to transpire. However, it is not wholly accurate.

As the election loomed in the distance, Wilson had not been anyone's first choice to run against One Feather. A number of people championed the cause of Dolores Swift Bird, who had been appointed an associate judge in the tribal court system in early 1971. She, however, had small children and felt that the presidency would be too demanding of her time. She declined to run, and Wilson stepped into the vacuum.[45]

Wilson was a thirty-eight-year-old plumber and father of six. During One Feather's administration, he represented Pine Ridge village on the Oglala Sioux Tribal Council, serving on the council's Law and Order, Education, Investigation, and Labor committees and acting on the last two as secretary and chairman respectively. His campaign manager was Barbara Means-Adams (cousin of AIM leader Russell Means). She maintains that Wilson emerged as One Feather's main competitor simply because he had the time and inclination. Not many people were really interested in running.[46]

With One Feather occupied by the duties of his chairmanship and mired in a string of controversies, capped by the Yellow Thunder affair, Wilson campaigned vigorously. He managed to pool together substantial resources, which opponents later speculated came from off-reservation sources. He visited people on evenings and weekends. He spent money on cookouts and picnics. And most importantly, he went after mixed-blood *and* full-blood voters.[47]

Dick Wilson was a mixed blood himself (5/16 by his own account), living in Pine Ridge village. He had numerous connections in the mixed-blood community, which was his natural voter base. Superintendent Lyman even noted once that Wilson did not "feel comfortable outside the mixed-blood society of Pine Ridge." Nonetheless, he made a concerted effort to court full bloods during the 1972 election.[48]

Gerald One Feather's policies had not been antagonistic to full bloods, especially when compared to some of his predecessors. But he did little to court them during the election, "and a chairman cannot do that without paying a heavy price for it," Oglala chief Frank Fools Crow later observed. In fact, one of the complaints levied against One Feather was that he spent too much time off-reservation, traveling frequently to Washington, D.C., and elsewhere. Many full bloods who were already apathetic toward the entire tribal council system were left feeling ambivalent about the incumbent. Additionally, One Feather was vulnerable in the full-blood community over his handling of the Yellow Thunder case. When the incident erupted, the entire federal bureaucracy, from the BIA on down to the tribal council, faced accusations of having been slow to act. After all, Yellow Thunder's sisters had gone to all of the pertinent federal institutions that were supposedly there to help Native people, including the tribal council. But the family felt it had been to no avail. Tribal attorney Ethel Merrival had eventually gone to Gordon to demand an investigation, but to some it seemed like the OST had waited too long to get involved. Lyman later admitted that "we did not move fast enough," and that inaction eventually hurt One Feather in the election.[49]

Wilson seized the opportunity to attract full-blood votes. In addition to his unrestrained campaign spending, Wilson painted himself as a supporter of the full-blood cause. He even wore his hair shoulder-length, something that to this day is often taken as a serious expression of full-blood values; far beyond the political statement long male hair made in America during the late 1960s and early 1970s, hair has a special meaning in Lakota culture. It is not viewed as mere dead cells, but as part of the living person. Strict adherents of Lakota culture and religion keep the hair they pull from their comb in a special receptacle. Cutting it regularly is anathema to them. On the other side, for some Indian men, keeping their hair short indicated an abandonment of past ways in favor of modern American values. Sporting his long hair, Wilson became an open advocate of community actions in Gordon. He was even a vocal supporter of the American Indian Movement, stating he was behind their efforts in Gordon "110 percent." Not too long after taking office, however, Wilson got a crew cut.[50]

Ellen Moves Camp was a full-blood elder who supported Wilson during the 1972 election, a decision she later came to regret. "It's really bad to say, but our people did go for the money and all the promises he made when he was campaigning," she said afterward. "Different men went out to these districts and told what Dick Wilson promised. They'd take a cow, butcher it, and feed the people. Our people must have been pretty hungry to elect him."[51]

When the election unfolded, Wilson had won a tight race. In taking five of the reservation's nine districts (see maps 4 and 5), the demographics had worked in his favor; the mixed-blood stronghold of Pine Ridge village favored him by a 3:1 ratio, and Wilson had gained enough ground to split the vote in more rural districts. For her efforts, Means-Adams received $7,000 after the victory, no small sum on a reservation where the average annual income was still under $1,000.[52]

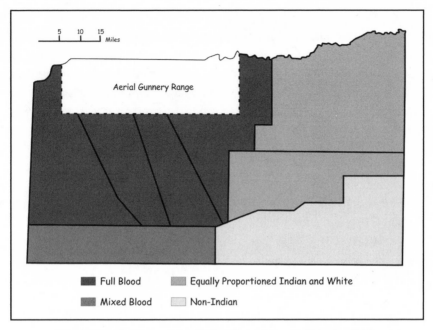

Ethnic Distribution on Pine Ridge Reservation by District, 1971.

Source: DeMallie, Raymond J. "Pine Ridge Economy: Cultural and Historical Perspectives," p. 267, in *World Anthropology: Economic Development.* Edited by Sam Stanley. Hague: Mouton Publishers, 1978.

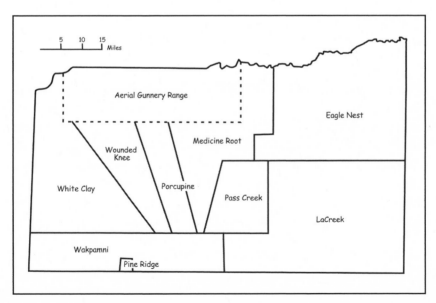

Pine Ridge Reservation Voting Districts, 1972

Dick Wilson's inauguration was held on April 10 at the Oglala Community School in Pine Ridge village. Lifelong Pine Ridge resident and unabashed Wilson supporter Bessie Cornelius got there early. She would later describe it as the "most impressive inauguration ceremony I have ever seen." Dignitaries from neighboring tribes, the state of South Dakota, and the federal government attended. Even AIM leader Russell Means was there. Planned as a two-day powwow with drum groups and singers from around the area, the event began with a buffalo dinner. Afterward, Jim Blue Bird of the Native American Church and respected full-blood elder Frank Fools Crow gave the opening prayers. In a time-honored tradition, Gerald One Feather offered a pipe to Wilson, who in turn donned a ceremonial feathered bonnet headdress and was administered the oath of office. Vice President Dave Long, who had won re-election, gave his opening remarks. Then the new chairman addressed the crowd that had assembled in the school's auditorium.[53]

"Let me reassure you that my campaign promises will serve as the blueprint for my administration," he pledged to them. "We will not be belligerent, we will not be quarrelsome. . . . The Oglala Sioux Tribe is all one family." It is unfathomable that anyone present could have predicted just how far from the spirit of these words Dick Wilson would stray over the course of the next four years.[54]

DISINTEGRATION

Dick Wilson's chairmanship was explosive, confrontational, and controversial from the very beginning. A point of contention still exists over whether Wilson always had little or no respect for the full-blood people who would come to make up the bulk of his political opposition and his true colors came to the fore once he took office or whether he was simply a man with a no-nonsense, caustic, adversarial personality whose autocratic tendencies and staggering lack of tact and statesmanship quickly alienated many of the full blood members of the reservation. What remains indisputable is that as the political tensions he inherited quickly worsened (much of it through his own mishandling), Wilson gravitated toward the reservation's mixed-blood constituency and the OSTC's federal sponsors, while simultaneously ruthlessly seeking to quash his emerging full-blood political opponents by any means necessary.[55]

The new tribal council officially met for the first time on April 11, 1972, at Billy Mills Hall in the town of Pine Ridge when President Dick Wilson called the meeting to order at 10:00 a.m. The open divisions and contentious issues that would come to mar the Wilson administration were apparent from the start. After Father Paul Steinmetz delivered the opening prayer, a dispute arose over the swearing-in process. Leo Wilcox, a representative from Pine Ridge village, advised Wilson to make sure all council members were sworn in. The comment was aimed at C. Hobart Keith, a tribal court judge and a fellow representative from Pine Ridge village.

Keith was an exceptional man. Fluently bilingual and well rounded in both Lakota and mainstream American cultures, he was given to quoting biblical chapter and verse as a means of criticizing the American legal system. "Many [bad] things are caused by that august body the United States Congress, state legislatures, and even tribal councils," he once observed. In response to Wilson, Keith stated that he had been previously sworn in by Pete Two Bulls. Wilson challenged the oath's validity and demanded that Keith should be sworn in at the regular meeting, as had the rest of the council members. Article III of the OST's bylaws does mandate a swearing-in oath and supplies the text, but it makes no mention of where or by whom it must be administered. After a brief debate, Keith acquiesced, and Wilson administered the oath of office. But the disagreement was only a harbinger of things to come.[56]

Later that morning, Representative Richard Little from the White Clay District questioned the legality of the election that had taken place in the Porcupine District. He was specifically referring to the seating of Orland Big Owl. But Wilson backed Big Owl, and the matter was closed. Shortly thereafter, C. Hobart Keith, along with Jake Little Thunder of Eagle Nest District, made a motion to postpone the election of the executive committee until 1:00 p.m., so that the council could consider the nominees. It was defeated by a vote of 6–12. The elections then commenced. However, in their midst, Little and Wilson Gay of Medicine Root District brought up the matter of Birgil L. Kills Straight.[57]

Kills Straight was not new to the task of serving Pine Ridge. In the late 1960s he had worked as the Information Coordinator for the reservation's branch of the federal Office of Economic Development. When the Office sponsored *War Cry,* a new reservation newspaper, he became one of the editors. He also served on the board of directors and as first vice president of the Tiospaye Federal Credit Union. In 1968, he began hosting a weekly radio show that aired Sunday afternoons on KOTA-FM Rapid City. With Pine Ridge then having no radio station of its own,[58] Kills Straight's program was dedicated to keeping listeners abreast of issues, news, and happenings relevant to the reservation.[59]

Kills Straight had been elected as the other representative from Medicine Root in 1972. Little and Gay asked that Wilson now swear him in as a recognized member of the Council. This had not yet happened. Wilson replied by requesting Kills Straight to provide written proof of his residency during the time of the election. The matter was subsequently tabled until later that afternoon. After lunch, the issue was brought up again. Wilson responded that he believed Kills Straight did not meet the residency requirements specified by OSTC election ordinances. The president maintained that this was because during the time of the election, Kills Straight had been living in Rushville, Nebraska, a border town south of the reservation. Since this would be a violation of the rules on candidate eligibility, Wilson refused to administer the oath. In addition, the chairman stated that the issue was being investigated, and he was waiting for a report.[60]

The dispute over Kills Straight's election finally came to a head when the council met on July 18. With Superintendent Lyman in attendance, C. Hobart Keith began the meeting by robustly attacking the entire IRA system and challenging the validity of not only the election ordinance Wilson was using to preclude Kills Straight, but indeed the entire OST constitution and bylaws. Wilson insisted that Kills Straight had lived in Rushville, Nebraska, before taking out a nominating petition for the election, and he even produced an affidavit from a Rushville landlord claiming that Kills Straight had rented one of his apartments. After further discussion, Richard Little and Keith moved to have Kills Straight seated. When the motion appeared to pass by receiving seven votes in favor, three against, and six abstentions, Wilson circumvented the apparent outcome by invoking the chair's prerogative: he nullified the result on the grounds that the plurality of seven votes did not constitute a simple majority of the sixteen total votes cast. Hoping to lure abstainers who may have been hesitant to vote against Kills Straight face-to-face, Wilson ordered a new vote by secret ballot. The plan backfired as the abstentions split evenly, and the motion carried 10–6. Displaying sour grapes, Wilson had Judge Dorothy Richards administer the oath to Kills Straight instead of administering it himself, just one day after his minor power struggle to force Keith to receive the oath from him in person.[61]

By the next meeting on July 25, the level of dissension within the Oglala Sioux Tribal Council had reached the point that at least one member felt the need to address it. Etta Youngman of White Clay District opened the meeting by noting that the larger issues confronting the reservation, such as land matters and tribal enrollment, were starting to compete with internal problems for the council's attention. She then admonished the council members to attend to their business, "so that they can look into the people's faces when they walk out of the Council hall." The OST heeded her advice for the mean time, dealing with several looming issues.[62]

On August 17, Wilson's paranoia about maintaining order was manifested in Ordinance 072–04, which passed by a vote of 18–0 and severely curtailed the public's right to assemble on Pine Ridge Reservation. The "Ordinance to Prevent Riots and Unlawful Assembly" prohibited public gatherings of as few as three people who merely had the vaguely defined "intent" to riot. Violation could incur a penalty of up to thirty days labor and/or up to a $100 fine, plus court costs. In addition, it gave police officers wide discretion in enforcing the ordinance, including the ability to employ virtually anybody and as many people as necessary to aid in the execution of a command to disperse.[63]

Despite the unanimity on 072–04, there was still serious friction in the council between what were emerging as two distinct camps: the chairman and his supporters versus those who were antipathetic toward the chairman. This rivalry would eventually bring out the worst in Wilson. For example, when the council began to debate a bilingual education program that South Dakota funded and the OST managed, Birgil Kills Straight took a position contrary to Wilson's stance. He made a motion to vote on the matter, and the motion was seconded by Richard Little. Wilson, however, flatly refused to recognize the motion on the rather vague grounds that it was not consistent with the OST constitution.[64]

Less than two weeks later, the OSTC Executive Committee passed a resolution requesting the Bureau of Indian Affairs to assume all responsibility for law enforcement on the reservation on the grounds that the tribe could no longer afford the cost. On September 5, Acting Superintendent R. W. Penttila (Lyman was out of town) forwarded the resolution to the BIA with his approval. Thus, for the lack of adequate funds did the OST cede one of the cardinal powers of sovereignty: a nation's ability to enforce its own laws.[65]

Many Oglalas felt that such an elemental step in the restructuring of the OST should not have been pursued by the five-member executive commit- tee. It seemed like the entire Oglala Sioux Tribal Council should have voted on the measure. This proclivity for minimizing democracy and the input of the people was just one of the ways in which Dick Wilson alienated numer- ous Pine Ridge citizens during 1972. He was also brusk and unforgiving in how he dealt with those people he viewed as political enemies. It was, of course, a self-fulfilling prophecy, as his enemies, perceived and real, were antagonized by his coarse behavior and tactless tactics. Many full bloods felt particularly betrayed as Wilson embraced the arbitrary power of his IRA office and seemed to use his position to play favorites.

"Right from the start, people resented him," Ellen Moves Camp later asserted. She had supported him during the election, but now she felt that she had been misled. "Ever since Wilson's been in office it's just been a one- man council. He's just some kind of dictator that got in there."[66]

By October, less than a year after Wilson's inauguration, talk was begin- ning to simmer on the reservation about a move to impeach the new tribal chairman.[67]

6

Full Force Gale

Oglala Politics and the American Indian Movement

URBANIZATION

BETWEEN 1930 AND 1970, Native Americans experienced a tremendous rate of urbanization that easily exceeded any other ethnic group in the United States. According to the census department, less than 10 percent of American Indians lived in urban areas in 1930. By 1970, this figure had nearly quintupled, reaching almost 50 percent.[1]

The first major force driving this change was World War II. Of the just under 400,000 American Indians at its outset, about 25,000 men enlisted, or roughly one-third of all able-bodied men age 18 to 50. Another 40,000 to 45,000 Native Americans worked off-reservation in the defense industry: one-fifth of all the women and nearly one-half of all non-enlisted men. After the war ended, most enlisted men returned home, and many of the Native industrial workers were let go. They usually returned to impoverished reservations. However, many of them had experienced a higher standard of living than they were used to, albeit ever so briefly. This experience led many Native people to leave reservations for cities after the war in an effort to recapture that standard. It also helped open the way for a postwar federal policy that would encourage Native Americans to leave reservations for large American cities.[2]

In 1950, Congress passed Public Law 474, also known as the Navajo-Hopi Act. It was aimed at developing the Navajo and Hopi Reservations in the Southwest and featured a $90,000,000 appropriation. However, beyond reservation development, it also provided for an off-reservation job-placement program. It directed the Bureau of Indian Affairs (BIA) to open offices in Los Angeles and Salt Lake City in 1951 and in Denver the following year, which were to oversee the placement of Navajo men in the labor market. A recruitment office in Gallup, New Mexico, encouraged men to leave their reservation for jobs in the three cities. By 1951, approximately 17,000 Navajos were working off-reservation, mostly in seasonal harvesting jobs or as unskilled railroad employees.[3]

In 1950, President Harry S. Truman appointed Dillon S. Myer Commissioner of Indian Affairs (CIA). Myer's previous qualification was running the War Relocation Authority (WRA), the odious government agency responsible for the administration of some 110,000 Japanese-Americans who had been rounded up by the armed services, banished from their homes along the Pacific coast, and forcibly removed to prison camps in the West during World War II. Now head of the BIA, Myer promptly used the new Navajo job placement program as a stepping stone to a broader approach. In 1952, he announced the start of Operation Relocation. The BIA would sponsor the movement of Native Americans to off-reservation jobs in urban areas as an alternative to developing the reservations themselves. The unfounded justification for this new policy was what the government called the excess population theory. It simplistically maintained that most reservations were lacking the resources necessary to support their superfluous populations. The BIA would solve this alleged problem by promoting off-reservation employment, augmented by job training and placement. Of course, while the BIA was insisting that a reservation like Pine Ridge, with 4,350 square miles and just over 10,000 people, was populated beyond the capacity of its resources, no one in the Interior Department was saying the same thing about the nearly 8,000,000 people living within the relatively minuscule confines of New York City's 444 square miles.[4]

After Dwight D. Eisenhower was elected president in 1952, he appointed Glenn Emmons to replace Meyer as commissioner. Emmons was a conservative New Mexico banker who embraced the new relocation policy and sought to expand it. He announced that the program would be open to any enrolled member of a BIA-sponsored reservation. However, a fiscally conservative Congress granted only a modest increase in funding, far short of Emmons's request of $8.5 million, and the program was stretched beyond its means.[5]

Accurate figures of relocations are hard to come by. Various sources indicate that in 1952, the Bureau oversaw the relocation of approximately 450 to 850 people nationally. The following year, without much more in the way of resources, it sponsored the migration of between 1,400 and 2,600 people. Field relocation offices designed to receive the migrants were opened in Oakland (1954), San Francisco (1955), San Jose (1956), and St. Louis (1956). In 1954, somewhere between 1,650 and 2,550 people moved to metropolitan areas via relocation. By 1956, those numbers were up to 4,300 to 5,300.[6]

The government continued to prop up its rather dubious population-based rationalization. Simultaneously, BIA officials engaged in the active recruitment of American Indians into the relocation program. Employing what amounted to little more than propaganda, they frequently provided misleadingly glowing portrayals of the lifestyle that supposedly awaited Native people in the cities. For their part, many Native Americans were eager to recapture the relatively high wages they had garnered during the war. The Bureau falsely led them to believe that this would be the case if they moved to a large city.[7]

The failure of the program to deliver what it promised contributed to disenchantment among many Indians. A report published by the Field Foundation in 1956 found numerous complaints, including inadequate training on reservations for adjustment to city life; inadequate screening of the unqualified, such as alcoholics or the mentally ill; understaffed relocation offices; inadequate follow-up procedures; and poor urban housing selection. Moreover, the Bureau's supposed "maximum" figures were actually quotas assigned to federal personnel who were pressured to treat them as minimal numbers to attain. These were but a few of the criticisms the report leveled at the program.[8]

Despite its shortcomings, relocation's expansion continued, largely unabated, for almost two decades. Receiving offices were added in such locales as Cincinnati, Joliet, Dallas, and Cleveland. As late as 1968, new offices were opened in Tulsa and Oklahoma City. By 1970, census figures indicated that there were 307,551 more Indians living in cities than there had been in 1930. A conservative estimate of the numbers who left reservations between 1952 and 1970 is 118,000.[9]

The upshot of such dramatic urbanization was the formation of Indian ghettoes, primarily in cities throughout the West. In 1970, the median income for American Indian families in urban areas was just $7,323, compared with $10,629 for their white counterparts. Likewise, 21 percent of urban Indian families lived below the government's poverty line, while that figure was just 6.9 percent for white urban families.[10]

Tribal governments had not been oblivious to these developments and had done what they could to ameliorate the situation. For example, the United Sioux Tribes of South Dakota[11] all contributed money to a fund that created employment offices in major cities to help Native people looking for work. Despite such efforts, however, Indian slums grew up in one American city after another during a quarter-century of rampant Native urbanization. This development, certainly notable in its own right, also came to have an indirect impact on Pine Ridge Reservation politics during the reign of Chairman Dick Wilson.[12]

THE AMERICAN INDIAN MOVEMENT

Clyde Bellecourt was born on May 8, 1939. One of twelve children, he hailed from the White Earth Ojibwa (Anishinaabe) Reservation in Minnesota, just south of the Canadian border. When he was still a child, his parents moved the family to Minneapolis. In trouble with the law at an early age, he was twice sent to the St. Cloud Reformatory. Eight months out of St. Cloud for the last time, he was convicted of burglary and sentenced to eight months at Minnesota's Stillwater State Penitentiary in 1962.[13]

While inside, Bellecourt earned a high school equivalency diploma and a license as a steam plant engineer. He also met a fellow Anishinaabe inmate named Eddie Benton Banai, and the two of them began to organize other Native inmates. In Bellecourt's words, the group attempted to instill an "education about being Indians, instead of just rotting in prison and making license plates." Bellecourt's and Banai's prison organizing was one of the seeds from which the American Indian Movement (AIM) germinated.[14]

After three stints behind bars for burglary and armed robbery, Bellecourt was finally paroled in 1964. He moved back to Minneapolis and began to organize. By 1968, he and Banai had teamed with two other Anishinaabe activists: George Mitchell, also from White Earth, and Dennis H. Banks.[15]

Banks was born into the Anishinaabe Pillager Band on Minnesota's Leech Lake Chippewa Reservation in 1932. At age eight, he was removed from his family and sent some 250 miles away to the Pipestone Indian School. Over the next three years, he ran away nine times (and was always caught), before finally being transferred to a junior high school in Whapeton, North Dakota. After two years there, he was transferred again to a large BIA school on the Santee Dakota Reservation in Flandreau, South Dakota. He ran away for the last time at age sixteen, making his way back to Leech Lake. Forced to speak only English at the boarding schools, he had lost the use of his Native tongue.[16]

He joined the Air Force in 1953 and spent three years in Japan, where he took a wife and had his first child. His experiences in the military, serving in an occupation force in a foreign country during the Cold War, and his marriage to a Japanese woman all contributed to his early politicization. The United States refused to recognize the marriage because his wife's family were socialists. After twice going AWOL with his family, Banks was court martialed, convicted, discharged, and sent back to America in chains. His family was forbidden from joining him.[17]

Upon his return stateside, he spent several years enduring unemployment, alcohol abuse, and petty incarcerations. In 1966, while trying to support a new wife and eight children on a minimum wage job, he was sentenced to five years for burglary. During his imprisonment, which included nine months of solitary confinement, Banks heightened his politicization. After obtaining an early release in May 1968, he teamed up with George Mitchell, a childhood friend from boarding school. They held a meeting to organize Indian residents of Minneapolis-St. Paul for civil rights actions. At their first public meeting, attended by about 200 people, one of the most vocal proponents for direct action was Clyde Bellecourt. The American Indian Movement was born.[18]

In a story that may be somewhere between apocryphal and legendary, someone (versions range from Mitchell to an anonymous woman) suggested that the new group call itself Concerned Indian Americans. It was not long, however, before the members realized that that acronym was already taken. They changed their name to the American Indian Movement and ushered in its much more telling acronym; in a catch phrase that would illustrate the organization's forthright and unapologetic approach to Indian civil rights, members boasted, "We AIM not to please." Influenced by the tactics and rhetoric of the Black Panthers, their early efforts included civilian patrols in Indian neighborhoods to monitor police abuse. They also fought discrimination in jobs and housing and set up alternative education programs called Survival Schools, which were designed to equip Indian children with life skills for the urban environment and to provide them alternative views of Native history unavailable in public schools.[19]

AIM's approach to these issues was vibrant and uncompromising. They placed action ahead of organization and planning. They were unabashed in their use of fiery rhetoric, unapologetic in their anger at anti-Indian racism, and overt in their advocacy of a intertribal nationalist philosophy. Their urban constituency represented innumerable Native nations, and they accordingly developed an ideology that stressed the connection between all Native peoples and their common resistance to domination by America's mainstream culture, society, and government. As the organization achieved early successes, it added key leaders and expanded across the country. Among them were Vernon Bellecourt, Russell Means, and John Trudell.[20]

One of Clyde's older brothers, Vernon Bellecourt had dropped out of school in the eighth grade and made his way to Minneapolis's Indian ghetto soon thereafter. At age nineteen, he preceded his brother at the St. Cloud Reformatory. In the late 1960s he moved to Denver with his wife and three children, ostensibly to enter the real estate business, but quickly found his calling with AIM. "I could see the pride in these young men and women. A new dignity, a new awareness, a new power, a strength," he later recalled. "Then I looked at myself. I was making money and living in White suburbia. I was assimilated into the mainstream of White America. And I was disenchanted." He promptly founded AIM's Denver chapter.[21]

Russell Means was born on November 10, 1939, on the Pine Ridge Reservation. Shortly after the outbreak of World War II, his family moved to Vallejo, California, where his father worked in the navy shipyards. Typical of many Indians in the defense industry, the elder Means was laid off after the war ended, and the family moved back to South Dakota. It was not long, however, before the Meanses returned to Vallejo before moving on to San Leandro, just south of Oakland, in 1954. Spending most of his time in the San Francisco area, Russell Means eventually married and had children. He took a job as an accountant on South Dakota's Rosebud Reservation in the summer of 1967. When the job did not work out, he and his family participated in the relocation program and ended up in Cleveland, Ohio, the following July. By 1969, he had co-founded the Cleveland Indian Center. In 1970, he joined AIM and established their Cleveland chapter. By the early 1970s, the press was often citing Means and Dennis Banks as AIM's two foremost leaders. The urban Indian roots of AIM were now obvious to all. "Russell Means is a product of this (urbanization process) if you want to get right down to it," observed BIA employee Wyman Babby, himself a Lakota.[22]

In the spring of 1970, a twenty-three-year-old Santee Dakota named John Trudell also joined AIM. During the previous year, he had been part of the recent takeover of Alcatraz Island by urban Indian activists in San Francisco, an event that garnered headlines and focused the nation's attention on modern Native issues. The occupiers had seized the abandoned prison in San Francisco Bay and turned it into a publicity coup by citing the provisions of an Arapaho and Sioux treaty that entitled the Indian signers to reclaim ceded property that the federal government let lapse into disuse. Trudell had eventually become one of the leaders of the occupation. A four-year veteran of the U.S. Navy, he also produced "Radio Free Alcatraz," a radio show broadcast on KPFA-FM, Berkeley's Pacifica station. The program was soon being aired in New York City and Los Angeles as well. Shortly after joining AIM, Trudell became their national spokesman, and he would eventually rise to national chairman in the mid-1970s.[23]

Major AIM chapters were subsequently added in Milwaukee, San Francisco, and Chicago.[24] By 1973, there were seventy-nine local chapters, including eight in Canada, and the Movement would claim some 5,000 members. As the 1970s opened, the organization and leadership that served to define the American Indian Movement was in place. Mostly first generation urban Indians, they coalesced from around the country and eventually began to set their sights on the place of their origin: the reservation. Several early unsuccessful attempts to make an impact on reservations were not enough to dissuade them. A suitable opportunity for them to make a positive impression on a significant portion of reservation full bloods appeared in early 1972 with the violent death of Raymond Yellow Thunder.[25]

ENTER AIM

When Raymond Yellow Thunder's sisters, worried about their brother's disappearance, sought help from their nephew Severt Young Bear, they were aware that he had two sets of political connections. As chairman of their district, he was heavily involved in OST politics. But Young Bear also had connections to the American Indian Movement. By early 1972, AIM had started to appear on the national stage with their robust and confrontational efforts on behalf of Indian people. In fact, when Yellow Thunder's sisters tracked Young Bear down on a Friday night after work, they appealed directly to his affiliations with the Movement. "You have some friends that are with AIM," one of the sisters reminded him. "I wonder if you could go to them, ask them that we want something to be done to the people that killed our brother, and we want a full investigation."[26]

That night, Young Bear obtained free gasoline from a sympathetic service station employee and drove the nearly six hundred miles to Omaha, Nebraska, where AIM was holding a meeting. Oglala Sioux Tribal Councilman Birgil Kills Straight, who also had AIM connections, had informed them that Young Bear was on his way. He arrived at AIM's hotel room late that night, and they conferred past dawn. The organization that had been founded by urban Indians and had cut its teeth working in the Native ghettoes of the Midwest, now resolved to intervene on behalf of a full blood family from a reservation on the Northern Plains. The organization chartered a bus. Filling it and several cars, they headed toward Pine Ridge. Along the way, they garnered additional supporters at the Winnebago Reservation in northeastern Nebraska.[27]

From AIM's point of view, their involvement in the Yellow Thunder affair was a tremendous success. They held a community meeting at Billy Mills Hall in the town of Pine Ridge, which was followed by a March 1 press conference where they announced that protests in Gordon would start on the sixth. With AIM marshaling the protesters, about 500 people descended on town. In addition to the marches, which lasted for three days, AIM fueled a boycott of Gordon's businesses and participated in meetings with state, county, and town officials. The meetings helped lead to the suspension of a notoriously racist Gordon police officer whom numerous people accused of raping Indian women, the creation of a human rights commission to monitor problems of anti-Indian racism in the region, and the second autopsy of Yellow Thunder.[28]

Press coverage of the American Indian Movement's activities in Gordon was generally favorable, helping to cement the group's national reputation. But more importantly, AIM's actions had made a profound impact on the opinion of many Pine Ridge full bloods. AIM had answered the request of Yellow Thunder's sisters, and in a matter of days the group had shaken up the little border town with a forceful display of Indigenous pride and fearless activism. Said Severt Young Bear, "When AIM came in and helped the family look into the death, that made the older people that are living out on the reservation, out in the country–they kind of lifted up their heads, and were speaking out then."[29]

If the American Indian Movement was energizing the Lakota people of Pine Ridge, then the inverse was also true; AIM was gaining momentum from its involvement on the reservation. Leonard Crow Dog became AIM's spiritual leader. Great-grandson of the man who shot Spotted Tail, he was born and raised on the Rosebud Reservation. A practitioner of the traditional Lakota Sun Dance spiritual ceremony and a member of the Native American Church, Crow Dog has gone so far as to state, "When the traditional Lakota and the city militants got together, that was the moment AIM took off." Dennis Banks concurred. "The march on Gordon changed things for Lakota People, for AIM, for American Indians everywhere . . . and we were elated. Among the Lakota people, many felt that Gordon was a turning point, that Indians didn't have to take the abuse anymore. Hundreds of them joined AIM.[30]

AIM was becoming increasingly enmeshed with the goings-on of Pine Ridge. Their activities at Gordon had brought about positive, tangible changes, and as noted previously, Chairman Dick Wilson was publicly supporting the organization. However, this was soon to change. AIM's next major endeavor would lead Wilson to make a complete about-face in his attitude toward the Movement. Ironically, it would take place a half continent away from Pine Ridge, in Washington, D.C.

When Leonard Crow Dog hosted a Sun Dance on his property (known as Crow Dog's Paradise) in August 1972, numerous AIM leaders were present. Talk inevitably turned political. When former Rosebud tribal chairman Robert Burnette brought up the idea of a march on Washington, D.C., it generated immediate interest. Indian activists on the West Coast had been contemplating a similar idea, and various wings of Native activism began to coalesce. Burnette dubbed the proposed march "The Trail of Broken Treaties." He went to New York City to begin organizing. The Winnebago leader Reuben Snake led the effort in the Midwest. Assiniboine Hank Adams, an advocate of Native fishing rights, orchestrated matters on the West coast. The idea was beginning to take shape: several caravans, moving from west to east, would travel across the country to bring national attention to the hundreds of treaties the United States had abrogated and otherwise violated over the years. Starting in Los Angeles, San Francisco, Seattle, Denver, and Rapid City, South Dakota, the caravans would stop at various reservations and spiritual sites, and pick up Native people along the way, before finally converging on the nation's capital during the last week of the 1972 presidential election. More than a dozen Native organizations signed on to take part in the Trail. After the Sun Dance, AIM leaders headed back to their base in Minneapolis to begin their own organizing efforts.[31]

In early October, the caravans slowly began to wind their way eastward. By the end of the month, they had all made their way to Minneapolis. There, the organizers huddled to refine their strategy. The result was "The Twenty Points Position Paper." Largely the work of Hank Adams, it voiced the march's ideology and outlined its goals, including exigencies for the federal government to revive the treaty-making process, the creation of a treaty commission to review violations and supply suitable compensation, and a call for the federal government to conduct its Native policy within the context of treaty relations. The organizers hoped to present the presidential candidates with the paper and to force Native issues to the forefront of the campaign. Shortly thereafter, the caravans resumed their eastward trek.[32]

When the marchers arrived in Washington on November 1, they found two disconcerting situations. First, housing arrangements for the more than a thousand participants were extremely inadequate, thereby fueling tensions. For example, some of the participants found themselves sleeping in the cold, dank, rat-infested basement of a local church. Worse yet was the government's attitude. That late in the campaign, the election seemed a foregone conclusion: Nixon was stampeding toward an easy victory over South Dakota Democratic Senator George McGovern. The protest organizers would have none of the political leverage that a competitive race would have produced. To make matters worse, personal meetings were unavailable, as both major candidates were gone, traveling across the country and shoring up votes during the final week before the election. Furthermore, the Nixon administration officials who met the protesters were not particularly sympathetic; by now they were suspicious of any activity in which the anti-establishment members of AIM participated.[33]

Amid these circumstances, the planned, peaceful protest spontaneously turned into a full-scale riot. The marchers assembled at the Bureau of Indian Affairs building on Friday, November 3. By 5:00 p.m., protesters were disillusioned and government officials paranoid, each side suspicious of the other. The poor housing had been partly the fault of the march's organizers, who had not properly anticipated the magnitude of the Trail's logistics, but many of the protestors presumed it was the government's fault. Thus far, nothing productive had come of their stay in Washington, and frustrations were mounting. At the last moment, it seemed like disaster would be averted, as the government stepped in and offered temporary accommodations at various locales and agreed to a meeting at eight that evening in the auditorium of the Labor Department building, several blocks away. What they had not told the marchers, however, was that some 200 municipal and federal law enforcement officers, equipped with riot gear, were stationed in the Bureau of Indian Affairs building in anticipation of trouble. Instead of anticipating it, however, they instigated it.[34]

At the conclusion of some rather fruitless talks between Indian leaders and government officials, the law enforcement officers received word that the Indians and their supporters were set to leave the building. The officers immediately appeared in the lobby and began to employ authoritarian measures to "encourage" their quick departure. By all accounts, what happened next was an extemporaneous reaction by the protestors. Already disenchanted with the situation, alarmed by the sudden appearance of the heavily armed officers, and incensed by their unnecessarily strong-armed tactics, the protestors revolted and a riot ensued. After several minutes, the police were regrouping out on the street, and the Indians had occupied the building.[35]

Although the Trail of Broken Treaties had been an event originally organized and manifested by more than a dozen Native groups from all over the country, once the situation turned chaotic and violent, the American Indian Movement took center stage. AIM organized a security detachment to guard against forced entry by police and to maintain order among protestors within the building. AIM also managed the ensuing negotiations with the federal government and dealt directly with news reporters from around the country. Largely unaware of the national scope of the Trail of Broken Treaties before the occupation, the press now interpreted the occupation as another rambunctious, AIM-driven protest.[36]

Louis Bruce, the Mohawk/Oglala Commissioner of Indian Affairs, stood in the midst of the turmoil. Personally supportive of the Trail, he was an appointee of the Nixon administration, which was now highly critical of the event and engaged in trying to extricate the occupiers. As noted in the prior chapter, Bruce was already surrounded by antagonistic Interior Department officials who resented his self-determination policies and were attempting to undercut his position. The commissioner now made a fateful decision. Against the wishes of the Nixon administration, he went to the BIA building and personally met with the protestors in an effort to jump start negotiations and bring about a peaceful resolution to the conflict. He was joined by LaDonna Harris, the Comanche wife of Oklahoma Senator Fred Harris. Not long thereafter, Bruce was relieved of his commissioner-ship.[37]

Negotiations sputtered, continuing in fits and starts. The occupation did not finally end until November 9, two days after Nixon's re-election victory. The Indians in the building were eventually granted partial amnesty and given more than $66,000 to defray the cost of transporting some of the elderly people back to various reservations around the country. By the time the protesters left, the building was in shambles. Despite its nominal role in the planning and initial execution of the Trail of Broken Treaties, the American Indian Movement had again gotten its name in newspaper headlines across the country. However, the aftermath of its participation in the ill-fated march would not be felt as acutely anywhere as it was on Pine Ridge.[38]

BACKLASH

One of Commissioner Louis Bruce's innovations had been the establishment of the National Tribal Chairman's Association (NTCA), a new organization whose purpose involved giving tribal chairmen from reservations around the country a forum to compare and contrast the various issues that confronted them, and to strategize for the future. The group was funded by the BIA's National Council on Indian Opportunity (NCIO). A number of Native people were suspicious of the NTCA on those grounds alone. Some critics felt that tribal chairmen were already dependent on the federal bureaucracy for their authority and standing. They wondered if this new organization would co-opt tribal leaders further.[39]

A few months before the Trail of Broken Treaties, the NTCA had received about $55,000 from the BIA for its annual conference, which was held in Oregon. Perhaps not surprisingly then, the NTCA's position on the Trail of Broken Treaties was effectively co-opted by the NCIO, and the Chairman's Association turned against Bruce during the BIA building takeover. As the occupation lingered on, the National Council prompted the NTCA to hold a press conference denouncing the protest. In fact, the NCIO went so far as to fly certain chairmen to Washington from around the country for that express purpose. Once gathered, they took turns condemning the "militants" who had allegedly staged this unwarranted, gratuitous display of lawlessness, and who really did not represent the sentiments of American Indians. After all, they pointed out, had not the chairmen themselves been elected to represent Native people?[40]

Pine Ridge Chairman Dick Wilson was a member of the NTCA. He was also one of the most vociferous Native critics of the Trail of Broken Treaties fiasco. Just months earlier, he had lauded AIM's efforts in the Raymond Yellow Thunder affair and had publicly voiced his support of the organization. Now, rather suddenly, he completely reversed himself.

The Oglala Sioux Tribal Council's final quarterly session of 1972 opened on November 8, just one day before the BIA building occupation in Washington, D.C., ended. This was a significantly late start for the council meeting. In fact, Article V of the Oglala Sioux Tribe's bylaws stipulates that the quarterly meetings are to be held in January, April, July, and October. However, Chairman Wilson's dictatorial tendencies were in full bloom by the autumn of 1972. The October meetings were not held when scheduled because he refused to call them into session. Wilson's critics charged that through such actions, the chairman was bypassing the Council in an effort to expand his own powers. Instead of working through the council, he increasingly governed his administration through the council's five-member executive committee. Within the executive committee, only Vice Chairman David Long was opposed to Wilson's centralizing policies and strong-handed techniques. Thus, by conducting his business in this manner, Wilson could be sure that his actions would be relatively unimpeded.[41]

Wilson's circumvention of the council was not merely guided by his desire to assert his own policies. He was also reacting to outside forces that were increasingly pitted against him. A grassroots effort to have him impeached was in motion by the fall of 1972. The Porcupine District Council had voted to ask their representatives on the OSTC (Orland Big Owl and William High Hawk) to initiate impeachment proceedings against the tribal chairman. Wilson was, of course, aware of all this, and his refusal to call the tribal council into session during October was probably guided in part by his efforts to make sure that such proceedings would not be initiated. The strategy worked, and the move to impeach Wilson was held in abeyance amidst accusations by frustrated Porcupine residents who contended that their councilmen had been either bought off or intimidated by the chairman.[42]

After securing his political position, Wilson finally relented and allowed the October Tribal Council session to be held in November. The president called the meeting to order on the eighth. His very first item for discussion was the recent events in Washington. Wilson now disavowed AIM, categorizing it as an illegitimate organization that the council should not recognize. The council responded by authorizing the chairman to send a telegram to the commissioner of Indian Affairs, secretary of the interior, and the president of the United States. It read: "The Oglala Sioux Tribal Council in Regular Session by unanimous decision has taken a stand November 8, 1972, to inform you that the Tribe does not condone or approve any and all action taken by the American Indian Movement in Washington, D.C., nor is any member of the American Indian Movement authorized to speak for and in behalf of the Oglala Sioux Tribe."[43]

Two days later, the topic of AIM again arose at the council meeting. This time there was fearful speculation that AIM might "hold a victory dance" on the reservation. In response to this anticipated trauma, the council voted 17–0 that "the President of the tribe should be given the overall authority to take whatever action that he felt would be necessary to protect the lives and property and to insure the peace and dignity of the Pine Ridge Indian Reservation." The council then provided Wilson "full assurance that [they] would give him their complete support on whatever action the president may have to take."[44]

The council then passed Resolution 072–55, "A Resolution of the Oglala Sioux Tribal Council to Protect Property, Interests, and Sovereign

Dignity of the Oglala Sioux Tribe." It singled out AIM for its "unjustified damage to Indian Bureau offices and to the destruction and damage and ultimate loss of records within these offices." The American Indian Movement, it said, "is not recognized by the Oglala Sioux governing body as an organization." Finally, it went so far as to forbid the use of any buildings under the OST's jurisdiction "by the AIM organization or for any so-called 'victory dancing.'"[45]

At Wilson's instigation, Chief Judge Theodore Tibbets of the Oglala Sioux Tribal Court issued a restraining order on November 20. It prohibited Russell Means and Severt Young Bear from joining *any* assembly during the next thirty days. AIM was now more or less banned from the reservation, and Wilson had it within his discretion to enforce that policy by any means he saw fit. Wilson added a taunt to the injunction. Now sporting a crew cut himself, he threatened to cut off Means's braids personally if the AIM leader set foot on the reservation. He also hung a poster on his office wall offering a $1,000 reward for Means's pickled body. When Dennis Banks turned up on the reservation, tribal police, now under BIA jurisdiction but acting at the chairman's behest, arrested the AIM leader and escorted him off the reservation. Young Bear and Means, however, could not be so easily removed. They were both enrolled members of Pine Ridge, the former a lifelong resident of the reservation. A stronger show of power would be needed. It came around Thanksgiving, when Vice Chairman David Long invited Means to attend and speak at a meeting of the Oglala Lakota Land Owner's Association. Means agreed. While there, Wilson had him arrested. Means took the hint and subsequently moved to the neighboring Rosebud Reservation.[46]

Wilson's change in attitude was as quixotic as it was sudden. Why did Wilson so fervently and immediately reverse his support of the American Indian Movement? Resolution 072–55's reference to lost and damaged records from Washington could hardly be the grounds for explaining it. In fact, many of the "records" to which the resolution referred had not been destroyed, damaged, or lost at all. To the contrary, they had been intentionally seized during the occupation. Guided by the advice of a sympathetic deputy commissioner from the Bureau of Indian Affairs, AIM took the opportunity to grab what they viewed as incriminating records that would detail BIA corruption and ineptitude. Documents on the issues of Native and/or reservation land tenure, finances, law-enforcement, health, and the

tribal councils were all salvaged and evacuated during the final hectic hours
of the occupation. They were eventually sorted out and given to nationally
syndicated columnist Jack Anderson, who used the material as the basis for
a series of devastating exposés of the BIA that appeared in newspapers
around the country. On January 21, 1973, the federal government was sufficiently embarrassed that it went so far as to arrest Les Whitten, one of
Anderson's researchers, for the possession of stolen government property.
Trail of Broken Treaties organizer Hank Adams, who abhorred the violence
in Washington, had also been arrested on the same charge as he was preparing to return those documents that he had tracked down. Both were eventually acquitted by a federal grand jury.[47]

However, concern over BIA documents hardly accounts for the sudden
and profound anti-AIM sentiments that Wilson now spouted. In fact, the
resolution against and about AIM "victory dances" on Pine Ridge may not
have even stemmed from any legitimate concerns. After the Trail of Broken
Treaties concluded, AIM split into three caravans: Dennis Banks led one
southward to North Carolina, John Trudell and Vernon Bellecourt headed
toward New York City, and Russell Means went westward with the final ret-
inue, initially returning to Minneapolis. Means spent several weeks traveling, continuing on to Arizona and California. The closest he got during that
time to "victory dancing" at Pine Ridge was his attendance of a United
Sioux Tribe meeting in Pierre, South Dakota (several hours east of the
reservation), where he received a chilly reception, but still managed to garner sizeable donations.[48]

One possible explanation for Wilson's vitriol may be his growing ties
with the federal government. As noted above, the National Tribal Chairman's Association, to which Wilson belonged, had harshly criticized AIM at
the federal government's behest. In fact, the government's attitude toward
the Movement in the aftermath of the BIA building occupation could be
seen clearly in Arizona. When Means led an AIM delegation to the Hopi
Reservation in that state during his westward trek after the Trail, news of
their arrival preceded them. In response, the federal government closed
down its agency and the superintendent left the reservation altogether. This
is not surprising, considering that the BIA was intimidated by AIM even
before the Trail of Broken Treaties. Indeed, during the protests in Gordon
over the death of Raymond Yellow Thunder, the BIA was already quite
wary of the urban activists. Charles Trimble, then head of the American

Indian Press Association (AIPA), later recalled that the Bureau went so far as to try to co-opt the AIPA. The BIA wanted them to present the situation as AIM outsiders simply "raising hell" in the little border town, and to ignore all of AIM's constructive work, as well as the fact that it was a largely local, grassroots protest.[49]

Barbara Means-Adams, Russell Means's cousin and Dick Wilson's former campaign manager, believes that federal influence motivated, at least in part, Wilson's furious antagonism. She maintains that an Interior Department official, with the surname of Alvarez, told Wilson after the BIA occupation that the chairman needed to cut his hair, renounce AIM, and denounce the Trail of Broken Treaties, or face massive cuts in federal funding.[50]

The U.S. government was incontrovertibly dedicated toward treating the American Indian Movement with enmity after the Trail of Broken Treaties.[51] But beyond federal prodding, the internal political dynamics of Pine Ridge also played an important part. As mentioned, Russell Means was an enrolled member of the tribe. In fact, he and his siblings had even inherited 190 acres of land on the reservation (although Means claims he stopped receiving payments from the standing lease agreement after joining AIM). In late 1972, as he and many others became increasingly disillusioned with Wilson, Means announced that he would seek the Pine Ridge chairmanship in 1974. He would pose a direct and personal threat to the power of the incumbent chairman. Discrediting and attacking AIM was now in Wilson's political interests.[52]

The two possible explanations for Wilson's anti-AIM attitude and behavior noted above (federal pressure and Means's political challenge to his regime) rely on external forces acting upon the Pine Ridge chairman, and the supposition that he reacted to them accordingly. However, a number of authors have offered another possible explanation that relies on internal forces. They have asserted that Wilson was personally antagonistic toward full bloods, with whom AIM was in the process of aligning, and that his own rancorous view of the world led him to act accordingly. Whatever ill feelings Wilson may have harbored toward his full-blood brethren might very well have played a role in determining his anti-AIM actions. However, there were also real political issues that should be considered. By dividing the reservation over the issue of AIM, Wilson may have sought to prop up his own flagging support.[53]

One may interpret his actions as designed to create an "AIM-scare" of sorts. Surely, AIM was a confrontational organization. But by November 1972, their efforts had been almost exclusively targeted at Euro-American institutions and power structures, not at men like Dick Wilson. And the Movement gave no clear indication that it was looking to put Wilson at the forefront of its agenda in the aftermath of the Trail of Broken Treaties. To the contrary, AIM's leaders focused their attention elsewhere during November. It was Wilson who seems to have instigated the serious contentiousness between himself and AIM. During the November council meeting, the chairman called many of the OST's employees to a meeting at Billy Mills Hall in the village of Pine Ridge. Once assembled, he told the group that the American Indian Movement was headed toward Pine Ridge Reservation and that the aforementioned "victory dancing" would be followed by AIM attacks against the reservation's BIA building and tribal government offices.[54]

In reality, there is virtually nothing in the historical record to indicate that AIM was planning to do any such thing. However, details about the BIA building occupation in Washington were still unclear so soon after the event's conclusion, and the scare tactic seemed to work. By the end of the meeting, many of the employees were convinced that a violent invasion by AIM was close on the horizon. In light of this and the political realities confronting him, Wilson may very well have decided to adopt an anti-AIM stance as a way of consolidating political support.[55]

CRACKDOWN

When the Oglala Sioux Tribal Council concluded its November session, council members Johnson Holy Rock and Richard Little made a motion to recess with the intention of coming back into session after Thanksgiving. However, Chairman Wilson would not call the council back to order until December 12. In the mean time, Wilson began to take steps to add muscle to his political position.[56]

First, he attacked his most immediate political opponent, Vice Chairman David Long. When Russell Means spoke at the Oglala Lakota Land Owner's Association, it was at Long's invitation. In reprisal for this act of defiance, which so blatantly flew in the face of Wilson's new anti-AIM policy, the chairman suspended Long from the vice presidency. It was a clear abuse of power on Wilson's part. The OST's constitution and bylaws make no provision for the suspension of OSTC officers, except as an intermediary step during the process of impeachment and removal, and Wilson had made no move to impeach Long. He simply unilaterally suspended him. To make matters worse, Wilson's dictatorial methods quickly spilled beyond the confines of the tribal council.[57]

Citing the extended powers granted him by Resolution 072–55, Wilson formed a new militia under the pretense of maintaining law and order on the reservation. Wilson's critics derisively labeled the new force the "Goon Squad." The members of the squad adopted the label, converting it into a patriotic acronym: Guardians Of the Oglala Nation. Now universally known as the GOON Squad, the group was to be the source of great controversy and violence during the remainder of Wilson's chairmanship.[58]

The origins of the GOON Squad are still speculated upon. One frequent assertion is that Wilson, with the federal government's blessing, misappropriated approximately $65,000 in federal funds that had been earmarked for highway development programs on the reservation, using the money to recruit and arm the unit. If this is true, it is quite ironic given that the Wilson's executive council had just recently relinquished reservation policing to the Bureau of Indian Affairs for lack of adequate funding. The chairman claimed that the tribal government's budget could not afford to fund the official reservation police force, instead transferring control of it to the BIA, but he somehow found the money to pay for a private armed force. As a result, Wilson now had something akin to a praetorian guard at his disposal.[59]

In fact, Wilson freely admitted that the initial money for the GOON Squad did indeed come from the BIA. There were also admissions that they were armed in part by local white supporters. Bessie Cornelius, a Catholic, mixed-blood Wilsonite whose daughter worked as Superintendent Lyman's secretary, sketched the GOONs as such: "Now if you were to take a composite of the goon, a goon would be an individual just like my husband. Self-educated or college educated, formally educated, trained, employed by the Bureau, by the tribe, self-employed . . . but every one of them Indian, and let me tell you, every one of them more Indian than Russell Means."[60]

Cornelius was a poster-child for the notion of a mixed-blood colonial elite on Pine Ridge. She was a fourth-generation Christian on the Indian side of her family. Her white father was a successful sheep rancher on the reservation. His family had previously profited on Pine Ridge by commercial farming and by raising sheep and cattle. She had an open antipathy for full-blood culture. She believed that the impoverished full bloods of the reservation had no one to blame but themselves; after all, she reasoned, all of her kids went to college, why couldn't theirs? The press called her husband's family "Dick Wilson's men."[61]

Wilson himself described the GOON Squad as an auxiliary police force, designed "to handle people like Russell Means and other radicals." The GOONs, he later told Congress, were, "a small group of people to protect our buildings, bureau offices, tribal offices." They would turn out to be much more than that.[62]

However, not all GOONS were even eager to serve on the squad. One Pine Ridge Oglala, an OST employee who repaired wells for the reservation water works, recounted the overtures he received to join the GOON Squad. Richard Wilson himself asked the man and his co-workers to stand guard at the BIA building and tribal offices. As the man's boss was George Wilson, the chairman's brother, the tribal employee felt that his job might be threatened if he did not comply. He and his co-workers were given basic instructions in riot control and hand-to-hand combat and then posted at various buildings in the village of Pine Ridge.[63]

The fact that the man's boss was the chairman's brother was not unusual. Dick Wilson had placed family members and friends in numerous positions throughout his administration. Amid the poverty of Pine Ridge, Wilson's brother Jim earned $25,000 per year as the head of the Tribal Planning Office, in addition to the $15,000 he earned in consulting fees. Wilson's wife had replaced the embattled Leland Bear Heels as the director of Head Start, and a nephew was installed as the tribe's personnel director, further building Wilson's political capital by extending his control over the reservation's scant supply of jobs. The head of the GOON Squad was Glenn Three Stars, a Wilson supporter with an unsuccessful employment record. Patronage politics was not new to Pine Ridge. There had been accusations of that nature throughout the reservation's history, right through to the One Feather administration, and the practice continues to this day. However, Wilson's manipulation of the system created unprecedented consequences.[64]

Issues of job security aside, there was quite clearly a number of GOON Squad members who were loyal to Wilson, militant in their attitude toward his opponents, and genuinely motivated to serve him. Under Wilson's guidance, they began a campaign of intimidation against the chairman's political opponents. Threats soon escalated into violence. Ellen Moves Camp, a full-blood elder, described the situation: "They [the GOON Squad] would go around and anybody that stated anything against Dick Wilson, why, they were automatically beaten up or threatened. . . . We have guns all over the reservation, threatening people, putting them in the hospital. You don't have no protection at all on the reservation. You have to carry a gun on this reservation now, ever since he's been in there. There's been homes burnt up."[65]

Russell Means remembers GOONs smashing car windows, slashing tires, and arresting people on dubious charges. One young lady had to leave her automobile to get help after accidently driving into a ditch on a reservation road. She was a Wilson opponent and her car had an AIM bumper sticker. When she returned, she found the car riddled with bullets to the point of rendering it inoperable. By the end of November, even OSTC Vice Chairman David Long noted, "I have bullet holes in my window and eight horses shot."[66]

The situation would only worsen in the years to come. By 1975, Walter Gallagher from the Pine Ridge town of Kyle would phone authorities with some very disturbing news. He had witnessed an attack on six white AIM supporters, men and women, who had driven onto the reservation. They were dragged from their car and beaten by fifteen to twenty GOONs. The beating took place under direct orders from President Wilson, who was present at the incident from start to finish.[67]

By using anti-AIM scare tactics, abusing the powers of his office, and increasingly employing threats and violence through the GOON Squad, Wilson sought to disengender support for the Movement and to squelch political opposition on the reservation. In the end, however, this strategy backfired as his opponents, both on the reservation and off, united against him.

ALLIANCE

Dick Wilson's coercive tactics helped to speed up a process that was already under way: a political alliance between full-blood residents of the reservation and the urban activists of the American Indian Movement. The two groups were drawn together by a set of reciprocal dynamics: AIM's desire to shed its image as mere urban activists and to define itself as an authentic Native organization, and the wishes of many full-blood people on Pine Ridge to find an ally in their burgeoning dispute with Wilson.

The search for viable alternatives to the IRA government had never ceased on Pine Ridge. In 1967, more than three decades after the installation of the OSTC and still five years before Wilson's election to the chairmanship, Pine Ridge Oglala Jake Herman had spoken on behalf of the disenchanted. "People want to return to the chiefs."[68]

From AIM's perspective, the reservation full bloods offered a direct link to traditional Native cultures, a link that had been diminished during the preceding decades of urbanization. It seemed not to matter that many of AIM's leaders were Anishinaabe and that Pine Ridge Reservation was inhabited by Oglala Lakotas who had been their enemies during previous centuries, spoke a completely unrelated language, and practiced a religion quite different from traditional Anishinaabe religion. Through the lens of AIM's intertribal ideology, the full bloods of Pine Ridge offered a connection to their Native roots and a chance for AIM members to achieve what Dennis Banks referred to as "re-identity."[69]

Leaders of the American Indian Movement had first made a strong connection with traditional Lakota culture when they accepted the spiritual guidance of the Crow Dog family, among whom were Henry and his son Leonard, Sichanghu medicine men on the neighboring Rosebud Reservation. Henry Crow Dog was the grandson of Crow Dog, the man who had shot Spotted Tail in 1881. He and his family lived on an allotment known as Crow Dog's Paradise. Dennis Banks had sought out the Crow Dog family as early as 1970, saying, "I've come because you people have something we city Indians have lost. We have an Indian organization that is doing fine, but it needs not only a political philosophy but also a spiritual meaning in order to be complete." The Crow Dog family accepted the young urban activist into their home, and Leonard Crow Dog became AIM's spiritual adviser.[70]

AIM's search for a cultural connection also had a generational element to it. The leaders of the American Indian Movement were typically in their thirties, and many of their members were even younger than that; AIM easily garnered the support of many young Native Americans on the reservations and in the cities, who were attracted to the Movement's defiant pride and unapologetic approach. The full-blood Lakotas from whom AIM sought guidance were frequently elders who could pass on not only Lakota language and religion, but history as well. Mary Brave Bird was a Rosebud Lakota who would later marry Leonard Crow Dog. She first encountered AIM at the 1971 Sun Dance at Crow Dog's Paradise. Then in her late teens, she immediately gravitated toward the Movement. But she also noticed how the alliance between AIM and the full-blood elders was already blossoming. "Something strange happened then. The traditional old, full-blood medicine men joined with us kids," she later recalled. "It was the real old folks who had the spirit and wisdom to give us. The grandfathers and grandmothers who still remembered a time when Indians were Indians, whose own grandparents or even parents had fought Custer gun in hand, people who for us were living links with the great past. They had a lot of strength and power, enough to give some of it to us."[71]

Perhaps not surprisingly given AIM's general orientation and the deteriorating situation on Pine Ridge, what started out as a relationship based on culture soon turned political. AIM won over many full bloods with their eager and effective participation in the protests over the death of Raymond Yellow Thunder. Even Dick Wilson had lauded their efforts at the time. However, as Wilson made himself a common enemy of many full bloods on his own reservation, as well as the entire American Indian Movement, the anti-Wilsonites on Pine Ridge increasingly allied themselves with AIM in the face of the chairman's repressive measures. Many full bloods realized that AIM could bolster their efforts with the enthusiasm and the sheer physical strength needed to fend off the increasingly outrageous actions of the GOON Squad.

Of course, not everyone was enamored with the alliance. "The deadbeats, the losers, those are AIM supporters," railed Bessie Cornelius. "The solid citizens have a lot to lose. They're already living and building the lives they want."[72] Reverend Howard Orcutt, an elderly Presbyterian minister living in the town of Martin, in Bennett County, claimed that most of AIM's supporters on the reservation were youngsters "who had no ambition other than to mooch off others." To him, they were ne'er-do-wells. At the same time, however, he had to admit that Wilson was "as big a crook as the rest of them." This was not an unenlightened opinion. Orcutt had known Wilson personally since 1952.[73]

During the 1930s and 1940s, full bloods had often bypassed the Oglala Sioux Tribal Council and dealt directly with the Office of Indian Affairs. This was possible in part because then Superintendent W. O. Roberts was somewhat sympathetic to their cause and cognizant of the fact that the new tribal council did not always work to the benefit of the Oglala people.[74] But bypassing the OSTC for the BIA did not appear to be a suitable strategy for full bloods in the early 1970s.

As the new federal policy of self-determination took hold in the late 1960s, the Bureau of Indian Affairs somewhat loosened its controls over tribal governments. The new superintendent of Pine Ridge Reservation in 1972 was Stanley David Lyman, a man who blindly followed the mandates of the self-determination policy and staunchly stood behind the OST chairman to the bitter end, despite the executive vulgarities of Wilson's administration. As late as April 16, 1973, six weeks into the forthcoming occupation of Wounded Knee, after nearly a half year of GOON Squad belligerence, Lyman proved himself incapable of understanding the complexity of the situation. Violence was springing from the Wilson administration. On that day Lyman observed what had by then become a common scene on the reservation: Wilson's Oglala opponents holding a demonstration. The superintendent confronted the protesters, asking them what they were upset about. The demonstrators were skeptical that he would be genuinely interested, but they informed him that the GOON squad had been harassing them. Lyman suggested that they sign a complaint form. The suggestion was clearly impotent; the GOONs were being funded by the federal government and led by Dick Wilson, a man with federal backing. Furthermore, the complaint would be reviewed by Lyman himself, a man who backed Wilson from start to finish. The protestors rejected the suggestion. Lyman thus concluded that the demonstrators "haven't even given the system a chance." It is difficult to perceive that a lifelong BIA employee such as Lyman could be so stunningly oblivious to not only the historical roots of the situation, but also the immediacy of the circumstances around him. Pine Ridge Lakotas had been under the suzerainty of the Indian Reorganization Act for nearly four decades and at odds with Wilson and agitating for his removal for more than a year. To dismiss their skepticism by saying they "haven't even given the system a chance" is disturbingly imperceptive at best. Nonetheless, this was the case.[75]

As a result, Wilson's opponents increasingly allied themselves with AIM in an effort to bolster their cause. Full-blood elder Ellen Moves Camp stated the matter clearly. "And with our brothers and sisters of the American Indian Movement, we feel stronger. We're not scared of them [the

GOON Squad]. This is what we needed—a little push more. Most of the reservation believes in the AIM, and we're proud to have them with us."[76]

By the end of 1972, Chairman Wilson had alienated a significant constituency on Pine Ridge Reservation, specifically many full bloods who viewed him as corrupt, antagonistic, and tyrannical. At the same time, he abruptly changed his attitude toward the American Indian Movement, transforming himself from a vocal supporter to an ardent enemy. In the process, he inadvertently helped increase the rate at which the cultural alliance between AIM and the Pine Ridge full bloods blossomed into a political alliance as well. As the full bloods, often led by female elders like Ellen Moves Camp, Gladys Bissonette, and Agnes Lamont, continued to protest the abuses of the Wilson regime, AIM increasingly joined with them.[77]

The legal scholar Vine Deloria, Jr., himself a former resident of Pine Ridge, eloquently described the situation on the eve of the occupation of Wounded Knee. "The coalition had finally been formed which was to shuffle Indian affairs beyond recognition," Deloria wrote. "Urban Indian activists seeking an Indian identity and heritage and traditional Indians buttressed by the energies of the young combined forces and made ready to push the Indians who had accommodated the white man off the reservations."[78]

7

"That Great Symbolic Act"

The Siege of Wounded Knee as a Grassroots
Political Protest

TOWARD THE END OF 1972, a new protest group formed on the Pine Ridge Reservation. The Inter-District Tribal Council was vocal in its opposition to Chairman Dick Wilson and Superintendent Stanley Lyman, demanding both of their resignations. Among their complaints was that Wilson was violating the Oglala Sioux Tribe's Constitution by not holding the mandated quarterly meetings of the Oglala Sioux Tribal Council (OSTC).[1]

Chairman Dick Wilson had pushed the October meetings of the Oglala Sioux Tribal Council back to November. After what was intended to be a brief Thanksgiving holiday recess, he finally called them back to order on the morning of December 12, 1972. The first thing he did was address the council on the issue of escalating tensions and violence on the reservation. In short, he justified his increasingly authoritarian measures, including the implementation of his private police force (the GOON Squad), as being "in line" with the powers accorded him under Council Resolution 072–55. After Wilson defended his actions, discussion turned to another matter: his impeachment. Antipathy between the chairman and his opponents had become sufficiently agitated that the latter were now calling for Wilson's removal from office. They accused him of, among other things, bribery, corruption, intimidation, graft, and nepotism.[2]

One of Wilson's chief opponents on the council was his own vice president, David Long. Wilson had stretched the boundaries of his office beyond recognition by unilaterally suspending Long because of the Vice President's association with the American Indian Movement. Not surprisingly, Long was now among those leading the charge to have Wilson impeached. After the council discussed how to handle impending impeachment hearings, Wilson renewed his political attack against Long, this time by proxy. He gave the floor to a tribal member and political ally named William Rooks.[3]

William Rooks and his brother Eugene were conservative, militantly anti-AIM, mixed-blood members of the John Birch Society. The two men periodically had Wilson's ear, and they actively encouraged his autocratic behavior and dictatorial tendencies by insisting that the American Indian Movement was actually a communist front organization, its members insidious soldiers in the Marxist-Leninist movement for world domination. Wilson now looked on as William Rooks attacked Long, reading a list of charges against the vice president.[4]

Some of the council members might have believed fantastic claims of AIM's alleged work on behalf of the Soviet Union and the People's Republic of China, but they knew better than to listen to insinuations about David Long, a man most of them knew personally. As discussions and debates centered specifically on the suspension of Long and more generally on the tense situation on the reservation, it became clear that the council as a whole thought Wilson had exceeded his authority in suspending his vice president, regardless of which side of the Wilson-Long dispute individual council members might come down on. After 3:00 p.m., council members William High Hawk and Paul Apple finally made a motion to lift the suspension and reinstate Long. It carried unanimously. An amendment was then added to the motion. It proposed that the two men shake hands and continue with their duties. Though largely cosmetic, the measure passed 14–2, with one abstention.[5]

The following day's session saw the day-to-day business of the council begin with an opening address by Paul Apple, who noted all of the good work the council had done despite its many "petty grievances." Petty or not, the more mundane business of the tribal council continued to be interspersed with the contentious issues that now colored the reservation on a daily basis. Council members Hobart Keith and Richard Little, who were both aligned against Wilson, brought up charges of corruption against the chairman. They made the claim on behalf of members of a local family, the Prados. Little and Birgil Kills Straight, another Wilson opponent, made a motion that the matter be heard in tribal court, with Keith acting as attorney for the Prados. The motion carried with sixteen for and two not voting.[6]

The following day's session was largely devoid of the highly politically charged issues that had surfaced during the previous two days. A number of economic development issues were tabled for further review. The council went into recess at 4:30 p.m. after a motion by Orland Big Owl and Florence Tibbetts that the meeting resume in one week, on the twenty-first of December. As tensions on the reservation increased, however, Dick Wilson would seek to minimize the input of a council that had just repudiated his suspension of Vice President Long. Bypassing the December date, the chairman would not reconvene the Oglala Sioux Tribal Council until February 1973.[7]

AIM RETURNS

By late November 1972, Dick Wilson's draconian measures had successfully dispersed AIM's leaders from the Pine Ridge Reservation. He was incapable, however, of keeping them out of the surrounding region. As the Northern Plains winter announced the arrival of 1973, the American Indian Movement engaged in a series of activities around Pine Ridge's borders, as if they were encircling the Oglala homeland as part of some ineluctable spiral that would bring them back to the troubled reservation.

In January, AIM went to the small Nebraska panhandle town of Scottsbluff to conduct a planning session with the New Congress for Community Development, a group devoted to defending the economic and civil rights of Chicano laborers and community members in the region. Mexican-Americans were heavily represented in the local agriculture industry, particularly as hard-working, underpaid seasonal laborers. On the night of January 13, Scottsbluff police arrested Russell Means and Pine Ridge resident Edgar Running Bear at the Park Motel after receiving complaints about noise. The authorities were quite aware of whom they were taking into custody. They also went out of their way to arrest Means's brothers: Dace

Means, for parking a car illegally in an alley, and Ted Means, for allegedly assaulting an officer as he intervened to prevent the police from manhandling his wife and child. Leonard Crow Dog was arrested for driving without a valid license. By Means's account, the police planted a gun on him once he was inside the jail and tried to fabricate a reason for shooting him in his cell by making it appear as if he were attempting an armed escape. Nothing of the sort came to pass, and Means was released on bail the following day.[8]

In retaliation for this treatment, AIM picketed the jail, harassed the police officers at their homes, and filed a $200,000 lawsuit against the sheriff, the chairman of the county board of commissioners, the county attorney, the Scottsbluff mayor and police chief, and the head of the Nebraska Highway Patrol. Ten days of protests concluded with AIM's departure, police and national guardsmen following them on the ground and by air until they left the state.[9]

Amidst the protests in Scottsbluff, another Pine Ridge Oglala had been killed by a white person in a reservation border town. On January 21, twenty-year-old Wesley Bad Heart Bull had gone drinking with some family members and friends at Bill's Bar in Buffalo Gap, South Dakota, a minuscule town about fifteen miles due west of Pine Ridge. Bad Heart Bull engaged in several quarrels with other patrons that night. One of the confrontations eventually spilled out onto the street, where it turned fatal. Darld Schmitz, a thirty-year-old local white man who had also been drinking, stabbed the young Lakota to death. Both men had checkered pasts (multiple arrests, histories of violence), and eyewitness accounts of the encounter varied over issues of provocation and whether or not Bad Heart Bull was armed when Schmitz knifed him to death. Schmitz, an Air Force veteran who worked as a gas station attendant in the nearby town of Custer, was subsequently charged with manslaughter and released on a $5,000 bond.[10]

The episode hardly mustered the moral indignation of the Raymond Yellow Thunder murder, but tensions were much higher in early 1973 than they had been in early 1972. Back then, Yellow Thunder's sisters had turned to AIM for help after being frustrated by a lackadaisical response from myriad state, local, and reservation officials. A year later, the Bad Heart Bull family did not even bother going elsewhere; Sarah Bad Heart Bull, the dead man's mother, went straight to AIM. She wanted to see Schmitz charged with murder instead of manslaughter. Many believed that such would have surely been the case if a Native American had stabbed a white person under identical circumstances. AIM responded quickly, and concern over the Bad Heart Bull killing soon piggybacked onto a previously planned protest in nearby Rapid City, South Dakota.[11]

Ron Petite was an American Indian Movement leader who had helped coordinate the Trail of Broken Treaties. Based in Rapid City, he also was in charge of the Sioux Indian Emergency Care and Rehabilitation Center. Earlier in the month, he had announced a plan for AIM to come to Rapid City and engage in a series of protests on behalf of Native people living there. Although this South Dakota tourism hub of 40,000 people at the base of the Black Hills and near Mt. Rushmore was sizably larger than most reservation border towns, American Indians there still felt the same stinging barbs of racism that were evident in places like Gordon and Scottsbluff. This bigotry had severely aggravated a tragic situation the previous spring. Rapid City had been flooded by fierce rains and melting snow that led Rapid Creek to burst its banks, killing well over 200 people and decimating countless homes and businesses. Among those devastated were Indian residents of the city, mostly Lakota, who typically lived in a south side slum known as Sioux Addition. Amid the disaster were accusations that relief efforts for Sioux Addition residents had been inexcusably slow and insufficient compared to aid given to their white neighbors. At the beginning of the year, Petite had urged AIM to protest this discrepancy, as well as discrimination in housing, jobs, and a lack of equitable services for Native veterans. Now, with one eye squarely set on the proceedings surrounding the arraignment of Darld Schmitz for the killing of Wesley Bad Heart Bull, the American Indian Movement moved its base of operations to Rapid City.[12]

AIM's leadership set themselves up at the Mother Butler Center, a former Catholic alcohol rehabilitation agency that now served more as a shelter. They orchestrated activities in Rapid City as the Movement's membership descended upon the town. There were boycotts and pickets of numerous businesses, ranging from K-Mart, Dunkin' Donuts, Piggly Wiggly, and a Coca-Cola bottling plant to the major utilities, including Northwestern Bell Telephone and Black Hills Power and Light. AIM members hung signs with slogans like "Welcome to the most racist state in the U.S.A.!" Eventually, a riot broke out between whites, who felt threatened by the forcefulness of the protests, and Indians, who were venting frustrations that had built up over generations. Local police arrested some 200 Indians and held them at the Pennington County Jail. At the height of the protests and violence in Rapid City, Russell Means announced that the American Indian Movement would caravan to South Dakota's Custer County courthouse on February 6, where AIM would meet with state officials and demand that Darld Schmitz be charged with murder for the killing of Wesley Bad Heart Bull.[13]

Means had urged AIM members from all over to converge on the town of Custer, and he confidently predicted that more than 1,000 people would show up. When the night of the sixth arrived, however, two factors served to keep the numbers down. First was a heavy snow storm around Custer. Second was a newspaper story: an unnamed government source had led *Rapid City Journal* writer Lyn Gladstone to report incorrectly that the rally had been called off. A February snow storm on the Northern Plains is to be expected. The misreporting, however, is more curious. Since the occupation of the BIA building in Washington, the American Indian Movement had come under intense scrutiny from the Federal Bureau of Investigation. The FBI would soon thereafter initiate a counterintelligence program[14] (COINTELPRO) designed to infiltrate, harass, incarcerate, and otherwise disrupt the American Indian Movement. Between the bad weather and the disinformation, only about 200 people showed up in Custer.[15]

The meeting took place inside the courthouse. Representing the state of South Dakota were two agents from the Division of Criminal Investigation, along with the Custer County sheriff and state's attorneys for Custer and Fall River Counties. Despite the facts that the courthouse was a public building and that press and television crews had already received access, the officials insisted that only five Native people from among those gathered would be allowed inside for the meeting. Thus, while the roughly 200 people assembled were left to mill about in the snow or wait in their cars, Russell Means, Dennis Banks, Leonard Crow Dog, and Dave Hill, a Choctaw AIM leader from Salt Lake City, went inside where Bob High Eagle was already present. Law enforcement officers in full riot gear guarded the entrance of the building, preventing anyone else, including Sarah Bad Heart Bull, from going inside.[16]

The Native delegation's goal at the meeting was to raise the charges against Schmitz to murder. The prosecution adamantly refused. With the two sides at loggerheads, Means and Hill went outside to address those who had gathered, hoping to rally them to more vocal protests. When the two leaders attempted to return to the meeting, police would not allow Hill to re-enter the building. Means created a distraction by grabbing one officer by the collar and throwing him to the ground, allowing Hill to slip back inside. This action, however, triggered more vocal confrontations between the police and protesters. When Sarah Bad Heart Bull got into a heated argument with a state trooper, he put her in a choke hold with his night stick. The scene quickly turned violent.[17]

As the crowd lurched forward up the steps of the courthouse, law enforcement officials engaged them with little restraint. Hand-to-hand fighting broke out all around. As the police launched tear gas canisters into the crowd, Indians responded with molotov cocktails. They also threw the canisters back into the building itself. As things turned chaotic inside, Banks briefly engaged a trooper, then threw a chair through a window and fled along with Crow Dog. While police quickly subdued Means and Hill, the conflict raged on for well over two hours. By the time it was finally over, thirty-seven people were arrested, including Sarah Bad Heart Bull. Destruction in the town of Custer was substantial. The chamber of commerce building had been burned to the ground, the courthouse was damaged by fire, two police cars were destroyed, and numerous other buildings were vandalized. AIM raised the $35,000 needed to free Russell Means the next day. Others were not so lucky. In a note of bitter irony, Sarah Bad Heart Bull would eventually spend more time in jail (five months) for protesting her son's death than the very man who killed him would; an all-white jury acquitted Darld Schmitz of second-degree manslaughter later that year.[18]

After the episode at the Custer County courthouse, AIM members returned to their temporary base in Rapid City. A number of those arrested at Custer were held at the Pennington County jail in Rapid City, and this became the focal point of renewed demonstrations. During the next several days, AIM leaders held numerous meetings with city and county officials with mixed results. The nights were frequently punctuated by confrontations between Indians and whites, which occasionally turned violent. In the meantime, however, AIM's efforts were focused solely on Rapid City and its outlying towns. The movement had not yet signaled when it might return to Pine Ridge. Chairman Dick Wilson was waiting for them nonetheless.[19]

BUILD-UP

On February 5, some six weeks late and just one day before the protests in Custer, Chairman Wilson finally called back into session the Oglala Sioux Tribal Council meeting that had recessed on December 14. At first, proceedings within the council were civil and businesslike. Among other things, the OSTC voted not to purchase tourist facilities in the Black Hills, a place that many Lakotas hold sacred, and the council received a briefing on various financial matters from a Washington, D.C.–based tribal attorney. However, the even temper of affairs within the council was the calm before the storm and provided a stark contrast to what was generally taking place outside the meeting hall.[20]

As winter's grip on the reservation tightened, the violence perpetrated by President Wilson's GOON Squad showed no signs of letting up. "They were constantly harassing us," recalled Lou Bean, a reservation elder and one of the women leading the charge against the Wilson administration. Her family endured threats and intimidation. "They broke the windows out of the car, they cut our tires, they chased my kids home from school, they called my kids all kinds of dirty names, when I go down town they follow me in the grocery store. And that cop, it got so he sat outside across the street watching the house all night long. It just went from bad to worse."[21]

On February 8, OSTC members C. Hobart Keith, Richard Little, and Birgil Kills Straight stepped outside the confines of the council meeting to make public a list of eight impeachment charges against Wilson that they had compiled and had notarized the previous day. Included were accusations of corruption, embezzlement, nepotism, and numerous abrogations of the Oglala Sioux Tribe's constitution and bylaws. At the same time, Wilson's opponents had started circulating a petition demanding his removal. They would eventually garner 1,450 signatures.[22]

The following afternoon, the ongoing saga of Vice President Long's suspension intruded upon the otherwise prosaic business of the council. Wilson's suspension of Long had not only been the byproduct of questionable judgement, but was also unconstitutional. Recognizing this, the council had reinstated him in December. Now, council members Johnson Holy Rock (himself a former OST chairman from 1960 to 1962 and 1966 to 1968) and Paul Apple introduced a motion that would retroactively pay Long for the time he had been wrongfully suspended and had his salary withheld.

The motion carried unanimously, but six members abstained, perhaps not wanting to side with Wilson's opponents, even symbolically.[23]

From there, the conversation turned to the subject of Wilson himself. Vice President Long and Council members Keith and Kills Straight (see Appendix C) officially introduced their impeachment charges against Wilson. The council then consented to having them read. "We charge you with gross incompetency, malfeasance and misfeasance in office and demand your immediate removal from office," stated a preamble, which was followed by the eight charges.[24]

The introduction of the written charges was an important step for the anti-Wilsonites. Article VIII, section 2 of Oglala Sioux Tribe's constitution specifies the following: "Any complaint against any officer of the council or any councilman must be in writing and sworn to by the complainant." Wilson's failure to submit a written complaint had been one of several factors that nullified his suspension of Long. Now that the charges against Wilson had been signed, notarized, and read into the council's official records, the effort to have him impeached was officially in motion and would have to be addressed. Both sides were now ready to marshal their forces for the battle ahead. Paul Apple and Robert Ecoffey made a motion to table the complaint until the next session. It passed by a 10–4 count. Keith and Little then made a motion that the council recess for one week. It carried unanimously. The impeachment hearing was scheduled for Wednesday, February 14.[25]

During the interim, Wilson moved to strengthen his position. To do so, he again played the AIM card. Under the pretext of fearing an invasion, the chairman turned to the federal government for protection and reinforcement. The American Indian Movement, he alleged, was preparing to storm Pine Ridge in an attempt to turn his impeachment hearing into a bloody coup. Or, he suggested, they might seek to incite violence on the one-year anniversary of the death of Raymond Yellow Thunder (ca. February 12). The claims were baseless and bordered on the nonsensical. Most of AIM's leaders were in Rapid City, battling mounting legal woes and enmeshed in that city's Indian civil rights campaign. Nonetheless, on February 11, more than sixty-five U.S. marshals arrived on the reservation. Agents from the Federal Bureau of Investigation soon followed. Wilson's Pine Ridge opponents were furious.[26]

In reaction to what they perceived as an unwarranted invasion by federal authorities, a number of Lakotas came together to form the Oglala Sioux Civil Rights Organization (OSCRO). Although most federal officials would perpetually hold the opinion that OSCRO was little more than a front organization for the American Indian Movement (which they believed was itself a communist front organization), the exact opposite was the case. OSCRO was a local, Indigenous, grassroots organization that opposed Wilson and Superintendent Stanley Lyman and resented the presence of armed federal law enforcement officers on their reservation. Only later would they turn to AIM for support.[27]

The driving force behind the Oglala Sioux Civil Rights Organization was a number of full-blood women elders. While men have traditionally held the sanctioned offices of power in Lakota politics, women have often guided the development of various policies and spurred the men on to action, especially when they have perceived their men to be halting. "What makes an Oglala woman militant," noted anthropologist Marla Powers, "is that she organizes with other women to help Oglala men face contemporary issues." Such was the case with OSCRO.[28]

Vernon Long, the OSTC vice chairman's brother, was president of OSCRO. Pedro Bissonette was vice president and Eddie White Wolf was secretary. But the real driving force behind OSCRO was women like Lou Bean, Ellen Moves Camp, Agnes Lamont, and Pedro Bissonette's adopted mother Gladys Bissonette (she was also his blood aunt). The elder Bissonette recalled when OSCRO first went into action, following the appearance of United States marshals on the reservation. "It was on the 11th of February, 1973, when my son came up to my house and said, 'Mom, there's busloads and busloads of people being unloaded at Billy Mills Hall. Go down and see,' he said. So I jumped in my car and got all of my grandchildren and I drove round and round and I noticed they were all in blue pajama outfits, like. They were all white, no, a few were colored, and I thought, well, I wonder what these people are up to." After realizing they were federal marshals, Gladys Bissonette consulted with other full-blood women elders. "It was on the morning of the 12th. Two of my women friends came in and said they wanted me. They were going to gather as many people as they could and protest against Dick Wilson. We decided to demonstrate because we wanted to know why those marshals were there."[29]

More than 90 percent of the ensuing protest group was comprised of Oglala women. They marched into the BIA building in Pine Ridge village and confronted Superintendent Lyman, demanding that he do something about Wilson's actions. Lyman feigned impotence, claiming that his hands were tied; he could not go over Wilson's head. This was, of course, patently untrue. In the spirit of the new self-determination policy emanating from Washington, Lyman might *choose* not to go over the chairman's head, but as superintendent he clearly had the power to do so. Superintendents had been periodically doing so ever since the OST's founding under the IRA nearly forty years earlier, and Gladys Bissonette knew that. Everyone on the reservation did. She admonished Lyman for being disingenuous and told him that if he was simply going to stand by and watch while Wilson ran amok, then he might as well leave the reservation altogether. "This is the kind of people they pick to guide the Indians," she harangued him. "Some hayseed like you that don't know nothin'." Instead of adressing the women's concerns, Lyman finally called in the BIA police, who used riot sticks to remove the protestors from his office by force, while marshals cordoned off Wilson's office.[30]

Lyman was largely unsympathetic toward the anti-Wilsonites. He stood behind the chairman until the end and was rather unwilling to acknowledge the legitimacy of complaints against the chairman. Part of Lyman's attitude stemmed from his genuine support for self-determination. He felt that the federal government should refrain, as much as possible, from interfering in the workings of tribal governments, regardless of a council's actions or agenda. Beyond these convictions, however, Lyman was clearly anti-AIM and mistakenly convinced that much of the unrest on Pine Ridge was the result of AIM machinations.[31]

In fact, Lyman never interpreted the presence of U.S. marshals and FBI agents on the reservation in the same way that Wilson's opponents did. While he did become disenchanted with them later during the siege of Wounded Knee,[32] he was at first quite impressed with their presence, which he believed would thwart AIM from coming to Pine Ridge. Whereas Gladys Bissonette belittled the federal forces, referring to them as wearing "blue pajama outfits," Lyman admired, "the smart-looking, blue-unformed marshals."[33]

While Gladys Bissonette was getting nowhere with Lyman, her son Pedro was likewise accomplishing little with the tribal chairman. After reaching him on the phone, Pedro inquired as to why the marshals were there and if they could be removed. "I have nothing to say," Wilson insisted. "I don't have anything to talk to you Indians about."[34]

Members of the Oglala Sioux Civil Rights Organization continued to protest over the course of the week, demanding that Wilson and Lyman resign and that the marshals and the FBI leave their reservation. While the demonstrators were vocal and adamant, they failed to turn back the tide. By the eve of Wilson's February 14 impeachment hearing, there were eighty marshals, twenty BIA police from outside reservations, and seventeen local BIA police officers stationed in Pine Ridge village. Relations between the protestors and the marshals were less than cordial at times. Lou Bean recalled the taunting she received from one marshal at a demonstration: "Us 75 marshals could whip you 300 Indians very easily." With a wide array of heavily armed federal officers on Pine Ridge at Wilson's behest and Superintendent Stanley Lyman giving the chairman his fullest support, OSCRO and other protestors were clearly pinning their hopes on Wilson's impeachment.[35]

On the morning of the fourteenth, approximately 300 marchers appeared in front of Billy Mills Hall, where the impeachment hearing was scheduled to take place. Oglala women bearing signs and placards comprised the majority of the crowd that soon surrounded the hall. Not long after chanting, drumming, and singing began, people learned that that Wilson had canceled the meeting on the grounds of bad weather and poor road conditions. Clearly, the weather had not been bad enough to prevent the protestors from traveling to Pine Ridge village and congregating outside. Consequently, they were suspicious. Many of them suspected the real reason the postponement was that Wilson wanted to buy time to allow the BIA police to receive more training from the United States marshals. Either way, the hearing was rescheduled for February 22. After protestors confronted Stanley Lyman over the sudden cancellation, the superintendent attempted to get Chairman Wilson to address them. He refused.[36]

IMPEACHMENT

In the week leading up to Chairman Dick Wilson's impeachment hearing, U.S. marshals spent extensive time training BIA police in a variety of violent crowd-control techniques. Lessons ranged from classroom lectures to instructions on how to use tear gas, .38-caliber pistols, and twelve-gauge shotguns.[37]

Meanwhile, the FBI was thoroughly incapable of ascertaining when, or even if, the American Indian Movement might come to Pine Ridge. AIM continued to focus its energies on Rapid City, South Dakota. Despite rumors of AIM's pending invasion of the reservation, which was Wilson's original justification for requesting federal reinforcements, AIM showed no signs of actually heading there. Consequently, the number of marshals assigned to Pine Ridge fluctuated over the course of the week. On February 17, forty marshals were allowed to leave Pine Ridge, with forty remaining in street clothes. On the twentieth, the FBI predicted that AIM would precipitate violence at the impeachment hearing. It turned out to be an incorrect presumption. The same day that it was made, Russell Means and Vernon Bellecourt were scheduled to appear on television in Rapid City, and Dennis Banks was spending several days camping in a rural area near Eagle Butte, South Dakota, after having addressed the state legislature in Pierre on the fifteenth. Nonetheless, the recently dismissed marshals returned.[38]

On February 22, the day of the impeachment hearings, Stanley Lyman recorded the following in his diary. "I spoke with U.S. Marshal Reese Kash who told me that AIM was definitely coming today. I questioned him about his source, as to whether or not it was reliable. He made a curious remark, something to the effect that, 'Well, I can't tell you that it is from a wiretapping because that is illegal. Let me just say that it is from a very reliable source.'" Lyman then made a revealing analysis of Kash's comment. In so doing, Lyman displayed a certain naivete that, perhaps more so than any real malice toward the full-blood coalition, may account for his backing of Wilson despite the chairman's obvious abuses of power. "Naturally, this made me wonder how the FBI and the U.S. Marshal Service manage to get some of the information they get," he mused. "They, of course, would not reveal this, but they *must* have wiretaps and they *must* have under cover people because otherwise there would be no way of knowing some of the things they know."[39]

That Lyman was an ingenue concerning illegal domestic intelligence activities such as wiretaps perhaps speaks well of his faith in the U.S. government. The same cannot be said of his faith in the Lakota people he was ostensibly serving. This was, after all, a man who encouraged Lakotas to abandon their reservations for cities, while simultaneously admitting that less than one-third of those who did leave made a good adjustment to city life. He also believed that for the majority of Lakotas who lived on Pine Ridge in dire poverty, such poverty was a "choice." Indians who left only to return, he felt, did so in order to be a big fish in a small pond, and he believed that Indians had a tendency to use their being Indian as an excuse for their failures. He had little respect for Lakota religion, equated the rural reservation life with an inability to achieve progress, and lauded the Lakotas' supposed natural abilities while doubting their ability to cope. Taken as a whole, Lyman's ideas and actions paint the portrait of yet another condescendingly paternalistic BIA bureaucrat who was well-meaning but, to put it mildly, extremely intellectually unsophisticated despite the bevy of his own experiences. In the end, Stanley Lyman earnestly believed he was working in the best interests of Lakota people, unaware that his good intentions were helping to pave a highly undesirable road.[40]

Regardless of the FBI's various information-gathering techniques, legal and otherwise, the Bureau was mistaken in its assertion that AIM was on its way to Pine Ridge. It was not. Most of the American Indian Movement had remained behind to pursue its agenda in Rapid City. One of their leaders, however, had arrived for the impeachment hearing. Russell Means, an enrolled member of the Oglala Sioux Tribe and a victim of Wilson's dictatorial measures, attended the proceedings at Billy Mills Hall. Before this, he had briefly returned to Pine Ridge earlier in the month. Along with Severt Young Bear, Pedro Bissonette, Vernon Long, and Edgar Running Bear, he met with Wayne Colburn, the then ranking marshal on the reservation. The five Lakotas quickly found any attempts to negotiate with Colburn fruitless. "If you guys try to get tough, we'll just shut you down," the marshal warned them. "We'll take care of you." Of course, neither AIM, OSCRO, nor any other anti-Wilsonites had attempted a bloody coup. Now Means was back to see if Wilson's opponents on the Oglala Sioux Tribal Council could pull off a bloodless one.[41]

By nine o'clock on the morning of the twenty-second, anti-Wilson protestors were gathering numbers at Calico Hall, situated about six miles north of Pine Ridge village. Around ten o'clock, a caravan of approximately 150 cars containing well over 300 people headed south and made its way to Billy Mills Hall in Pine Ridge village, where the hearing was scheduled to take place. They circled the hall three times before parking and setting up their demonstration. Entire families were in attendance. There were drummers and singers. Spiritual leaders conducted ceremonies with the *can nunpa* (sacred pipe). Protesters were equipped with signs and placards. Superintendent Lyman noted that OSCRO's protest had started "right on schedule, perfectly peaceful, but with some fairly inflammatory signs—not really inflammatory, I guess, just critical. One of the signs was really quite clever; it said, 'Lyman, we don't want your Dick,' meaning . . . Dick Wilson."[42]

The protestors may have been peaceful, but there was no question that they were facing the threat of brute force from the federal government. Marshals had set up numerous positions around the BIA building in Pine Ridge village. They patrolled three different sandbagged positions on the roof alone. A nearby warehouse was teeming with uniformed marshals, and BIA road employees removed cars from the area for fear that AIM could use them as firebombs. Inside the BIA building, an armed command post in the south wing featured grenade launchers, sniper rifles, gas masks, and gas grenades. The regional director of the FBI and the U.S. attorney for South Dakota were both present, and communications equipment and personnel were in contact with the director of marshals in Washington, D.C., on an hourly basis. OSCRO members derisively dubbed the site "Fort Wilson."[43]

Inside, the meeting did not finally convene until 11:50 a.m. Respected full-blood elder and medicine man Frank Fools Crow gave the opening prayer. Wilson began the meeting by insisting that the council watch a film, *Anarchy–USA*. Produced by the John Birch Society, it interspersed violent footage from the People's Republic of China and Algiers with clips from America's urban riots of the 1960s in order to make the claim that the American civil rights movement was nothing more than a cover for communist agitation designed to bring about a Marxist regime in the United States. Many people inferred that the purpose of the film was an effort to link AIM and OSCRO to a broader communist conspiracy; both organizations operated under the banner of civil rights. The absurdity of this theory on the American civil rights movement aside, the American Indian Movement was not even present en masse at the hearing, making any connection to it somewhat irrelevant. The Oglala Sioux Civil Rights Organization was present in full force. However, the notion that these full-blood Lakota denizens of Pine Ridge Reservation, who had organized in opposition to what they viewed as Wilson's corrupt and violent regime, were somehow the pawns of a global communist conspiracy was likewise absurd.[44]

After the showing of *Anarchy–USA*, the council discussed the issue of where to hold the meeting. In order to accommodate the hundreds of people, it would have to be moved to the gymnasium of Billy Mills Hall. The alternative was to hold it in a smaller room and broadcast it over closed circuit television to outside observers. Upon hearing that the citizens of Pine Ridge might be banned from the hearing, Pedro Bissonette made his feelings known, insisting that the people had a right to attend in person. Birgil Kills Straight and Maurice Wounded offered a motion that the meeting be held in the gymnasium. It passed 19–0 with one abstention. Before the move to the gymnasium was made, however, more conversation ensued within the council. Some members were concerned that the audience in attendance might become vocal, perhaps interrupting the meeting to voice their discontent. This had happened in the past at some of the more contentious OSTC sessions. The council forged a compromise. They would hold the meeting in the Bill Mills gymnasium, but a second motion that passed 17–0 with two abstentions ruled that the council would go into a closed meeting if there was any interference from those in attendance. With the logistics decided upon, the council recessed at 12:50 p.m.[45]

As the council broke for lunch, the several hundred people who had come to witness the hearing assembled inside the gymnasium. Estimates measured the crowd at nearly 700 people.[46] The council reconvened at 2:10 p.m. After a prayer by full-blood medicine man Ellis Chips and a roll call of members, Wilson brought the impeachment charges to the floor and submitted his written responses.[47]

The first charge was nepotism in hiring OST personnel. Wilson's statement read, "In hiring personnel for the many different programs operated by the Oglala Sioux Tribe, the Personnel Office has the responsibility of advertising the positions and the Program Directors usually hire the people they feel are qualified. This is done based on the recommendation of the Personnel Office. There is no doubt that some of my friends and relatives have jobs but so has every administration. Records prove this."[48]

The second charge was operating the OST without a budget. "During the month of August 1972 the Oglala Sioux Tribal Council adopted a budget. Records will prove this," Wilson countered. However, he produced no such documents.[49]

The third charge accused him of using tribal money to pay for a band at a private party at his home. "The band that I am accused of hiring with tribal funds is not true. I paid this Band out of my own pocket."[50]

With regards to misappropriating the tribal station wagon, he stated: "I have used the tribal wagon at times and have also parked the station wagon at my house at times. As president of the Oglala Sioux Tribe I have had to attend meetings in most of the surrounding towns and if the station wagon is available I use it."[51]

The fifth charge cited him for failing to compel the treasurer to make a report. "The first thing I did upon taking office as President I asked for an Audit. The Superintendent can vouch for this as well as other members of the Executive Board. The treasurer can make a report any time the Council asks for it."[52] He did not produce the report or any related documents.

The sixth charge cited his failure to call the quarterly sessions of the OSTC as mandated by the OST's bylaws. "The October session of the Oglala Sioux Tribal council was called in October and the October session is still in effect, as we have never adjourned." In fact, the October session had not been called until November. It was now February, and he made no mention of the January meeting, which was as of yet still uncalled.[53]

The seventh charge accused him of using the executive committee to circumvent the tribal council's eight-member housing authority board. "Since taking office as tribal President it has been impossible to get a quorum of the Housing Authority and as a result we have been doing the best we can under the circumstances."[54]

The final count accused him of having wrongfully arrested council member C. Hobart Keith; members are immune from arrest while conducting council business. "Mr. Keith came into my office and yelled at me and called me out for a fight. Mr. Keith violated Section 74 of the Oglala Sioux Tribal [Law and Order] Code, so I signed a complaint against him. How he was arrested I don't know. If Mr. Keith conducted himself according to the office he holds as Councilman, them Mr. Keith would never have been arrested."[55]

After the reading of Wilson's written defense, the council engaged in extensive discussion over several procedural matters. Foremost was the issue of when the actual impeachment trial would take place. Wilson, in a surprise move, chose to waive the twenty-day waiting period to which he was entitled. This caught his opponents off guard. They had anticipated using the three weeks to prepare their case and insisted that the trial not take place immediately. However, Robert Ecoffey and Orland Big Owl introduced a motion that the council accept the charges as they had been filed and that the matter be settled that very day. Their motion passed 11–7 with two abstentions.[56]

The next debate concerned the issue of who would be the presiding officer, as the chairman was ineligible to preside over his own impeachment. No volunteers were forthcoming. James Iron Cloud was nominated, but he withdrew his name on the grounds that his hearing was not very good. Moot Nelson, Pete Swift Bird, Anthony Whirlwind Horse, Johnson Holy Rock, Gerald One Feather, and OST Chief Judge Theodore Tibbits were also mentioned, but all of them declined. "Well, god damn it," Wilson shouted. "[N]obody wants this hot seat of mine?" After two hours, the council still had not selected someone. Wilson could not help gloating: "I don't know why you are trying to throw me out when you can't get anyone else to sit in this hot seat." Finally, Vincent Thunder Bull accepted a nomination, and the council approved him with a unanimous vote of 20–0. After assuming the office, Thunder Bull entertained a motion to recess at 5:30.[57]

The next morning, Superintendent Lyman returned to Pine Ridge village and noticed that "the law was all over the place." Marshals were busily readjusting their sandbags and other defensive equipment to make their positions less visible to the public. "That's where the bags should've been yesterday as well," he lamented.[58]

The session reconvened at 10:35 with Vincent Thunder Bull presiding. The opening prayer of the previous day had been given by Frank Fools Crow, a Lakota medicine man. This day it was offered by Reverend Sidney Martin. Fools Crow, however, did make an opening address to the council. Fools Crow's very presence was symbolically important to the anti-Wilsonites. Then in his eighties, he was one of the most respected elders and medicine men on Pine Ridge. Many considered him the premier ceremonial chief of the Pine Ridge Lakotas, and a supporter of the full-blood community, most of which was aligned against the tribal chairman. Wilson himself was largely antagonistic toward Fools Crow, treating him with a fair amount of enmity and refusing to recognize him as ceremonial chief.[59]

The chairman had shown up on the second day of the hearing looking rather dapper. Superintendent Lyman commented on his appearance. "It was the first time I had ever seen Dick Wilson wearing a suit. He looked good. He seldom wears a pants-and-jacket combination." The change in attire, however, did not reflect a change in attitude. Wilson was contemptuous of the entire process. "It makes it really difficult to get something done while you're being harassed by the village idiot," he muttered to a reporter.[60]

Despite Fools Crow's presence, the anti-Wilsonites were in poor shape. The chairman had cleverly outmaneuvered them when he waived the twenty-day waiting period, and they were caught ill-prepared. The first issue of the day dealt with whether Wilson was entitled to an attorney. Wilson had brought a lawyer named Bat Richards to represent him. However, a 1941 OSTC ordinance had ruled that an officer facing impeachment would not be entitled to an attorney. Wilson, who generally conducted himself in the name of tribal sovereignty and derided civil rights, now cited the 1968 Civil Rights Act as entitling him to representation, and Stanley Lyman concurred. This was especially ironic given Wilson's showing of *Anarchy–USA* the day before and the fact that later during the siege of Wounded Knee, Wilson would accuse his opponents of "hiding behind the skirts of civil rights, and yet it has never been adopted by this tribe. We have no mechanics whatsoever to initiate the Civil Rights Act of '68 at all."[61]

In the end, Vincent Thunder Bull ruled that the accused was in fact entitled to representation. Perhaps feeling confident, however, Wilson now elected to represent himself. As the proceedings got under way, Council member Richard Little led the prosecution and Wilson began to give oral enhancements of the written defense he had submitted the previous day. Initially, the crowd applauded every time the prosecution made a point. However, after Thunder Bull issued a stern warning to clear the room, they desisted and sat quietly. Later on, anti-Wilsonites accused Wilson of sending several *agents provocateur* into their seating area to stir up noise, with the purpose of goading Thunder Bull into closing the meeting. The alleged tactic did not work. Wilson's opponents chased off the noisemakers, whoever they were, and the meeting remained open. The council broke for lunch at 12:15 p.m.[62]

After the recess ended at 1:40, Richard Little resumed questioning Wilson, but the lack of preparation showed. While Wilson had not brought any records for his defense, the prosecution did not have many records of their own to introduce as evidence. What few they had were original documents. Not wishing to submit originals, Little and Birgil Kills Straight summoned Superintendent Lyman so he could take them to his office to have copies made. Lyman recorded a telling moment as he escorted the men to the BIA offices: "The marshals were shocked at the entry of two obviously AIM types, but I assured them that these were respected councilmen."[63]

Once inside the office, Lyman was stingy, insisting that the "respected councilmen" make only one copy of each document. In another revealing moment, the superintendent confessed, "Dick Wilson sure as hell would be mad at me if he knew I was doing this. Nevertheless, I do have to provide any service that can be offered to either side in this issue."[64]

After returning to the meeting, Little requested that he be allowed to introduce additional charges against the chairman. He and Kills Straight argued that the original complaint had been worded in a way to allow for the introduction of future charges. Thunder Bull denied the request on the grounds that the proceedings had already begun. Hobart Keith was particularly upset about these developments, charging that the plaintiffs were facing a stacked deck. "I'll take this to federal court," he shouted. With that, Kills Straight, Keith, and Little staged an impromptu boycott and stormed out of the building. They were joined by council member Morris Wounded of Wakpamni District. Several hundred pro-impeachment attendees followed the councilmen out; most of them were upset that Wilson had been allowed to chair the proceedings of the previous day. They believed that Thunder Bull had been bought off or had at least knuckled under to Wilson during the hearing, and they felt that the entire proceedings had a pro-Wilson bias from start to finish. By exiting the proceedings, many of them were voting with their feet in true Lakota fashion, just as many Oglalas had done nearly forty years earlier by abstaining from the referendum to reorganize.[65]

Amid the bustle, Russell Means took the opportunity to berate Orland Big Owl and William High Hawk, the two OSTC representatives from his home district of Porcupine. He implored them to join the boycott. When they refused, Means stormed out of the gymnasium, taking more followers with him.[66]

After the departure of the councilmen and a sizable portion of the crowd, Thunder Bull ruled the hearing closed and offered to step down as presiding officer. Staunch Wilson supporters Emma Nelson and Leo Wilcox made a motion to that effect, which the remaining councilmen passed unanimously, 14–0 with one abstention. Dick Wilson re-assumed his position of chairman.[67]

With the forementioned councilmen still in absentia, the OSTC quickly passed two more resolutions unanimously. The first ordered the council to request the FBI to audit the Oglala Sioux Tribe's financial affairs. Such activity does not generally fall within the FBI's realm, but an audit was in fact eventually conducted by a subcontractor of the Interior Department. The second resolution, sponsored by Wilcox and Robert Ecoffey, requested the U.S. attorney general to make a full investigation of all "subversive activities on the Pine Ridge Reservation." This was clearly aimed at the Oglala Sioux Civil Rights Organization and the American Indian Movement.[68]

Shortly after the passage of the two resolutions, Birgil Kills Straight and Richard Little returned to the meeting. Emma Nelson and Elizabeth Roubideaux quickly made a motion to adjourn. It carried 15–0. Kills Straight and Little did not vote.[69]

Thus did the October 1972 meeting of the Oglala Sioux Tribal Council, originally convened in November, finally come to an end at 2:45 p.m. on Friday, February 23, 1973. Chairman Dick Wilson had dodged impeachment.[70]

AFTERMATH

Immediately after the council meeting, about several hundred protestors,[71] many of them OSCRO members, marched on the BIA building down the street from Billy Mills Hall. C. Hobart Keith and David Long both addressed the crowd. Unhappy with Vincent Thunder Bull's conduct, Keith called for a new hearing with an impartial judge.[72]

Law enforcement officials reacted to the protest by going into full alert. Dick Wilson was escorted out of Billy Mills Hall by BIA police and taken to the BIA building with his family. Once inside, Wilson and others received gas masks to wear. On the roof, marshals were moving sandbags back into a visible position to serve as parapets.[73]

Oglala Nation News, the reservation's weekly newspaper during this period, described the scene as "tense at times," but no serious violence broke out. Chief U.S. Marshal Reese Kash addressed the crowd, attempting to reduce tensions by joking with them. Hobart Keith responded with an sharp tirade. One marshal on the roof was hit by a sling shot pellet. Five members of OSCRO attempted to hold a meeting with federal officials inside the building. Superintendent Lyman was prepared to meet with any two of them, but Kash denied entrance to all of them. Later that night, U.S. marshals escorted Wilson's family off the reservation. Lyman's wife had left the state earlier in the day. The superintendent then called Nebraska authorities and had them shut down all of the bars in the border towns.[74]

The immediate effect of the aborted impeachment hearing was to galvanize the two sides: those opposed to Dick Wilson and those who supported him. After the spontaneous protest in front of the BIA building, his opponents re-assembled at Calico Hall, the site north of Pine Ridge village that had become their unofficial meeting place. During the next week, they would meet there almost continually to air their grievances and consider plans of action. By the end of the night of failed impeachment, OSCRO had gained some 800 new members.[75]

As for Wilson, he felt secure now that the threat of impeachment had passed. The marshals were going to remain on the reservation, and the chairman was prepared to confront and attack his opponents. Even Stanley Lyman, one of Wilson's biggest supporters, did not feel safe from Wilson's wrath. After Wilson and his escort arrived in the BIA building, Lyman learned that the chairman wanted to see him in the superintendent's own office. "I started back to the office thinking, 'Well, the son of a bitch! Now that he has won he is going to start cleaning house, and the first thing he is going to do is clean out the superintendent!'" As it turned out, this was not the case, though Wilson's fury would soon descend on those he did view as his enemies.[76]

Over the next two days, hundreds of Pine Ridge Lakotas gathered at Calico Hall to discuss their options. In addition to members of the Oglala Sioux Civil Rights Organization and other opponents of Dick Wilson, there were traditional medicine men from respected families like Black Elk, Chips, Crow Dog, Catches, Young Bear, and Wounded. Significantly, seven of the eight traditional chiefs most respected by the full-blood community were also there: Frank Fools Crow, Tom Bad Cob, Eddie Iron Cloud, Sr., Frank Kills Enemy, Weasel Bear, Matthew King, and Charles Red Cloud.[77]

The impeachment process had failed. Those gathered considered what to do next, discussed various alternatives, and consulted with the chiefs and medicine men. They also basked in their Lakota culture, turning the event into an extemporaneous powwow. Drum groups performed while people danced. A communal kitchen sprang up to feed everyone. After his reinstatement, Chairman Wilson had reminded people of OSTC Resolution 72–04, which defined a riot as any public disturbance involving three or more people. However, neither his GOON Squad nor the BIA police moved to prevent the hundreds of Lakotas who were now gathering at Calico Hall.[78]

As the people continued to hold meetings during the four days between the end of the impeachment hearings (February 23) and the eventual occupation of the town of Wounded Knee (February 27), the U.S. marshals, South Dakota State Patrol, and BIA police (from Pine Ridge and other reservations) went through a series of escalations and de-escalations as they tried to guess what might happen next. It would all prove to be for naught. None of the various law enforcement agencies, including the FBI, were ever able to predict the occupation of Wounded Knee. Until the very end, federal officials were consumed by the idea that the American Indian Movement would storm the BIA building in Pine Ridge village. When the seizure of Wounded Knee finally occurred, federal authorities were caught completely off guard. Their inability to correctly prognosticate either the date or location of the occupation stemmed largely from the fact that the takeover was a spontaneous grassroots event that could not have been predicted, no matter how deeply the FBI infiltrated AIM or how many informants reported to the marshals from Calico Hall. This did not, however, stop federal officials from trying.[79]

While neither Wilson, the BIA Police, nor the marshals took any direct action against those assembled at Calico, the protestors had been under intense surveillance by federal officials, and even the not-so-subtle GOON Squad. Then, on February 25, the FBI received a tip that AIM was keeping a large cache of hidden weapons at Calico Hall. In response, marshals invaded the hall and conducted an extensive search. The Bureau's intelligence turned out to be erroneous. They found nothing.[80]

Insulted by the invasion of Calico Hall, the full-blood opponents of Dick Wilson had had enough. That night they made the decision to officially invite the American Indian Movement back to the reservation to help their cause. It was not an easy decision. While AIM had impressed many with their actions at Gordon and even on the Trail of Broken Treaties, the organization's activities had always attracted controversy and occasionally violence. In addition, the federal government was clearly targeting AIM, so to invite AIM was to invite federal antagonism. But with Dick Wilson firmly entrenched with the full support of the BIA, the GOON Squad running rampant, and the FBI and marshals showing no signs of leaving the reservation, the Movement seemed like the strongest ally available to the full-blood community of Pine Ridge. "We decided that we did need the American Indian Movement in here because our men were scared, they hung in the back," OSCRO member Ellen Moves Camp explained. "It was mostly the women that went forward and spoke out. This way we knew we had backing, and we would have more strength to do what we wanted to do against the BIA and Dick Wilson. All the people wanted it." All seven of the traditional chiefs gave the decision their blessing. Russell Means recorded a taped message imploring Dennis Banks to come down to the reservation as soon as possible. He immediately gave the tape to messengers who set out to find Banks. They would eventually track him down on February 27 at Red Scaffold near Eagle Butte where he was camping with some twenty people.[81]

The following day, the entire reservation shut down for the funeral of highly respected Oglala medicine man Ben Black Elk. He was the son of Nick Black Elk, the Oglala holy man who had participated in the Battle of Greasy Grass Creek (Little Big Horn) as a boy, remembered the carnage of Wounded Knee, and had been immortalized with the publication of *Black Elk Speaks*. Wilson's opponents and supporters alike came out to pay their respects.[82]

The previous night, there had been reports that BIA police were intimidating people at Black Elk's wake. After the funeral, OSCRO members and their full-blood allies again convened at Calico Hall as prominent AIM members were making their way to the reservation. Dennis Banks was on his way. BIA police attempted to serve the Bellecourt brothers with a restraining order but failed to intercept them. Russell Means was already on Pine Ridge. As an enrolled member of the tribe, he was immune to expulsion from its confines. However, at 2:40 the following afternoon, he was cornered by two GOONS at the Sioux Nation grocery store in Pine Ridge village: Poker Joe Noble and Glenn Three Stars, the man Dick Wilson had personally appointed as head of his GOON Squad. After roughing up Means, they assaulted Gary Thomas, a legal aide lawyer sympathetic to OSCRO.[83]

On the twenty-seventh, some twenty AIM members, including most of its major leaders, joined the more than 300 anti-Wilson protestors at Calico. The hall was packed to capacity, with onlookers spilling out of the doorway on a late February afternoon. Banks and Means quietly went across the street to the basement of the Holy Rosary Mission Catholic Church where they joined a small group of OSCRO leaders and traditional leaders who had gathered there, including Frank Fools Crow and Pete Catches. Ready to make a show of force to protest the situation on the reservation, they discussed their plan of action. A move on the heavily armed BIA building ("Fort Wilson") in Pine Ridge village, they realized, would be suicidal. Further up the road from Pine Ridge village was the small town of Wounded Knee. That, they decided, was where they would make their stand.[84]

The large group at Calico Hall was organized. Most of them knew that they were on the verge of engaging in a major protest, but very few of them were privy to the actual destination. "To tell the truth," Mary Crow Dog later testified, "I had not joined the caravan with the notion that I would perform what some people later called 'that great symbolic act.'" Meanwhile, two carloads of experienced AIM personnel went ahead to secure the hamlet and procure firearms and ammunition from the Wounded Knee trading post. The larger caravan of more than fifty cars filled with protestors followed shortly thereafter. They drove right through the village of Pine Ridge and by the BIA building, at first alarming the marshals before leaving them confused. As the head of the caravan arrived in Wounded Knee, Frank Fools Crow led a prayer ceremony. There would be no organized protest, however. Chaos was not far behind. Soon, the younger members of the caravan were ransacking the trading post. Before long, federal authorities had figured things out. They quickly sealed off the perimeter. The seventy-one-day occupation of Wounded Knee had begun.[85]

8

Conclusion

Connecting the Past

A PAIUTE INDIAN from Nevada named Wovoka was the original prophet of the Ghost Dance religion. Known to the local white settlers as Jack Wilson, he began to proselytize in the late nineteenth century. Wovoka's message was millennial, stressing the onset of a new, atavistic world to soon dawn: wild game would return in bounty, the earth would be rejuvenated, and people would be reunited with the dearly departed. This would all come to pass, he said, if people would subscribe to his unique blend of traditional Native (Paiute and others) and Christian ideology and ritual. The people should take to heart his message of love and dance the Ghost Dance for hours on end, the culmination of which would be a trance wherein dancers temporarily "died" and received visions from the world beyond.[1]

The Lakota people first received Wovoka's message in 1889, after sending several emissaries to see him in Nevada. With the harsh new realities of colonial conquest still fresh upon them, many Lakotas gravitated toward the new religion. They also interpreted it slightly differently, expanding and customizing Wovoka's vision. For them, the earth reborn as a paradise also meant that perhaps the dreaded *wasichu* (white people) would disappear in the process. Many Lakota adherents also came to believe that the sacred Ghost Dance shirts, which one was to wear while dancing, might have the properties necessary to fend off bullets.[2]

Up on the Standing Rock Reservation, which straddles the border of North and South Dakota, the Hunkpapa medicine man and resistance leader Tatanka Iyotanka (Sitting Bull) received word of the new religion that was sweeping up many of his Lakota brethren. His personal opinion of the Ghost Dance as a spiritual endeavor is not clear; he may have accepted aspects of it, or he may have been a skeptic. Regardless, he at least recognized in it a mechanism for galvanizing his people, for raising their confidence, and for restoring their will. Whatever his personal convictions, he encouraged the activity and sponsored dances on his property near the Grand River.[3]

The Office of Indian Affairs agent on Standing Rock at the time was a man named James McLaughlin. Agent McLaughlin had a disturbingly patronizing view of Native Americans that was typical for the turn-of-the-century. He later dedicated his autobiography "To my friend the Indian, whose good parts survive as a monument over the graves of a vanishing race." In addition to his patronizing paternalism, McLaughlin was also a mortal enemy of Sitting Bull, posthumously describing the Lakota leader as "crafty, avaricious, mendacious, ambitious . . . I never knew him to display a single trait that might command admiration or respect." In their own language, the Lakota people called McLaughlin "Young Man Afraid Of Lakotas."[4]

Already perturbed by the new display of resilience and sense of independence that the Ghost Dance engendered in many Lakotas, McLaughlin was especially alarmed at Sitting Bull's willingness to use the religion as an energizing force among his people. In November, the agent ordered Sitting Bull to desist from hosting the celebrations, and he autocratically banned them altogether from the reservation.[5]

Despite McLaughlin's efforts, however, which included spying, propaganda, police harassment, and forbidding Sitting Bull to leave the reservation, the Hunkpapa leader continued to sponsor the dances. As McLaughlin persisted in his attempts to suppress the new religious movement, he informed his superiors that he believed Sitting Bull to be a threat and that the Hunkpapa leader and several of his followers should be sent to a military prison. In the pre-dawn hours of December 15, 1890, a detail of Indian Police, working under the auspices of the Office of Indian Affairs and the U.S. Army, raided Sitting Bull's home for the purpose of arresting him. When a tussle broke out, the police quickly assassinated Sitting Bull.[6]

In the immediate aftermath of Sitting Bull's murder, government forces commenced rounding up various bands of Lakotas throughout the reservations. Big Foot's band of Miniconjous, encamped on the Cheyenne River, were a high priority for the government's repression, as they had been active in the Ghost Dance. Fearing reprisals, Big Foot and his followers fled southward toward Pine Ridge. When a reconstituted version of George Custer's erstwhile Seventh Cavalry intercepted them near Cankpe Opi Wakpala (Wounded Knee Creek) on December 28, the soldiers encircled the Miniconjou families and mounted artillery on a nearby hill. There they stayed the night while the cavalry waited for further orders. The following morning, soldiers separated the men from their families and began to search tipis for weapons. When one soldier tried to disarm a man named Yellow Bird, the Lakota resisted. In the ensuing scuffle, the cavalryman was accidentally shot. The soldiers immediately fired on the Lakota men, killing about half of them in the first volley. What followed was little short of butchery: men, women, children, and the elderly were indiscriminately hunted down and slaughtered by the soldiers, with corpses later found upwards of eight miles away. Perhaps as many as 300 Lakotas were wantonly slaughtered that day. Another sixty soldiers were killed, most of them from friendly fire.[7]

As the cavalry retreated, the wounded Indians were left to fend for themselves as a South Dakota blizzard began to brew. After the storm subsided on New Year's Day, 1891, the army and an array of volunteers came out to retrieve the dead, about two-thirds of whom were women and children. As a result of the debilitating cold, many of the bodies were frozen into contorted, mangled poses. A number of women were found with shawls covering their faces, as if to hide their eyes from the point-blank muzzle of a soldier's rifle. White souvenir hunters scavenged the corpses while they dug a trench. Others posed for photographs, as if standing by game trophies. The bodies, many of them naked, were thrown into a common grave near the creek. The members of the Seventh Cavalry received medals.[8]

The massacre at Wounded Knee is, quite understandably, a highly traumatic event in the history of the Lakota people. When the opponents of Dick Wilson gathered at the town of Wounded Knee on February 27, 1973, many observers concluded after the fact that the site had been preselected because of its powerful symbolism. Already ingrained in the consciousness of many Native Americans, Wounded Knee had also come to the attention of wider mainstream America with the appearance of *Bury My Heart at Wounded Knee*, a popular history book by dime store novelist and University of Illinois librarian Dee Brown.[9] Borrowing its title from a poem by Stephen Vincent Benet, this runaway 1971 bestseller featured a graphic and critical interpretation of the United States' ethnic cleansing of the American West in the mid-nineteenth century, concluding with a chilling description of the 1890 massacre. Not exactly a paragon of professional history, the book nonetheless brought the 1890 episode back to the forefront of national consciousness on the eve of the 1973 incident. Wounded Knee being chosen as a protest site in 1973 for its historical symbolism therefore seemed to be the logical presumption for outsiders who understood little else about the conflict. Historian Francis Paul Prucha, for example, has asserted that "the site was consciously chosen as a symbol because of the disastrous confrontation there between the Sioux and the Seventh Cavalry in 1890."[10]

Certainly, the historical significance of Wounded Knee was not lost on the Lakota protestors who occupied the small town near the creek and mass grave. There were few Lakotas at that time who had not lost a relative or ancestor at Wounded Knee, or who did not know someone who had. For example, Dick Fool Bull, the uncle of AIM spiritual adviser Leonard Crow Dog, had survived the massacre as a boy. He had seen the soldiers hunt down the women and children who tried to hide in ravines. However, Prucha's analysis is off target. As outlined in the previous chapter, the siege of Wounded Knee in 1973 was a rather spontaneous event and anti-Wilson protestors chose the site at the last moment in lieu of the well-fortified town of Pine Ridge.[11] But there is more to it than that. Beyond the very important historical legacy of the 1890 massacre, there were also several important modern issues that shaped Lakota perceptions of Wounded Knee; for the people of Pine Ridge, there was an additional layer of symbolism that was more immediate and dynamic.[12]

Clive Gildersleeve's trading post in the tiny town of Wounded Knee was a critical and controversial part of the landscape. Wounded Knee, in the minds of many Pine Ridge residents, was as deeply marked by the immediate presence of Gildersleve, his family, and the institution that they owned, as it was by the massacre that had bloodied the ground nearly three-quarters of a century earlier.

THE MODERN SYMBOL

Clive A. Gildersleeve was born near Pickert, Indiana, in 1899. In search of better income, Gildersleeve's father moved to the Fort Berthold Indian Reservation in North Dakota in 1910, where his brother-in-law was a teacher for the Indian Service. The family soon followed, and young Clive attended a reservation day school with mostly Indian students. Not long after, the family again moved, this time southward to the Pine Ridge Reservation, where Clive attended Reservation Day School Number 15 and eventually completed the eighth grade.[13]

Clive Gildersleeve spent parts of 1914 and 1915 working as a ranch hand, tending to cattle and horses on a pasture 800 to 900 acres in size near the reservation town of Porcupine. In addition to his stint as a cowboy, he worked part time at the trading post in Porcupine. After a term of service in the navy, he returned to Pine Ridge and worked full time at the Porcupine trading post from 1920 to 1923. He bought a small share in the operation from owner W. E. Thomas. It would prove to be the beginning of a long and controversial career in retail and commerce on Pine Ridge.[14]

Gildersleeve was soon the sole proprietor of the trading post and doing very well. His father joined him in the venture, and they used their profits to purchase the trading post in the town of Wounded Knee, thereby creating a relative commercial giant in the highly marginalized reservation economy. In 1934, they acquired from the federal government forty acres of land surrounding the business. As the only store for miles around, business at Wounded Knee was steady, with people coming from far and wide. Indian customers would arrive on horseback or on a wagon led by a team, and the entire hitching rail out front was often in use. While the reservation-wide prohibition of selling alcohol remained in place, the ban on selling firearms would eventually be lifted and the trading post offered most basic goods from food to hunting rifles. The store also doubled as the local post office. And Gildersleeve kept his hand in ranching as well. By 1949, he owned twenty-nine head of cattle.[15]

As proprietors of the only commercial outpost in the area, Clive Gildersleeve and his wife Agnes were able to use monopolistic practices, including highly inflated prices. This was a difficult burden for customers on a reservation that was, in a word, impoverished (see chapter 3). In this environment, the Gildersleeves were more than willing to extend credit to their customers. While the availability of credit was crucial to impoverished reservation denizens, it was accompanied by truculent business practices. Beyond high prices, there were also high interest rates for purchases made on credit; high finance charges for cashing government checks; buying Native crafts far below fair market value (and selling them to tourists for a substantial profit); and demanding inequitable trades during barter transactions on the cash–poor reservation by taking items at wholesale value and offering compensatory items at monopolistic retail value. The Gildersleeves went so far as to bring poorly substantiated claims against Indians who died intestate as a way of procuring money, belongings, and even land. And profits garnered from the economic exploitation of local Oglalas was eventually supplemented by outside revenue streams. As operations expanded after World War II, the Gildersleeves sold gasoline, food, and souvenir items to passing tourists.[16]

Beyond, to put it modestly, shrewd business practices, Clive Gildersleeve also displayed racist tendencies. His opinions of Indian people, which were given to gross generalizations, were informed by views that were quite determinist. "An Indian makes a very excellent cowboy if he is working for a man that knows his way around cattle, if he is told what to do and when to do it. The Indian is an excellent cowboy," Gildersleeve once observed. "But to do it on his own unaccustomed [to the] job of managing a ranch, he simply can't do it. It isn't his line." Upon hearing this, Gildersleeve's interviewer pressed him. After all, Gildersleeve himself had learned to manage a ranch with little prior experience. Why could Indians not do likewise? "No. You see, it takes more than just being able to rope and ride. It takes knowing markets, when to sell cattle." And why could Native Americans not learn? "Well, there you enter into the Indian nature. The Indian nature is sort of a freedom that you can't have and be a businessman. If an Indian knows where they're going to have a powwow or some get-together, they love to have a get-together in bunches, and that desire and that tendency is so strong that nothing will hold them. They will walk away and leave a bunch of cattle at the wrong time. They just have to do things that they do."[17]

In addition to their economic stranglehold on two reservation towns and questionable determinist views about the "nature" of Indian people, the Gildersleeves engaged in activities that many felt degraded the massacre victims. By the 1960s, highways within a roughly seventy-five-mile radius of their post were strewn with tasteless billboards that urged tourists to come gawk at the site many Lakotas considered to be the most sacred place on the reservation. "See the Wounded Knee massacre site," they beckoned. "Visit the mass grave. Post cards, curios, don't miss it!" The Gildersleeves were profiteering at the expense of the memory of the dead. "All credit cards accepted," the billboards assured travelers. Among the "curios" one might find at the trading post were postcards that featured photographs of the dead or pictures of American settlers several days after the massacre posing with shovels and smiles next to the mass grave they had dug. This was the pit that the victims were piled into en masse.[18]

The Wounded Knee trading post and tourist shop also featured a log cabin that the Gildersleeves referred to as a "museum." It was a collection of various objects made by Lakota people, ranging from clothing to artwork to sacred religious objects. Clive Gildersleeve had begun trading in Native craft work early in his career. Indeed, he was an earnest admirer the talent and skill of Lakota artisans. "I think the Sioux people are the very finest in beadwork and quill work," he once stated. He had bought many Indian custom-made objects, often as part of the credit system his stores offered. In essence, he was doubling as a pawn broker. And to Gildersleeve, such commerce offered positive opportunities for the reservation and its people; he believed it was to the benefit of his customers. "And lots of times, I find that they do not have money, so we can still get groceries to them by trading for what they do have. And during a lot of years, we have traded for hay, wood, horses, cows, garden produce, bones."[19]

In collecting objects for their museum, the Gildersleeves occasionally bought items outright. Other times they kept them in return for unpaid debts. They also developed a network of associates that supplied them with numerous items. They acquired items from a mixed-blood doctor named Ralph Hubbard and from Clive's brother-in-law Wilbur Egart, who used to dig up flints, arrowheads, and numerous stone artifacts as far away as the Cheyenne River Reservation on the other side of the state.[20]

Clearly, such a business was driven, in part, by the despair of the reservation's poverty and the attendant social problems that arise in such a situation. One Lakota woman had loaned the museum a fully beaded dress. She had made it herself, an extremely labor intensive product. The woman was afraid to keep it in her home because her grandson had once stolen the dress and hocked it. Upon retrieving the dress, she elected to place it with the museum, an act borne more from dire circumstances than any desire to enhance the museum's collection. And some of the items, many local Oglala Lakotas felt, did not belong in the Gildersleeves' possession at all, much less on display.[21]

At one point, the museum exhibited a ceremonial altar of the Native American Church. Members of the church, which uses peyote as a religious sacrament, repeatedly informed Gildersleeve that his keeping of the holy religious article was objectionable and that he should return it. In an effort to placate them, he feigned joining the church, sitting through a night-long service that he later reminisced about.

> We had a most wonderful peyote party. . . . I ate peyote, three or four times that night, and it didn't affect me in any way. I sat through the entire night, and I enjoyed every bit of it. I took four spoons, three spoons, two spoons, and one . . . it's a fairly large soup spoon . . . but I told them I would join them. And I made up my mind that I would join them, because I meant to keep this in the museum. I wanted to know the truth about it, I wanted to understand what I was talking about. That was the only way to do it.

While he did not return the altar, he did come away with a tolerant view on peyote. "Everybody frowns on [peyote]. But it's much milder; you can't say it's the dope that everybody says it is. But it's mild. It never bothered me, never fazed me in any way."[22]

This eyebrow-raising affair clearly demonstrates that the museum represented something quite different to Clive Gildersleeve than it did to many Oglalas. It seems that to him, the collection was endowed with a sense of legitimacy, by his own actions if need be. But many Lakotas did not accept this view, and Gildersleeve seems to have been, to a certain extent, in a state of denial about that. The establishment's very name is an indicator. The

Gildersleeves dubbed it the Crazy Horse Museum. While perhaps meant as a compliment, it is certainly hard to imagine that Tasunka Witko (Crazy Horse), perhaps the foremost embodiment of Oglala nationalism, independence, and resistance, would ever have countenanced such an institution, much less approved of his name being associated with it. But even after the siege of Wounded Knee, which led to the complete demolition of the trading post and museum, Gildersleeve would assert, "We've had a very good relationship with all our Indians; there's never been any problems encountered along the way." His use of the possessive pronoun "our" is perhaps telling. In this context, he continued to profess sympathy for Pine Ridge's Lakotas, despite his ongoing parasitic actions.[23]

Clive Gildersleeve's self-perception as a friend of the Lakotas, despite actions to the contrary, can be seen in certain other of his opinions. As early as the late 1940s, he was highly critical of the U.S. government's oncoming termination policy.[24] He rightly deemed it to be unethical and a disservice to Native peoples. That, however, did not stop him from seeking to capitalize on it at the expense of Indian people. In 1949, when the policy was still being formulated, he received a tip from federal representatives that Pine Ridge would soon be terminated and deprived of any financial support from the United States government. "I knew they were tipping me off," he admitted. Evaluating the potential fallout of the situation, he determined that Lakotas would be in dire need of money. He bought yet another trading post, this one in the reservation town of Kyle. He then formulated a plan: by offering credit through his stores to select, land-holding Indians, he could put himself in a position to leverage their debt when federal assistance ceased. He calculated that about $550 worth of credit per Indian would be enough to force them to sell their land to him in order to pay off their debts. He figured the turn around time for resale of the land, the final step to making profits, would be about three months. He put the scheme into action, extending more credit than usual to select Lakotas. His justification, in his own words, was that his actions would not "hurt the Indians any more than they are hurt, and I can make myself a bunch of money." However, his plans went awry because Pine Ridge Reservation was never terminated by the federal government. Gildersleeve ended up carrying substantial debt from the credit he had extended, some of which he never recouped. And the lesson he learned from the whole, sordid affair? "Never to believe Washington."[25]

In addition to badmouthing termination, he also judged the accompanying relocation program,[26] which encouraged Indians to emigrate to distant cities, to be a complete failure. However, it is thoroughly worth noting that he had a vested interest in that policy's failure; the successful off-reservation relocation of a large number of Lakotas to distant cities would have clearly hurt his business. Nonetheless, he did occasionally draw an ethical line in the prairie sod, so to speak.[27]

In 1949, a local white rancher approached him with a scheme to defraud Lakotas out of their cattle. Gildersleeve would call in his debts on Lakotas who owned competing herds. The Lakota ranchers would then have to sell their cattle to cover their debts, and the white rancher would buy them well below market value. How? The white rancher would have one of his mixed-blood Lakota employees submit very low bids to create the illusion of competitive Indian bids at auction and thereby gain government approval of the sales. Gildersleeve flatly refused to participate in the scam. It was moments of genuine ethical behavior such as this that allowed him to wax rhapsodically philosophic about Native people.[28]

"We've been very, very crude toward the Indian," he opined in an assessment of American history. "We have taken everything away from the Indian. . . . We took his land, then we condescended to give him a hundred-sixty acres back; and then we further made a very serious blunder by allotting to an individual Indian instead of the tribe. In other words, this is an open reservation [rather] than a closed; the land can be sold and is being sold and has been sold in big quantities for the simple reason that the Indian had no way of making a living."[29]

Gildersleeve also had his supporters. For them, the trading post and its operators did not symbolize the economic and cultural exploitation of an impoverished and vulnerable reservation society. Mixed-blood Pine Ridge resident Bessie Cornelius stood up for the Gildersleeves. To her, the trading post credit system represented a form of welfare system that worked to the benefit of the Indians. "I don't know how some of the people would have gotten along if it weren't for the people at Wounded Knee['s trading post]," she asserted. And in her estimation, Clive was, "I think, one of the finest persons I've known." Then again, Ms. Cornelius was not exactly a fountainhead of sympathy. "I think they were exploiters in a certain sense. But good grief, if you allow yourself to be exploited, you're going to be exploited, aren't you?" And she did admit to some of the Gildersleeves' more questionable business practices. "I had a little misgiving, I think it's the women that were out there [Agnes Gildersleeve and her daughters], were watching their finances real closely, let's just put it that way. They bought the finest beadwork. I don't know if they gave the best price for it." Nonetheless, as far as Cornelius was concerned, the Gildersleeve operation symbolized a positive force in the life of local Oglalas.[30]

Clive Gildersleeve's family and business associates have been able to garner substantial support and sympathy from the general nonreservation, non-Indian public in the surrounding areas of Nebraska and South Dakota that border Pine Ridge, much of it stemming from the destruction of their store during the Wounded Knee occupation. However, many critics, Indian and non-Indian alike, have been more pointed in their assessments. To John Neihardt, an outsider who spent a substantial amount of time on Pine Ridge during the mid-twentieth century, the Wounded Knee trading post represented the tacky commercialization of America and the exploitation of Native culture. Neihardt, who penned Black Elk's autobiography and religious vision[31] in the early 1930s, voiced his disgust in 1970 when asked specifically about institutions like the Gildersleeve museum and trading post. "Oh they make me sick. I hate to go to places like that. Wherever they start tourism, then you've got the cheapest characteristics of the human race. . . . I stay away as much as I can from such places. . . . it's just a fad."[32]

By the end of the 1960s, the Gildersleeves' daughter Jan and her husband James A. Czywczynksi had taken over much of the day-to-day operations after Clive Gildersleeve sold them a share of the store. While decades of working and living on Pine Ridge had garnered the Gildersleeves a modicum of cachet on the reservation, James and Jan Czywczynksi were relative newcomers, and their exploitative proprietorship dispensed with the social connections that had bound Clive and Agnes to the community. In addition to a litany of ongoing complaints, the operation was increasingly plagued by tighter credit, higher prices, and a seemingly naked capitalist ambition that was now devoid of the notion that the post was somehow a positive force on Pine Ridge; the Czywczynksis had forsaken the paternalistic niceties with which the Gildersleeves had tried to cloak their operation.[33]

The Gildersleeves' blend of greed and spiritual degradation reached a queer apex in 1969. Clive Gildersleeve and James A. Czywczynksi teamed with a Rapid City motel owner and a Custer, South Dakota, tourist attraction operator to conceive the ultimate insult: a $10-million, privately owned, Wounded Knee Massacre tourist site with a motel and stores. The centerpiece would be a Grecian marble monument: an obelisk, from the base of which ran red *terrazzo* blood across a marble platform and down its steps. Rounding out the hodgepodge of misplaced cultural symbols, the design also featured an eternal flame reminiscent of the one by President John F. Kennedy's tomb in Arlington National Cemetery. It was the ultimate effort by Gildersleeve and his associates to commodify Wounded Knee, to cash in on what, indeed, might rightly be termed "the cheapest characteristics of the human race." And it may very well have attracted tourists who were willing to purchase this version of Wounded Knee, had it come to fruition. But the matter came to a penultimate head almost immediately. After plans for its concept and construction were revealed, one South Dakota writer referred to it as "the most ambitious and bizarre chapter yet in the white man's exploitation of Indian misery and misfortune." Another called it an "esthetic monstrosity." To most Lakotas, this latest attempt to misappropriate Wounded Knee was an unfathomable indignity. Years later, that sentiment was concisely echoed by Claudia Iron Hawk Sully, then president of the Pine Ridge Wounded Knee Survivors Association. "We don't want our deceased relatives exploited by those people whose sole aim is to make money off the Massacre Site."[34]

As might be suspected, there were no Native Americans on the business commission planning to erect the monument and commercial structures. When the first planning commission stumbled, a second, non-profit commission named the Wounded Knee Memorial Association, again with no Native members, emerged with a new, slightly more sophisticated plan. Attempting to put a positive spin on the project, the commission claimed that the monument would somehow make amends for the unpaid debt that white America owed its forlorn Indigenous population. In essence, the second commission attempted to incorporate American guilt over the colonial subjugation of Indians, thereby attempting to veil the naked, crass commercialism of the proposed venture. It too began to sputter when it was unable to procure the land that held the grave site.[35]

The planning commission finally crossed the point of no return when it began exploring options to exhume the dead and move the mass grave. At that point, the Oglala Sioux Tribal Council and relatives of the massacre victims stepped in. They made their feelings known to Father Zuern, whose Holy Rosary Mission owned the land on which the grave was located.

Accordingly, he declined to sell the land to the developers. Single-minded in its zeal, the planning commission went so far as to try to intimidate the priest by threatening to squeal on him to his Jesuit superiors. However, Father Zuern stood firm, and he even offered to hand the land over to the Oglala Sioux Tribe. Thus was the debacle eluded.[36]

Then, on March 9, 1972, less than a year before the occupation of Wounded Knee, Lakota resentment over financial exploitation and spiritual degradation at Wounded Knee came to a head amid the outrage over the death of Raymond Yellow Thunder (see chapter 5). In an atmosphere of heightened sensitivity and rising anger over the Yellow Thunder affair, problems began to develop at the Wounded Knee trading post. Local Lakotas and their AIM supporters accused James Czywczynski of having badly mistreated a fourteen-year-old Indian boy from the Red Feather family. The Czywczynskis claimed the boy had made fun of Jan and instigated a curse-laden exchange with James. The boy claimed that Czywczynski had grabbed him by the throat in the process of throwing him out of the store, and he was quite shaken up by the assault. A group of Oglalas confronted the Gildersleeves and Czywczynksis about the incident. In the heady atmosphere surrounding the protests in Gordon, tensions ran high. As the exchanges heated up, the trading post proprietors were hardly conciliatory. Some Indians in the crowd voiced the idea of burning down the post. Clive Gildersleeve allegedly spit on an Indian, instigating a fracas. In the melee that erupted, Lakotas made off with some of the museum's belongings, including a number of spiritual items that many felt should not have been for sale or even on display to begin with. Gildersleeve later claimed the losses were valued at $50,000.[37]

After the incident, Gildersleeve innocently beseeched an Eastern newspaper reporter while surveying the damage. "I can't believe Indians did this. Why?" He then made a public plea: "And we do hope that the people who took them [the museum items] will return them so they will again be back in the museum where they belong."[38]

Clive Gildersleeve wanted to blame AIM for the changes bubbling on the reservation. He was unwilling to admit to himself that his own actions had played any role, or that there was seething resentment against him and his family over their exploitative and shameful actions during the previous four decades. Like the supporters of Dick Wilson's regime, he chose to deprive local Oglalas of their historical agency and point the finger at AIM for being foreign instigators. In his interpretation of events, they were the disruptive force, the outsiders who were riling up "his" Indians and upsetting the otherwise placid status quo. "I do think that the militant group who has come onto the Pine Ridge Reservation recently could do well to sit around and get acquainted with some of the people they are condemning instead of just barging in and trying to upset everything and trying to upset some very fine relationships between the Indian friends and their white friends who have been together so many, many years."[39]

But the relationship was not "fine," as the events during the siege of Wounded Knee would soon attest. The trading post would be all but destroyed during the seventy-one-day stand off, and most of the items on display at the museum were taken away or destroyed. After the 1972 mini-riot that began after the dispute with the Red Feather boy, the *Oglala Nation News* was amazingly prophetic in its reporting. "Contrary to what many authors have written that 'Wounded Knee was the last stand for America's Indian people,' it is now the beginning of a new movement which may rival the tragedy itself for historical significance."[40]

To the extent that this reservation newspaper spoke for its Indigenous constituency, it is clear that for Pine Ridge Lakotas the symbolic meaning of Wounded Knee resonated in the present and even the future, and was not uniformly trapped in the tragedy of the past. Indians were vividly aware that to many Americans, the 1890 massacre represented the final violent episode in the Western Indian wars. But to many Pine Ridge Lakotas, Clive Gildersleeve's Wounded Knee trading post represented the poverty, exploitation, and frustration of their ongoing colonial subjugation.

FROM BAD TO WORSE

As the siege of Wounded Knee progressed, the agenda of the full-blood community, which had engaged and now supported the standoff, evolved. An act of protest originally born from the frustration of living under Dick Wilson's autocratic and violent regime now transformed into something larger. No longer just a remonstration against one tribal chairman and his administration, it became an indictment of the entire tribal council system of government installed by the Indian Reorganization Act. On March 11, 1973, the besieged issued a proclamation. In an assertion of Lakota sovereignty, the statement publically announced the existence of the Independent Oglala Nation (ION). Refuting the IRA and all other mechanisms of America's colonial authority, the document declared that the 1868 Second Treaty of Fort Laramie would now be the basis for nation-to-nation negotiations with the United States. Furthermore, ION intended to send a delegation to the United Nations. Frank Fools Crow and Frank Kills Enemy would attend. Matthew King would be their interpreter. The declaration was forthright about the desire of the protestors "to abolish the Tribal Government under the Indian Reorganization Act. Wounded Knee will be a corporate state under the Independent Oglala Nation."[41]

In a show of support for ION and as an act of protest against Dick Wilson, several members of the Oglala Sioux Tribal Council boycotted the OSTC altogether. The council members in question were C. Hobart Keith, Birgil Kills Straight, Richard Little, Jake Little Thunder, Morris Wounded, and Vice Chairman David Long. Meanwhile, Lakotas from all walks of life continued to hold demonstrations in Pine Ridge village. Superintendent Stanley Lyman reacted with typical obtuseness, and Dick Wilson with predictable autocracy.[42]

For the most part, Lyman was unable to grasp why Lakotas were even upset and tended to view things in black and white. For example, when the anti-Wilsonites had broken into a spontaneous protest at the conclusion of the February 23 impeachment hearings, the superintendent was befuddled by what he saw. It was not just those that he referred to as "AIM-type people." Oscar Hollow Horn, a former member of the OST's law enforcement committee, was protesting. Indeed, so was Lyman's own secretary, Jo Cornelius, along with her brother Roger. "I knew that they were not part of a destructive force, but anyway, they were right there in front!" he observed with incredulity. As the protests continued, he was hampered by his own lens of perception. On one hand, as most people would, he felt that personal attacks against him were unwarranted; before March 11, he and Wilson were the focus of most of the political dissent. On the other hand, as the protests developed into an anti-IRA movement, he never gave the protestors credit for having the vision to effectuate a structural revision of the political system on Pine Ridge. Instead, he patronizingly viewed them as sincere but misguided, honest but ignorant.[43]

If the BIA superintendent, the federal government's local representative on the reservation, had such a dim understanding of the protestors' motives and abilities, one could hardly expect better from the more distant, primary power figures of the federal government. Interior Secretary Rogers Morton later indicated that President Nixon spoke to him only once about the occupation during its entirety. Nixon had inquired as to the expenditures for reservations and what percentage of it was going to Pine Ridge. When informed of the numbers, which were relatively sizeable for Pine Ridge, he is reported to have responded, "Well, what the hell are they making all the trouble for?" It simply never seems to have occurred to him that many Lakotas were not merely dissatisfied with their stake in the system, but rather they were dissatisfied with the system itself.[44]

During the siege, Dick Wilson moved to centralize his power even more so than he had previously. He rarely called the Oglala Sioux Tribal Council into session. After adjourning the October 1972 meeting the following February, he never called the January 1973 meeting. After a special session in March, which did little more than extend the chairman's powers, he called the April meeting, but the council issued no resolutions or ordinances. The July meeting was not held until August. In fact, between March and August of 1973, the OSTC took no official action as a governing body whatsoever. Part of the problem was that the boycott of the council by certain members made it very difficult to achieve a quorum. Fourteen of the twenty members were needed to reach the required two-thirds, but five of them were boycotting. When councilman Leo Wilcox died, it meant that every non-boycotting member would have to show up.[45]

Beyond minimizing the already hamstrung council, Wilson purged his adversaries. On April 4, he signed an executive order firing seven tribal employees who had demonstrated against him. He even fired his former campaign manager Barbara Means-Adams from her job of court clerk, accusing her of "advocating the overthrow of the elected government of the Oglala Sioux Tribe." On April 16, he disregarded official procedure and unilaterally suspended David Long for the second time after the vice chairman's boycott of OSTC meetings reached its seventh week.[46]

When the siege of Wounded Knee finally ended on May 8, 1973, it was not a victory for the besieged. More than 200 people were arrested, and the tribal council system was still in place. The remainder of Wilson's tenure on Pine Ridge, which did not end until 1976, was nothing short of a civil war.[47]

In 1974, the house of Oglala spiritual leader Frank Fools Crow was burgled and set ablaze. Fools Crow had been a vocal critic of Dick Wilson, and he suspected that the thievery and arson were retribution for his stance.

Property damage, however, was the least of problems for many of the chairman's opponents. Fools Crow received death threats from Wilson supporters the following year. For many others, there were more than threats.[48]

During the three years after the siege of Wounded Knee, Wilson's GOON Squad and the BIA police unleashed a reign of terror on the tribal chairman's adversaries. More than seventy of Wilson's opponents died violently: gunshots, arson, beatings, and inexplicable vehicular deaths. The Pine Ridge murder rate during these years was 17.5 times the national average. Charges were almost never brought against the perpetrators as very few of the killings were even investigated. Among those slain was Oglala Sioux Civil Rights Organization leader Pedro Bissonette, who was unarmed when BIA police shot him to death on October 17, 1973. Evidence that Wilson was behind the violence could be found on the night of February 26, 1975, when the tribal chairman personally ordered and oversaw the beating and knifing (not fatal) of six lawyers representing the American Indian Movement.[49]

Amidst the chaos came the June 26, 1975, shooting deaths of two FBI agents and one of Dennis Banks' bodyguards on the property of Harry Jumping Bull near the reservation town of Oglala. The federal government used the incident as an opportunity to arrest AIM's leaders, despite the fact that they had had nothing to do with the shootings. After failing to make cases against Russell Means or Dennis Banks, they indicted Leonard Peltier, the head of AIM security. In a trial of dubious validity, the government intimidated witnesses, tampered with and manufactured evidence, withheld exculpatory evidence, and engaged in other sundry practices in order to convict Peltier. He was sentenced to two consecutive life terms. Incarcerated for three decades, his case has attracted international attention, and Amnesty International currently lists him as one of the world's foremost political prisoners. No charges were ever filed over the shooting death of Joe Stuntz Killsright, the AIM bodyguard killed that day.[50]

The U.S. government continued to openly support Dick Wilson during this period of anarchy. Thus, it was of little consolation when federal investigations corroborated many of the original grievances Pine Ridge residents had levied against the chairman.

In 1973, Congress contracted the international accounting firm of Touche, Ross and Co. to conduct a review of the policies, procedures, and transactions of the Wilson administration. Among other things, the report was designed to review the council's compliance with OST regulations as well as its managerial efficiency and effectiveness. The firm submitted its findings on July 26 of that year.[51]

The report found that flagrant violations of recordkeeping had made it impossible to determine whether a number of tribal transactions were legitimate. There was no evidence that expenditures were going toward the goods and services for which they had been authorized or that payments for such were even in the correct amount. Nor were there any records to indicate that the tribe was receiving the goods and services for which it had paid. It was likewise impossible to ascertain if tribal employees were being paid the correct amounts, or if they were performing services for which they had been contracted. Banking practices were also highly irregular. Without making specific allegations, it noted that there was room for, and the possibility of, widespread corruption. "In general," the report concluded, "the Tribal Government is not functioning efficiently or effectively."[52]

In 1974, political opponents lined up in an attempt to dislodge Wilson from the OST presidency. Amid the turbulence, no less than a dozen Lakotas ran against the incumbent for the office of chairman. This was especially telling given the Wilson administration's undeniable willingness to use violence to intimidate and silence Wilson's opponents. A case in point was Roger Cornelius, the man who would eventually become Wilson's 1974 campaign manager. While driving across the reservation with University of South Dakota Professor Joseph Cash one day in July 1973, he passed Vice President David Long walking along the road. Cornelius told Cash in no uncertain terms that Cash's presence in the vehicle was the only reason he did not run Long off the road and into a ditch. Cash believed him. Vying for political office in this environment, the leading contenders were none other than AIM leader Russell Means and former chairman Gerald One Feather.[53]

Candidate Means was openly proclaiming himself as the champion of the reservation's full-blood constituency. In a speech he issued shortly after the siege of Wounded Knee, he cited Oglalas' "dissatisfaction with the tribal government, which has been imposed on people and which has been governing the Pine Ridge people the last forty years. And it just continues to get worse all the time and it cannot work and it will not work the way it's structured. . . . The people recognize that fact."[54]

By this time, AIM in general and Means in particular were highly dissentious subjects on the reservation. Whereas the Movement and its Oglala leader had once been heralded for their actions in Gordon, Nebraska, following the death of Raymond Yellow Thunder, their role in the violence now engulfing the reservation alienated many. "This thing has even divided families," noted Pine Ridge resident Edison Ward.[55]

Means's personality and style had antagonized some from the beginning. As early as 1972, Mona Montgomery of Pine Ridge had quit AIM soon after joining. "I don't really care for AIM," she said. Part of the reason was she felt Means was a hypocrite. And he had other weaknesses as a candidate. Though born on Pine Ridge, he had been raised in California and had returned to the reservation only recently. Many on the reservation still perceived him as an outsider. "If he is gonna come down here and run, he better quit talking national issues, start talking local issues," Mike Her Many Horses warned before the election.[56]

Despite his obvious political vulnerabilities, Means won the 1974 presidential primary on the divided reservation. Wilson was the first runner-up, meaning they would face each other in the February 7 general election. One Feather had come in third. When One Feather had faced Wilson in the general election two years earlier, there had been accusations of electoral corruption. In 1974, there would be more than accusations.[57]

Despite his earlier victory, Means lost the general election by exactly 200 votes: 1,714–1,514. Corruption had been widespread. Shortly after the election, the United States Civil Rights Commission issued a report that found "widespread irregularities took place before, during and after the election, and concludes that the results of the election are therefore invalid." Saying that the election was held "in a climate of fear and tension," the commission lambasted Wilson for numerous infractions. Wilson unduly influenced the selection of the election commission that counted the ballots and approved the results. He also failed to call the tribal council into session during the election as he was constitutionally required to do. Election judges and clerks were appointed inappropriately. Ballots and ballot boxes were tampered with. Most pervasive was the number of ineligible voters who took part. Reservation wide, the commission examined almost one-fourth of all the ballots and found nearly 20 percent of them to be invalid. In Wilson's base of support, Pine Ridge village, more than 30 percent of the ballots were cast by people who were not enrolled members of the Oglala Sioux Tribe.[58]

In the LaCreek District, there was much confusion over the official voting rolls. One woman even compiled her own unofficial roll in an effort to clarify the issue, but to no avail. The final tally in the district, where Means was expected to be very competitive, had him receiving only 51 of some 250 total votes. All of these gross irregularities, the report stated, had taken place right under the BIA's nose, but the Bureau had done nothing about it. Despite the commission's findings and its recommendation that a new election be held, the federal government chose to uphold the results and recognize Dick Wilson as chairman of the Oglala Sioux Tribe for a second consecutive term.[59]

Facing a stacked deck from the Oglala Sioux Tribe and finding no recourse from the BIA despite the civil rights commission's findings, Russell Means brought the issue into federal court. His lawyers claimed that the election fraud was a violation of the 1968 Indian Civil Rights Act. The initial decision in *Means v. Wilson* went against the AIM leader. However, Means had that dismissal successfully reversed in the eighth circuit court of appeals. The majority decision held that Means did have grounds for suit and remanded the case back to the lower court, allowing Means to proceed with charges against Wilson, GOON Squad leader Glenn Three Stars, and GOON enforcer Bennie "Tote" Richards. However, the circuit court did not finally issue its opinion until August 1975, rendering the decision somewhat moot; by the time a new hearing would be concluded, Wilson's term in office would be over or nearing its conclusion.[60]

The violence on Pine Ridge did not die down until Wilson was finally defeated in the more rigorously regulated 1976 election. The victor was Al Trimble, a man who ran as a moderate and received substantial support from full bloods. The rejection of Wilson in an honest election was not surprising. However, by 1976, AIM had also lost a degree of credibility among some full bloods. Part of it was guilt by association: AIM was intimately connected to the reservation-wide violence of the Wilson years, even if the chairman and his allies were responsible for instigating much of it. Nonetheless, AIM's own actions, which at times were brash, needlessly confrontational, and irresponsible, were also to blame for the disaffection felt by some. "I am not a member of the American Indian Movement," Oglala Lewis Bad Wound explained in 1974. "I'm a traditional." That same year, Frank Fools Crow was still standing by AIM. "If Dennis Banks and Russell Means go to jail for supporting the dignity of the Sioux Nation," he declared at a Congressional hearing, "[Y]ou must be ready to send us all to jail." By 1976, however, he referred to AIM members as "radical Indians" and said whites were justified in being angry at them. He did not disavow AIM completely, but he certainly curtailed his earlier support.[61]

Shortly after losing the 1976 election, Dick Wilson left Pine Ridge Reservation. He died of kidney failure and an enlarged heart in 1990.[62]

BOOKENDS

Part I of this work analyzed the establishment and development of the tribal council system on the Pine Ridge Reservation in the 1930s and 1940s. Part II examined the evolution of the council and its political development during the late 1960s and early 1970s, culminating with the occupation of Wounded Knee. From the outset, the contention has been that the establishment of the former is tied to the outbreak of the latter; the installation of the tribal council system is directly linked to the occupation and siege of Wounded Knee. The two events themselves may be viewed as bookends to the mid-twentieth-century efforts of Pine Ridge Lakotas to resist the colonial authority of the United States as it was manifested through the tribal council system.

Reorganization was a contested issue from the beginning. Specifically, many full bloods were suspicious of the new system and fearful that it would come to be dominated by mixed bloods who did not share their interests. This is important because much of the full-blood community continued to have little faith in the Oglala Sioux Tribal Council during the four intervening decades. Several scholars have pointed this out.[63] As recently as 1986, thirteen years after the siege, anthropologist Marla N. Powers observed that full-blood Oglalas "have no allegiance to the tribal council, except to the extent that temporary alliances with council officials may serve the immediate interests of individuals, because the true allegiance is between kinsmen whose locus of organization is out in the districts."[64]

What is more important than scholarly observations, however, is that numerous Pine Ridge Oglalas themselves have openly voiced their displeasure. "This Tribal Council Government is a substitute for our way," Grace Black Elk said in 1973. "It's run by white people's laws." Gladys Bissonette echoed her sentiments. "We want an independent sovereign Oglala

Sioux nation. We don't want no part of the Government, Tribal or BIA. We have had enough of that."[65]

Although John Collier had promised Frank Fools Crow and Charles Red Cloud in 1934 that the new tribal council would have substantial powers, this did not turn out to be the case. Instead, the Office of Indian Affairs initially retained most of its power during the first ten years of the Oglala Sioux Tribe's existence. This aspect of *realpolitik* was not lost on Pine Ridge Lakotas who continued to petition the OIA for help with matters large and small. When the council did attempt to exert its authority on the reservation, the new political situation was frequently what many had feared: the tribal council was often dominated by mixed-blood interests, particularly under the tenure of the initial chairman, Frank G. Wilson. The early council's actions were mitigated, however, by a reservation superintendent (W. O. Roberts) who, though his motives may have been suspect, was at least nominally sympathetic to the position of the full-blood community and increasingly leery of the tribal council's agenda.[66]

By the early 1970s, tribal councils around the country had expanded their authority under the Nixonian policy of self-determination. However, Lakotas continued to recognize the supremacy of the Bureau of Indian Affairs. Sicanghu Lakota Mary Crow Dog, from the neighboring Rosebud Reservation, noted that "the tribal governments, such as they were, had very little real power. Power remained always in the hands of the white superintendent and the white BIA bureaucrats. He had the support of Washington. In a conflict between the tribal president and the white superintendent, it was always the white superintendent who came out on top."[67] Mary Crow Dog's assertion is almost identical to Marla Powers' statement that "In a larger sense one might say that tribal government is merely an arm of the BIA, since BIA superintendents maintain almost absolute power over newly elected tribal councils." More recently, scholar Taiaiake Alfred stated in no uncertain terms that "the imposition of Western governance structures and the denial of indigenous ones continue to have profoundly harmful effects on indigenous people." Alfred views Native people "who possess authority delegated by . . . the United States government [as] less leaders (with apologies to the rare and admirable exceptions) than tools of the state."[68]

In addition, full bloods on Pine Ridge continued to be suspicious of the entire system, leery of the values it promoted, and wary of mixed-blood domination. "These puppet governments are oftentimes the most corrupt governments around and bring out the very worst in the whiteman system of governments," Frank Fools Crow said in 1976. "Councilmen on these puppet governments always represent the view of the white man because they are indoctrinated by the white man to act like this. These types of people are on the council because very few of our traditional people vote in these elections . . . These councilmen do not represent the majority of the people on the reservation."[69]

In the early 1970s, full-blood discontent with the system boiled over during the presidency of Dick Wilson. Wilson's administration, like a number of previous administrations, was antagonistic toward full bloods. However, several factors combined to make his regime worse. First, his dictatorial style was divisive, and his autocratic tendencies alienated and upset many full bloods and certain members of his own tribal council. Second was the willingness of the federal government to give Wilson a free hand, in effect handing over much of its political currency to him prior to the occupation of Wounded Knee. This occurred for two reasons: the superintendent during Wilson's tenure (Stanley Lyman) blindly supported the edicts of self-determination and was himself extremely patronizing toward the full-blood community; and Wilson became virulently anti-AIM, a position that echoed the federal government's own policies.

With reservation constituencies polarizing (Wilson's administration and its supporters versus the full-blood community and its supporters) at almost exactly the same time that national constituencies were polarizing (the federal government versus the American Indian Movement), the coalitions as they developed on Pine Ridge in the early 1970s seem predictable in hindsight. The culmination was the failed attempt to impeach Wilson, which directly led to the occupation and siege of Wounded Knee.

STILL

While visiting Pine Ridge in the spring of 1999, I went looking for the mother of a friend of mine. She is from the reservation town of Porcupine, a traditional hotbed of full-blood agitation. When I stopped by her house, a family member told me that she was at the tribal council meeting. Sessions of the OSTC are now rotated from site to site around the reservation, no longer held exclusively in Pine Ridge village as they were under Dick Wilson.

I made my way back to the town of Kyle, where I previously had been engrossed in a seemingly endless collection of documents at the archives of Oglala Lakota College. When I got to the meeting hall, she was not there. I asked around and got some hard stares and pointed questions. Clearly, my association with her was not a positive attribute in the minds of some councilmen. One member was more sympathetic. He grinned and told me that she had been raising a bit of a ruckus over the way the council was conducting its business and that some other members were trying to keep her from speaking at the open meeting on the grounds that her topics of discussion were not on the council's agenda. For now, though, he did not know where she was.

After another stint in the archives, I returned to the meeting. By then it had broken up, and my friend's mother was standing outside. "They can't keep me quiet," she said. By winter, she was no longer an army of one.

On January 16, 2000, another grassroots political protest took place on Pine Ridge. A local organization called Grass Roots Oyate (*oyate* translates as "nation" or "people") occupied the Red Cloud building, the OST's administrative center. Many of the occupiers were elderly full bloods. They were again upset with perceived corruption in the tribal council, this time under the administration of Chairman Harold Dean Salway. They erected a sacred Lakota altar and declared themselves sovereign under the Second Treaty of Fort Laramie of 1868. They demanded the removal of OST Treasurer Wesley Jacobs; a five-year forensic audit of the OST; audits of land holdings by the Bureau of Indian Affairs and First National Bank of Gordon, Nebraska; a five-year suspension of the entire Oglala Sioux Tribal Council; and a referendum to abolish the IRA system of government altogether.[70]

As happened during the Wilson years, the members of the Oglala Sioux Tribal Council divided, most of them spurning the local protestors. Chairman Salway tried to suspend all but four of the tribal council members. They, in turn, tried to suspend him. Although a number of the protestors supported Salway in his dispute with the council, the federal government sided with the council against him. Federal authorities informed the chairman that they would not recognize his declaration of a state of emergency and that he was suspended outright. "You have no authority whatsoever to order any tribal employee to do or not do anything," Assistant Secretary for Indian Affairs (the new name of the commissioner of Indian affairs) Kevin Gover wrote to Salway in a March 23 letter.[71]

Understandably frustrated, and perhaps forgetting that his office exists only at the discretion of a sixty-five-year-old piece of federal legislation (something that the full bloods have never forgotten), Salway was indignant. "We are a sovereign nation," he declared. "How can he tell me what to do?" Salway's suspension may have been a clear illustration of the IRA system as colonialism in action, but it was not a victory for Grass Roots Oyate. In fact, it was Salway who had previously suspended the OST treasurer to whom Grass Roots Oyate objected. Nor could the protestors hope for sympathy had there only been Indians in high places: Gover is an Oklahoma Pawnee. To his mind, "Salway was a bad guy," and "the Grass Roots Oyate had very little support in the community." When some urged him to take the building back by force, he ignored them. When Grassroots Oyate demanded the Black Hills back, he ignored them, too. The protest eventually ended peacefully. Salway lost his office in the next election.[72]

In a political coda of sorts, Russell Means again ran for the chairmanship of Pine Ridge in 2004. Once again, he finished first in the primary. And once again, he lost the run-off. This time, the victor was Cecilia Fire Thunder, the first woman ever to gain the reservation's presidency.

President Fire Thunder soon ran into her own controversy while running the IRA-sponsored Oglala Sioux Tribe. When the state of South Dakota legislated severe restrictions on access to abortions, the chairwoman proposed opening a women's clinic on Pine Ridge that would offer abortions. She maintained that the state would have no jurisdiction over the reservation on this matter. However, many Lakotas believe that abortions do not coincide with their values. Just as Chairman Wilson before her, Fire Thunder was now finding herself in a dispute with a sizeable portion of her constituency over how the government should act in reflecting Oglala ideals.[73]

Leading the charge against Fire Thunder were Councilmen Will Peters and Garfield Steele. They filed a complaint citing Fire Thunder for not informing the OSTC of her plans to open a women's clinic, an act for which she would require the council's approval. The tribal council held an impeachment hearing on June 29, 2006. With thirteen of its eighteen members present, the council voted 9–4 to remove Fire Thunder from office and elevated Vice President Alex White Plume to the OST presidency for the duration of the two-year term scheduled to end in December 2006. Fire Thunder sought redress in Oglala Sioux tribal court. She filed for an injunction against her removal on the grounds that the council had acted improperly in removing her. She contended that the impeachment hearing was unconstitutional since, among other things, the council did not provide evidence against her and she was denied access to an attorney. She also maintained that two-thirds (twelve total) of the entire council must vote to impeach her, not just two-thirds of those present.[74]

Tribal Judge Lisa Adams initially concurred, reinstating Fire Thunder July 17 and scheduling a formal tribal court hearing on the complaint for July 28, 2006. However, council members immediately approached Adams and insisted that the tribal constitution did not allow a tribal judge to issue a restraining order against the OSTC. Adams vacated her injunction the very same day and recused herself from the case. Fire Thunder was out and White Plume was in.[75]

These very recent political disputes on Pine Ridge will no doubt be taken up by historians in the future, and it would seem likely, given the nature of previous historical events, that in some way it will be interpreted as yet another example of ongoing Oglala unhappiness with the IRA system of government. However, Pine Ridge is not the only tribal council government in America to endure leadership problems in recent times. The Eastern Cherokees of North Carolina recently impeached their council chairman, and a former chairman of the Crow nation in Montana resigned his office in September of 2002 and pleaded guilty to fraud, receiving a three-year prison sentence for bribery. Charges of corruption are also seen across the foty-ninth parallel, levied against First Nation governments operating under the auspices of the Canadian government.[76]

At the same time, however, it should be noted that there are any number of tribal councils that function quite well and have not had the same historic dysfunction that has plagued the OST. Anthropologist Loretta Fowler has shown how Arapahos have successfully adapted to the tribal council system, molding it where possible to fit their Indigenous political institutions. Likewise, historian Paul Rosier has acknowledged the controversies that have surrounded the Blackfeet Business Council, but in the end concludes that "Blackfeet interest groups assiduously pursued their right to make [the IRA] conform to their respective goals and to use its tools to construct their version of an Indian-American community." The new governing systems have hardly been perfect in either case. In fact, Rosier's observations on some of the problems springing from the development of Blackfeet IRA government are quite similar to the ones arising from the advent of Pine Ridge's IRA government. The difference is that, unlike the measured adaptative successes of the Arapahos or Blackfeet, the Oglala Sioux Tribal Council has been a near constant source of contention among Oglalas; its successes on Pine Ridge have been limited, while its numerous failures have ranged from the mundane to the combustible.[77]

Regardless of any final tally on tribal governments, endless examples of corruption and other shortcomings can be found in various branches of the United States' local, state, and federal governments as well as countless governing bodies around the world. In other words, Pine Ridge hardly has a monopoly on political discord. But the fact persists that on America's Indian reservations, Indigenous people do not live under Indigenous governments. They rule themselves through foreign, Western political institutions that are subject to federal authority. Such is the legacy of colonialism. On Pine Ridge, that has led to resentment, frustration, and problems that persist to this day.

By July 1973, some two months after the conclusion of the siege, Chairman Dick Wilson was the living embodiment of Native contention over the nature of IRA-sponsored governments. There was no more vocal advocate of the IRA system, but even *he* was starting to show signs of skepticism. "I'm strictly a tribal government man," he asserted. He then went on to consider the meaning of this and made a candid confession. "It's not really the best system and we know it. But it is the system and we choose to work through it." On Pine Ridge, however, the word "we" was no longer a simple one.[78]

Appendix A

Preambles of the Constitution of the Oglala Sioux Tribe,
1921 and 1936

Constitution and By-Laws Oglala Sioux Tribe Pine Ridge Reservation, South Dakota: Preamble (1921)

We, the members of the Sioux Tribe of Indians of the Pine Ridge Reservation, South Dakota, in order to establish a more perfect unity amongst us, to obtain justice, insure domestic peace, to secure the common defense, to promote our welfare and self interest, to enjoy the blessings of rights, do ordain and establish this constitution for the Oglala Tribal Council.

Constitution and By-Laws of the Oglala Sioux Tribe of the Pine Ridge Reservation of South Dakota: Preamble (1936)

We, the Oglala Sioux Tribe of the Pine Ridge Reservation, in order to establish a more perfect organization, promote the general welfare, conserve and develop our land and resources, secure to ourselves and our posterity the power to exercise rights of home rule not inconsistent with federal laws and our treaties, and in recognition of God Almighty and His Divine Providence, do ordain and establish this constitution for the Oglala Sioux Tribe.

Appendix B

Members of the Oglala Sioux Tribal Council, 1936

Executive Council

President: Frank Wilson
Vice-President: Harry Conroy
Secretary: George Pugh

Representatives

EAGLE NEST DISTRICT

John Goes in Center
Robert Two Elk
William Young

PASS CREEK DISTRICT

John Ruff
William Fire Thunder
George Dull Knife

LACREEK DISTRICT

Walter Conroy
John Means
Egon Lessert

MEDICINE ROOT DISTRICT

Frank Apple
James Clifford
Charles Under Baggage

Otto Chief Eagle

PORCUPINE DISTRICT

John Rock
Oliver Jealous of Him
George Stirk
Thomas Conroy

WOUNDED KNEE DISTRICT

Charles Shot to Pieces
Richard Afraid of Hawk
William Ghost Dog
George Respects Nothing

WAKPAMNI DISTRICT

James LaPoint
Richard Whalen
Henry Standing Bear
James H. Red Cloud

WHITE CLAY DISTRICT

Grant High Whiteman
Samuel Stands
Ivan Star

Critic: Ted C. Craven

Appendix C

Members of the Oglala Sioux Tribal Council, April 1972

Executive Council

President Dick Wilson
Vice President David Long
Secretary Lloyd W. Eaglebull
Treasurer Emma T. Nelson
Fifth Member Everett Lone Hill

Representatives

PINE RIDGE VILLAGE

Emma T. Nelson
Elizabeth Robideaux
Leo Wilcox
Robert Ecoffey
C. Hobart Keith

WAKPAMNI DISTRICT

Maurice Wounded
Henry White Calf★
Peter Janis

WOUNDED KNEE DISTRICT

Paul Apple
Edward Stover

PORCUPINE DISTRICT

Orland Big Owl
William High Hawk

PASS CREEK DISTRICT

Florence Tibbitts

LACREEK DISTRICT

Emma Bettleyoun

MEDICINE ROOT DISTRICT

Wilson Gay
Birgil Kills Straight

WHITE CLAY DISTRICT

Etta Youngman
Richard Little

EAGLE NEST DISTRICT

Stephen Red Elk
Jake Little Thunder

Critic: Burgess Red Kettle
Sergeant-At-Arms: Henry Brown

★Henry White Calf resigned shortly after the election. He was replaced by former OST Chairman Johnson Holy Rock.

[219]

Appendix D

Presidents of the Oglala Sioux Tribe, 1936–2006

1936–38 Frank G. Wilson	1974–76 Richard Wilson
1938–40 Frank G. Wilson	1976–78 Albert W. Trimble
1940–42 Henry Jumping Eagle	1978–80 Elijah Whirlwind Horse
1942–44 William Fire Thunder	1980–82 Stanley Looking Elk
1944–46 William Fire Thunder	1982–84 Joseph American Horse
1946–48 James Roan Eagle	1984–86 Newton Cummings
1948–50 William Fire Thunder	1986–88 Joseph American Horse
1950–52 Henry Conroy	1988–90 Paul Iron Cloud
1952–54 Charles Under Baggage	1990–92 Harold Dean Salway
1954–56 Moses Two Bulls	1992–94 John Yellow Bird Steele
1956–58 Frank G. Wilson	1994–96 Wilber Between Lodges
1958–60 Frank G. Wilson	1996–98 John Yellow Bird Steele
1960–62 Johnson Holy Rock	1998–2000 Harold Dean Salway
1962–64 William Whirlwind Horse	2000–02 John Yellow Bird Steele
1964–66 Enos Poor Bear	2002–04 John Yellow Bird Steele
1966–68 Johnson Holy Rock	2004–06 Cecilia Fire Thunder
1968–70 Enos Poor Bear	2006 Alex White Plume
1970–72 Gerald One Feather	2006 John Yellow Bird Steele
1972–74 Richard Wilson	

Notes

Foreword

1. Vine Deloria, Jr., and Clifford Lytle, *The Nations Within: The Past and Future of American Indian Sovereignty* (Austin: University of Texas Press, 1984), 183.

2. Paul Chaat Smith and Robert Allen Warrior, *Like a Hurricane: The Indian Movement from Alcatraz to Wounded Knee,* (New York: New Press, 1996), 190–268.

3. Vine Deloria, Jr., and David E. Wilkins, *Tribes, Treaties, & Constitutional Tribulations* (Austin: University of Texas Press, 1999), 3–20.

4. Stephen Cornell and Joseph P. Kalt, *What Can Tribes Do? Strategies and Institutions in American Indian Economic Development* (Los Angeles: American Indian Studies Center, University of California at Los Angeles, 1992), 9–10.

5. Robert K. Thomas, "Colonialism: Classic and Internal," *New University Thought,* 6 (1966–67): 34–43.

Chapter 1

1. For an adequate in-depth chronicle of the siege of Wounded Knee that is unsympathetic to the besieged, see Rolland Dewing, *Wounded Knee: The Meaning and Significance of the Second Incident* (New York: Irvington, 1985). For an interpretation that is hostile to the Wilson administration and the federal government, see Ward Churchill and Jim Vander Wall, *Agents of Repression: The FBI's Secret War Against the Black Panther Party and the American Indian Movement* (Boston: South End Press, 1990), 181–260. For a more balanced view, see Pal Chaat Smith and

Robert Allen Warrior, *Like a Hurricane: The Indian Movement from Alcatraz to Wounded Knee* (New York: New Press, 1996).

2. For analyses of the press coverage, see: Michelle D. Dishong, "*New York Times* Coverage of the Occupation of Wounded Knee, South Dakota." M.A. thesis, Washington State University, 1996; Terri Schultz, "Bamboozle Me Not at Wounded Knee: The Making of a Media Event That Had Everything But the Truth." *Harper's* (June 1973): 46–56; Judith Anola Vick, "The Press and Wounded Knee, 1973: An Analysis of the Coverage of the Occupation by Selected Newspapers and Magazines." M.A. thesis, University of Minnesota, 1977; Natalie P. Wells, "Television News Coverage of the American Indian Occupation of Wounded Knee, South Dakota: An Analysis of Network Newscasts, February–May, 1973." M.A. thesis, San Francisco State University, 1982.

3. Oyate is Lakota for "The People" or "The Nation."

4. Name withheld interviewed by Tom Short Bull, April 4, 1973. South Dakota Oral History Center, Institute of American Indian Studies, University of South Dakota, Vermillion, SD. American Indian Research Program [hereafter, AIRP], 606 (no transcript) [copy of interview also in author's possession].

5. Ibid.

6. Ibid.

7. Ibid.

8. Richard Wilson interviewed by Joseph Cash, July 17, 1973. AIRP, 918 (no transcript).

9. Ibid.

10. Ibid.

11. Ibid.

12. Ibid.

13. Ibid.

14. Ibid.

15. Ibid.

16. Ibid.

17. Press Conference with Rogers C. B. Morton, July 18, 1973. AIRP, 914 (no transcript).

18. Ibid.

19. Ibid.

20. For discussions of the *Oceti Sakowin* see Guy Gibbon, *The Sioux: The Dakota and Lakota Nations* (Malden, MA: Blackwell, 2003), 2–3, 220; William K. Powers, *Oglala Religion* (Lincoln: University of Nebraska Press, 1982), 3–5; James R. Walker, *Lakota Society*, Raymond J. DeMallie ed. (Lincoln: University of Nebraska Press, 1982), 10–11, 14–18.

21. Gibbon, 3–6; Catherine Price, *The Oglala People, 1847–79: A Political His-*

tory (Lincoln: University of Nebraska Press, 1996); Richard White, "The Winning of the West: The Expansion of the Western Sioux in the Eighteenth and Nineteenth Century,*"Journal of American History* 65 (September 1978): 319–43; Jeffrey Ostler, *Plains Sioux and U.S. Colonialism from Lewis and Clark to Wounded Knee* (New York: Cambridge University Press, 2004), 13–39.

22. Gibbon, 105–33; Ostler, 40–243.

23. The seven subdivisions of the Lakotas are the Oglala, Sichanghu (a.k.a. Brule), Miniconjou, Hunkpapa, Itazipco (a.k.a. Sans Arc), Oohenunpa (a.k.a. Two Kettles), and Sisapa (a.k.a. Blackfeet; not to be confused with the Blackfeet Confederacy of the Northern Rockies, an unrelated group of people).

24. United States, *Statutes at Large,* 48:984 (1934).

25. Tom Holm, "The Crisis in Tribal Government" in Vine Deloria, Jr., ed., *American Indian Policy in the Twentieth Century* (Norman: University of Oklahoma Press, 1985), 135; Mario Gonzalez and Elizabeth Cook-Lynn, *The Politics of Hallowed Ground: Wounded Knee and the Struggle for Indian Sovereignty* (Urbana: University of Illinois Press, 1999), 219; Troy Johnson, Duane Champagne, and Joane Nagel, "American Indian Activism and Transformation: Lessons from Alcatraz," in Troy Johnson, Duane Champagne, and Joane Nagel, eds., *American Indian Activism: Alcatraz to the Longest Walk* (Urbana: University of Illinois Press, 1997), 35–36; Marla N. Powers, *Oglala Women: Myth, Ritual and Reality* (Chicago: University of Chicago Press, 1986), 143; Dewing, 354; William O. Farber, "Representative Government: Application to the Sioux," in Ethel Nurge, ed., *The Modern Sioux* (Lincoln: University of Nebraska Press, 1970), 123, 138; Ernest L. Schusky, "Political and Religious Systems in Dakota Culture," in Nurge, ed., 144; Paul M. Robertson, *The Power of the Land: Identity, Ethnicity, and Class Among the Oglala Lakota* (New York: Routledge, 2002), 200.

26. For a good overview of varying opinions on the IRA see Kenneth R. Philp, ed., *Indian Self-Rule: First-Hand Accounts of Indian-White Relations from Roosevelt to Reagan* (Salt Lake City: Howe Brothers, 1986).

27. Price, *The Oglala People;* Ostler, *Plains Sioux and U.S. Colonialism;* Thomas Biolsi, *Organizing the Lakota: The Political Economy of the New Deal on the Pine Ridge and Rosebud Reservations* (Tucson: University of Arizona Press, 1992); Robertson, *The Power of the Land.*

28. Dewing, *Wounded Knee;* Warrior and Smith, *Like A Hurricane;* Leonard Crow Dog and Richard Erdoes, *Crow Dog: Four Generations of Sioux Medicine Men* (New York: HarperPerennial, 1996); Mary Crow Dog with Richard Erdoes, *Lakota Woman* (New York: Harper Perennial, 1990); Russell Means with Marvin J. Wolf, *Where White Men Fear to Tread* (New York: St. Martin's Press, 1995); Bill Zimmerman, *Airlift to Wounded Knee* (Chicago: Swallow Press, 1976).

29. The post–Wounded Knee conflict on Pine Ridge, including details on the

Peltier case, which has since garnered substantial international attention, are covered in Churchill and Vander Wall, 261–388 and Peter Matthiessen, *In the Spirit of Crazy Horse*, rev. ed. (New York: Viking Press, 1991).

30. Lawrence M. Hauptman, "The Indian Reorganization Act" in Sandra L. Cadwalder and Vine Deloria, Jr., eds., *The Aggressions of Civilization* (Philadelphia: Temple University Press, 1984), 143.

31. Gonzalez and Cook-Lynn, 219; Gibbon, 173; Smith and Warrior, 171–268; Biolsi, 182–84.

32. Clyde D. Dollar, "The Second Tragedy at Wounded Knee: A 1970s Confrontation and Its Historical Roots," *American West* 10 (1973): 4–11, 58–61; Stanley David Lyman, *Wounded Knee 1973: A Personal Account*, with a foreword by Alvin M. Josephy (Lincoln: University of Nebraska Press, 1991), xv, 67–68, 131–32; Dewing, *Wounded Knee;* Francis Paul Prucha, *The Great Father*, 2 vols. (Lincoln: University of Nebraska Press, 1985), 2:1119; Dick Wilson, "Real Indians Condemn AIM," in John R. Maestas, ed., *Contemporary Native American Address* (Provo: Brigham Young University Press, 1976), 63–5.

33. A strong and cogent rejection of indirect colonial models of governing Indigenous people in both Canada and the United States can be found in Taiaiake Alfred, *Peace, Power, Righteousness: An Indigenous Manifesto* (Don Mills, Ontario: Oxford University Press, 1999). Studies that have contributed to the literature on the politics of specific reservations include David R. M. Beck, *The Struggle for Self-Determination: History of the Menominee Indians Since 1854* (Lincoln: University of Nebraska Press, 2005); Vine Deloria, Jr., and Clifford Lytle, *The Nations Within: The Past and Future of American Indian Sovereignty* (New York: Pantheon Books, 1984); Loretta Fowler, *Arapaho Politics, 1851–1978: Symbols in Crises of Authority* (Lincoln: University of Nebraska Press, 1982); Loretta Fowler, *Shared Symbols, Contested Meanings: Gros Ventre Culture and History, 1778-1984* (Ithaca: Cornell University Press, 1987); Loretta Fowler, *Tribal Sovereignty and the Historical Imagination: Cheyenne-Arapaho Politics* (Lincoln: University of Nebraska Press, 2002); Michael Joseph Francisconi, *Kinship, Capitalism, Change: The Informal Economy of the Navajo, 1868–1995* (New York: Garland Publishing, 1998); Erin Hogan Fouberg, *Tribal Territory, Sovereignty, and Governance: A Study of the Cheyenne River and Lake Traverse Indian Reservations* (New York: Garland, 2000); Rebecca Kugel, *To be the Main Leaders of our People: A History of Minnesota Ojibwe Politics, 1825-1898* (East Lansing: Michigan State University Press, 1998); James J. Lopach, Margery Hunter and Richmond L. Clow, *Tribal Government Today: Politics on Montana Indian Reservations* (Boulder: Westview Press, 1990); Nicholas Peroff, *Menominee Drums: Tribal Termination and Restoration, 1954–1974* (Norman: University of Oklahoma Press, 1982); Paul C.

Rosier, *Rebirth of the Blackfeet Nation: 1912–1954* (Lincoln: University of Nebraska Press, 2001).

Chapter 2

1. The six reservations, scattered across North and South Dakota, are Cheyenne River, Crow Creek, Lower Brule, Pine Ridge, Rosebud, and Standing Rock.

2. United States, *Statutes at Large*, 25:888 (1889); Paula L. Wagoner, *"They Treated Us Just Like Indians": The Worlds of Bennett County, South Dakota* (Lincoln: University of Nebraska Press, 2002), 39–46; Thomas Biolsi, *Organizing the Lakota: The Political Economy of the New Deal on the Pine Ridge an Rosebud Reservations* (Tucson: University of Arizona Press, 1992), 6, 9.

3. Wagoner, 39–46; Biolsi, 6, 9. It is worth noting that in 1976, which is slightly after the scope of this book, Washbaugh County was subsumed into Jackson County to the north.

4. The OIA has since been renamed the Bureau of Indian Affairs (BIA). The CIA is more recently known as the assistant secretary of the interior for Indian affairs.

5. Catherine Price, *The Oglala People, 1841–1879: A Political History* (Lincoln: University of Nebraska Press), 173–75; Rupert Costo in *Indian Historian Today* 1 (winter 1968): 4–8, 87; Marla N. Powers, *Oglala Women: Myth, Ritual, and Reality* (Chicago: University of Chicago Press, 1986), 32, 141. For a published memoire by an early agent to the Lakotas, see: James McLaughlin, *My Friend the Indian*, with an introduction by Robert M. Utley (New York: Houghton Mifflin, 1910; reprint ed., Lincoln: University of Nebraska Press, 1989).

6. House Resolution 25242, "Right of Indians to Nominate Their Agent," June 21, 1912. Reprinted in Vine Deloria, Jr., editor, *The Indian Reorganization Act Congresses and Bills* (Norman: University of Oklahoma Press, 2002),3–5; Statute 5335, "A Bill Conferring upon Tribes the Right to Recall Their Agents or Superintendents," May 2, 1916. Reprinted in Deloria, ed.

7. John Collier, *From Every Zenith: A Memoir and Some Essays on Life and Thought* (Denver: Sage Books, 1963), 15–21, 115–20, 124–26, 223; Lawrence C. Kelly, *The Assault on Assimilation: John Collier and the Origins of Indian Policy Reform* (Albuquerque: University of New Mexico Press, 1983), 38–42, 118–37.

8. For a general discussion of assimilation, see: Frederick Hoxie, *The Final Promise: The Campaign to Assimilate the Indians, 1880–1920* (Lincoln: University of Nebraska, 1984) and Francis Paul Prucha, *The Great Father: The United States Government and the American Indians*, 2 vols. (Lincoln: University of Nebraska Press, 1984).

9. Collier, 169–84, 340–53.

10. Ibid, 340–41, 351.

11. Ibid, 341–42.

12. Ibid, 345 [emphasis Collier's].

13. Ibid, 346 [emphasis Collier's].

14. Ibid, 173–75.

15. Prucha, 2:666–71; John. R. Wunder, *Retained by The People: A History of American Indians and the Bill of Rights* (New York: Oxford University Press, 1994), 67.

16. Prucha, 2:666–71; Wunder, 67.

17. The Five Nations, once patronizingly known to Americans as the "Five Civilized Tribes," are the Cherokees, Chickasaws, Choctaws, Muscogees (Creeks), and Seminoles. The Haudenosaunee (Iroquois) Confederacy League of Nations is composed of the Ganiengehaga (Mohawks), Oneidas, Onondagas, Cayugas, Senecas, and Tuscaroras.

18. Lawrence C. Kelly, "The Indian Reorganization Act: The Dream and the Reality," *Pacific Historical Review* 44 (August 1975): 296.

19. Ibid; Congressman Benjamin Reifel, interviewed by Joseph H. Cash, Summer, 1967, in *The Plains Indians of The Twentieth Century,* ed. Peter Iverson (Norman: University of Oklahoma Press, 1985), 110; Floyd Taylor interviewed by Joseph H. Cash, August 9, 1968. South Dakota Oral History Center, Institute of American Indian Studies, University of South Dakota, Vermillion, SD. American Indian Research Program [hereafter, AIRP], 50:1.

20. Reifel in Iverson, 110; Taylor interviewed by Cash, 50:1; Kelly, "The Indian Reorganization Act", 296.

21. United States, *Statutes at Large,* 48:984 (1934); Kelly, "The Indian Reorganization Act", 279–98.

22. United States, *Statutes at Large,* 48:984 (1934); Prucha, 2:695; Wunder, 70.

23. Kelly, "The Indian Reorganization Act", 301–4.

24. Charles J. Kappler, ed., *Indian Treaties 1778–1883* (Washington, DC: Government Printing Office, 1904; reprint ed., New York: Interland Publishing, 1972), 2:998–1007.

25. Thomas Spotted War Bonnet interviewed by George Nielsen, July 7, 1971. AIRP, 734 (no transcript). One should note that regardless of the given merits and shortcomings of various academic debates, Lakotas themselves (and indeed, many other Indian people) continue to use terms such as "progressive," "half-breed," "mixed blood," "traditional," "skin," and "full-blood," to describe not only genetic lineage, but also social and cultural orientations. For discussions by an academic see Wagoner; Paul M. Robertson, *The Power of the Land: Identity,*

Ethnicity, and Class among the Oglala Lakotas (New York: Routledge, 2002), 11–39. For Indian points of view, see Maria Campbell, *Halfbreed* (New York: Saturday Review Press, 1973) and Mary Crow Dog with Richard Erdoes, *Lakota Woman* (New York: HarperPerennial, 1990), 49, 56. For discussions by journalists, see Peter Matthiessen, *In the Spirit of Crazy Horse* (New York: Viking, 1983; rev. ed. with epilogue, 1991) and Joe Starita, *The Dull Knifes of Pine Ridge: A Lakota Odyssey* (New York: Berkley Books, 1995).

26. Taylor interviewed by Cash, AIRP, 50:1–3.

27. Verna Larvie interviewed by Herbert Hoover, August 17, 1974. South Dakota Oral History Project, South Dakota Oral History Center, Institute of American Indian Studies, University of South Dakota, Vermillion, SD. American Indian Research Program [hereafter SDOHP], 1172:1–4; Elaine Quiver interviewed by author, August 27, 2004; Virgnia Irene (Kain) Lautenschlager, *A History of Cuny Table, South Dakota 1890–2002*, edited by Katherine Bahr (Chadron, NE: Chadron State College, n.d.), 10–14, 19–23, 25–31.

28. Sarah Trechter, "White between the Lines: Ethnic Positioning in Lakhota Discourse," *Journal of Linguistic Anthropology* 11, no. 1 (2001): 24; Thomas E. Mails, *Frank Fools Crow* (Garden City, NY: Doubleday, 1973; reprint ed., Lincoln: University of Nebraska Press, 1979), 46; Robertson, 63; Wagoner, 63.

29. Wagoner, 44–45; Robertson, 63–64.

30. Thomas Conroy interviewed by Joseph H. Cash, Summer 1967. AIRP, 63:2–3; Jake Herman interviewed by Joseph H. Cash, Summer 1967. AIRP, 38:9–10; Agnes Gildersleeve interviewed by John S. Painter, July 21, 1981. AIRP, 1861:36; Reifel interviewed by Cash in Iverson, ed., 110; Powers, 144; Biolsi, 80–81; Robertson, 172–73; Edward Lazarus, *Black Hills White Justice: The Sioux Nation Versus the United States, 1775 to the Present* (New York: HaperCollins Publishers, 1991), 162–63.

31. Agnes Gildersleeve interviewed by Painter, AIRP, 1961:2, 18; Biolsi, 1, 68–73.

32. Agnes Gildersleeve interviewed by Painter, AIRP 1961:16–19; Eagle Hawk to Roe Cloud, quoted by Reifel in Kenneth R. Philp, ed., *Indian Self-Rule: First-Hand Accounts of Indian-White Relations from Roosevelt to Reagan* (Salt Lake City: Howe Brothers, 1986), 55–56.

33. Reifel interviewed by Cash in Iverson, ed., 110; Benjamin Reifel in Philp, ed., 54–57, 81; Benjamin Reifel interviewed by John Painter, October 8, 1980. AIRP, 1854:32–33; Biolsi, 1, 68–73; Collier to Reifel quoted by Reifel in Philp, ed., 57.

34. Herman interviewed by Cash, AIRP, 38:9–10; Thomas Conroy interviewed by Joseph H. Cash, Summer 1967. AIRP, 63:1, 4; Agnes Gildersleeve interviewed

by Painter, AIRP, 1961:27–29; Mildred Young interviewed by Joseph H. Cash, Summer 1967. AIRP, 64:1; Reifel in Philp, ed., 57; Biolsi, 68–73.

35. Biolsi, 78; Lazarus, 163.

36. Mike Her Many Horses interviewed by Joseph H. Cash, July 18, 1973. AIRP, 915, side 2 (no transcript); Biolsi, 82; Matthiessen, 27; Powers, 141; Robertson, 172.

37. Mails, 85, 105–7. Fools Crow quoted in Mails, 146.

38. Roger Bromert, "The Sioux and the Indian New Deal, 1933–1944." Ph.D. dissertation, University of Toledo, 1980, 174, 183.

39. Biolsi, 82; Matthiessen, 27.

40. Oglala Council, "Constitution and By-Laws", April 26, 1921, Box 13, Unmarked Folder, Records of the Oglala Sioux Tribe, Oglala Lakota College, Kyle, Pine Ridge Reservation [hereafter OLC]; Benjamin Reifel interviewed by John Painter, May 29, 1979, AIRP, 1795:5–6, 13; Agnes Gildersleeve interviewed by Painter, AIRP, 1861:19–20; Reifel interviewed by Cash in Iverson, ed., 111; Biolsi, 52–59; Robertson, 167–72.

41. Collier, 257.

42. Biolsi, 92–98.

43. Akim D. Reinhardt, "A Crude Replacement: The Indian New Deal, Indirect Colonialism, and Pine Ridge Reservation," *Journal of Colonialism and Colonial History* 6, no. 1 (spring 2005): 39–42.

44. Biolsi, 92–98; Reifel interviewed by Cash in Iverson, ed., 109–10; Taylor interviewed by Cash, AIRP, 50:4; Oglala Sioux Tribe, "Certification of Adoption" in "Constitution and By-Laws of the Oglala Sioux Tribe of the Pine Ridge Reservation of South Dakota," December 11, 1935.

45. Biolsi, 98; Benjamin Reifel interviewed by Thomas Biolsi, August 1984. AIRP, 1882:8.

46. "Pine Ridge" is still the name of the reservation. The "Oglala Sioux Tribe" was the name given to the new political entity, and the "Oglala Sioux Tribal Council" its governing body. For some readers it is perhaps best understood as the difference between "America" (a place), the "United States" (a sovereign state), and "Congress" (a governing body).

47. Oglala Sioux Tribe, "Constitution and By-Laws of the Oglala Sioux Tribe of the Pine Ridge Reservation of South Dakota," December 11, 1935; Biolsi, 98–108.

48. "Minutes of the Meeting of the Oglala Tribal Council January 9–10, 1936," Box 23, Folder 6, OLC.

49. Ibid.

50. Ibid.

Chapter 3

1. Field Aide Francis F. Fielder to Mr. Joseph Short Bear, December 30, 1940, Box 141, File 003.2 Indians of Porcupine and Red Shirt Table District. Main Decimal File 1900–65, General Correspondence, General Records Pine Ridge Agency, Pine Ridge, South Dakota, Records of the Bureau of Indian Affairs, Record Group 75, National Archives and Records Administration–Kansas City, MO [Hereafter NARA-MDF]; Agricultural Extension Agent Rex D. Kildow to Fielder, April 7, 1941, Box 141, File 003.2 Indians of Porcupine and Red Shirt Table District, NARA-MDF.

2. Fielder to Short Bear, December 30, 1940; Kildow to Fielder, April 7, 1941.

3. Kildow to Fielder, July 22, 1941, Box 141, File 003.2 Indians of Porcupine and Red Shirt Table District, NARA-MDF; Fielder to Superintendent W. O. Roberts, August 20, 1941, Box 141, File 003.2 Indians of Porcupine and Red Shirt Table District, NARA-MDF.

4. Fielder to Roberts, August 20, 1941, Box 141, File 003.2 Indians of Porcupine and Red Shirt Table District, NARA-MDF; Kildow to Fielder October8, 1941, Box 141, File 003.2 Indians of Porcupine and Red Shirt Table District, NARA-MDF.

5. Lawrence C. Kelly, "The Indian Reorganization Act: The Dream and the Reality," *Pacific Historical Quarterly* 44 (August 1975): 311; Henry F. Dobyns, "The Indian Reorganization Act and Federal Withdrawal," *Applied Anthropology* (spring 1948): 35–44; Vine Deloria, Jr., *Custer Died For Your Sins: An Indian Manifesto* (New York: Macmillan, 1969), 205–7; Taiaiake Alfred, *Peace, Power, Righteousness: An Indigenous Manifesto* (Don Mills, Ontario: Oxford University Press, 1999), 3.

6. Robert K. Thomas, "Powerless Politics" (Washington, DC: Department of Interior, 1966); reprint, *New University Thought*. University of Chicago (winter 1966-67), 3; Karl H. Schlesier, "Reply to Deloria, DeMallie, Hill, and Washburn," *American Anthropologist* 81 (June 1979): 561–63.

7. Thomas Biolsi, *Organizing the Lakota: The Political Economy of the New Deal on the Pine Ridge and Rosebud Reservations*. (Tucson: University of Arizona Press, 1992), 184–85; Paul M. Robertson, "The Power of the Land: Identity, Ethnicity, and Class Among the Oglala Lakota." Ph.D. dissertation, Union Institute, 1995, 258. Note: Robertson's initial statement against Biolsi came in the dissertation, which was later revised into book form, Paul M. Robertson, *The Power of the Land: Identity, Ethnicity, and Class Among the Oglala Lakota* (New York: Routledge, 2002). Aside from this note, all other citations of Robertson refer to the book of 2002, not the dissertation.

8. Fielder to Kildow, December 17, 1940, Box 141, File 003.2 Indians of Porcupine and Red Shirt Table, NARA-MDF.

9. Kildow to Fielder, January 22, 1941, Box 141, File 003.2 Indians of Porcupine and Red Shirt Table, NARA-MDF; Mrs. Charlotte Huebner to Roberts, December 4, 1940, Box 142, File 003.2 Indians of Wakpamni District 1938–1941, NARA-MDF; Roberts to Huebner, December 6, 1940, Box 142, File 003.2 Indians of Wakpamni District 1938–1941, NARA-MDF.

10. U.S. Department of the Interior, *Statistical Supplement to the Annual Report of the Commissioner of Indian Affairs* (Washington, DC: Government Printing Office, 1939), 76.

11. Ibid, 22, 25.

12. Details of this development are covered in the chapter entitled "The New Deal and Artificial Economies: Reinforced Dependence," in Biolsi, 109–25.

13. U.S. Dept. of Interior, *Statistical Supplement,* 25, 76, 88–90.

14. For an overview of this program, see the chapter entitled "Whither the American Indian?" in Richard Lowitt, *The New Deal and the West* (Norman: University of Oklahoma Press, 1984. 1993), 122–37.

15. "Resident Pine Ridge Indian Income for Calendar Year of 1938," Box 173, File 052 General Statistical Records and Reports (1 of 2). Ordinances, 1936–1939 and Administrative Records, General Records of the Oglala Sioux Tribal Government, General Records Pine Ridge Agency, Pine Ridge, South Dakota, Records of the Bureau of Indian Affairs, Record Group 75, National Archives and Records Administration–Kansas City, MO [hereafter NARA-AR]; U.S. Dept. of Interior, *Statistical Supplement,* 28, 66, 76.

16. Hudson Bird Head to Roberts, December 2, 1939, Box 141, File 003.2 Indians of Allen District, NARA-MDF; Agricultural Extension Agent R.F. Coulter to Bird Head, December 29, 1939, Box 141, File 003.2 Indians of Allen District, NARA-MDF

17. Agnes Gildersleeve interviewed by John S. Painter, July 21, 1981. South Dakota Oral History Center, Institute of American Indian Studies, University of South Dakota, Vermillion, SD. American Indian Research Program [hereafter, AIRP], 1861:48; Biolsi, 15–17, 191n31.

18. Benjamin Reifel interviewed by Thomas Biolsi, August 1982. AIRP, 1882:55–6; Agnes Gildersleeve interviewed by Painter. AIRP, 1861:12–13, 22–4.

19. Memorandum, Kildow to I.I.M. Office, June 16, 1942, Box 143, File 003.7 Memoranda, NARA-MDF; United States Department of Interior. Office of Indian Affairs. "Individual Indian Money Purchase Order, Margaret Blue Bird Conroy," July 19, 1941, Box 141, File 003.2 Indians of Manderson District, NARA-MDF.

20. Jerome Brown Bull to Whom It May Concern, May 15, 1943, Box 141, File

003.2 Indians of Kyle District, NARA-MDF; Biolsi, 15–16. Though not dealing with Lakota land sales, a thorough accounting of the ridiculously undervalued payments northern Plains Indians received during the late nineteenth century can be found in David Wishart, *An Unspeakable Sadness: The Dispossession of the Nebraska Indians* (Lincoln: University of Nebraska Press, 1994).

21. Memorandum, Kildow to Charles D. Parkhurst, Law and Order, September 22, 1942, Box 143, File 003.7 Memoranda, NARA-MDF; Memorandum, Kildow to IIM, Forestry, and Land Divisions, May 27, 1942, Box 143, File 003.7 Memoranda, NARA-MDF.

22. Field Aide Peter Cummings to Samuel, Nellie, and Elaine Kills In Water, no date, Box 141, File 003.2 Indians of Manderson District, NARA-MDF.

23. Roberts to Fielder, March 30, 1942, Box 143, File 003.5 Extension Staff, NARA-MDF.

24. Ward Churchill and Jim Vander Wall, *Agents of Repression: The FBI's Secret War Against the Black Panther Party and the American Indian Movement* (Boston: South End Press, 1990), 114–18; Robertson, 123–55.

25. Vine Deloria, Jr., and Clifford Lytle, *The Nations Within: The Past and Future of American Indian Sovereignty* (New York: Pantheon Books, 1984), 10; Donald J. Berthrong, "Legacies of the Dawes Act," *Arizona and the West* 21 (winter 1979): 354.

26. "Treaty With the Sioux-Brule, Oglala, Miniconjou, Yanktonai, Hunkpapa, Blackfeet, Cuthead, Two Kettle, Sans Arcs, and Santee and Arapaho, 1868," in Charles J. Kappler, ed., *Indian Treaties 1778–1883*. 3rd ed. (Washington, DC: Government Printing Office, 1904; reprint ed., New York: Interland Publishing, 1972), 998–1007; Edward Lazarus, *Black Hills/White Justice: The Sioux Nation Versus the United States, 1775–Present* (New York: HarperCollins Publishers, 1991), xx–xxiv, 48–53, 105–114, 381–402, 451–57.

27. U.S. Dept. of Interior, *Statistical Supplement,* 31.

28. Ibid, 33, 86. For a chronology and analysis of the IRA's somewhat tortured Congressional journey and numerous revisions from draft to bill, see Kelly, 291–312 and Graham D. Taylor, "The Tribal Alternative to Bureaucracy: The Indian's New Deal: 1933–1945," *Journal of the West* 12 (January 1974): 128–42.

29. U.S. Dept. of Interior, *Statistical Supplement,* 33, 42; Robertson, 123–55.

30. U.S. Dept. of Interior, *Statistical Supplement,* 33, 42; Robertson, 123–55.

31. U.S. Dept of Interior, *Statistical Supplement,* 25, 65, 76.

32. Memorandum, Range Supervisor George V. Hedden to All Division Heads, February 26, 1940, Box 143, File 003.7 Memoranda, NARA-MDF.

33. Roberts to Fielder, August 20, 1941, Box 141, File 003.2 Indians of Porcupine and Red Shirt Table District, NARA-MDF.

34. Roberts to Farm Agent Max C. Jensen, May 13, 1941, Box 141, File 003.2 Indians of Kyle District, NARA-MDF.

35. Roberts to United Sates Senator Harlan J. Bushfield, November 5, 1945, Box 141, File 003.2 Indians of Porcupine District, NARA-MDF.

36. Roberts to Agricultural Extension Agent R.B. McKee, March 19, 1945, Box 141, File 003.2 Indians of Manderson District, NARA-MDF.

37. Mark R. Ellis, "Reservation *Akicitas:* The Pine Ridge Indian Police, 1879–1885" *South Dakota History* 29 (Fall 1999): 190–210; Sidney L. Harring, *Crow Dog's Case: American Indian Sovereignty, Tribal Law, and United States Law in the Nineteenth Century* (New York: Cambridge University Press, 1994), 176, 185–92; John R. Wunder, *"Retained by The People": A History of American Indians and the Bill of Rights* (New York: Oxford University Press, 1994), 65.

38. Harring, 134–41; Wunder, 36–7.

39. Wunder, 65–6.

40. Ibid; Harring, 108–41,190–91.

41. Fielder to Kildow, December 30, 1940, Box 141, File 003.2 Indians of Porcupine and Red Shirt Table District, NARA-MDF; Harring, 108–10.

42. Kildow to Fielder, January 22, 1941, Box 141, File 003.2 Indians of Porcupine and Red Shirt Table District, NARA-MDF.

43. Wunder, 132, 139.

44. The eleven crimes reported are: arson, assault, adultery/incest/rape (counted as one), desertion and non-support, drunk and disorderly, liquor law violation, larceny/burglary/forgery/embezzlement (counted as one), murder/manslaughter (counted as one), perjury, narcotics (including marijuana), and miscellaneous.

45. U.S. Dept. of the Interior, *Statistical Supplement,* 83.

46. Ibid, 84.

47. Coulter to Clerk of Court Alex Winters, July 27, 1939, Box 142, File 003.2 Indians of Wakpamni District 1938–1941.

48. Clyde Ellis, *To Change Them Forever: Indian Education at the Rainy Mountain Boarding School, 1893–1920* (Norman: University of Oklahoma Press, 1996), xi–xii; K. Tsianina Lomawaima, *They Called It Prairie Light: The Story of Chilocco Indian School* (Lincoln: University of Nebraska Press, 1994), xi–xv, 1–8.

49. Clyde Ellis, 1–27; Lomawaima, 1–8.

50. U.S. Dept. of the Interior, *Statistical Supplement,* 22–25; Wunder, 65.

51. U.S. Dept. of the Interior, *Statistical Supplement,* 20, 22, 25.

52. "Statistical Report of the Superintendent of Indian Education," 11, in Superintendent of Indian Education George C. Wells to Roberts, October 12, 1942, Box 172, File 052.5 Day School Inspectors, NARA-AR.

53. Ibid, 5, 12, 14.

54. Pete Catches interviewed by Ed McGaa, Summer 1969. AIRP, 459:1, 9–11.

55. Mildred McGaa Stinson interviewed by Edward McGaa, August 23–24, 1968. AIRP, 523:3–5, 9; Marion Bilbroth Dreamer interviewed by John Watterson, July 19, 1973. AIRP, 163 (no transcript).

56. Mildred McGaa Stinson interviewed by Edward McGaa, AIRP, 523:6–7.

57. U.S. Dept. of Interior, *Statistical Supplement*, 20; Leonard Crow Dog with Richard Erdoes, *Crow Dog: Four Generations of Sioux Medicine Men* (New York: HarperPerennial, 1995), 71–81; Joe Starita, *The Dull Knifes of Pine Ridge: A Lakota Odyssey* (New York: Berkley, 1995), 254–60.

58. Wunder, 64–5.

59. Biolsi, xx–xxi, 175–78, 182–86.

60. Ibid, 83.

61. Ibid, 82–3.

62. Roberts to Mrs. Lucille LeClair, April 22, 1941, File 003.2 Indians of Porcupine District, NARA-MDF; Farm Aide Henry Cottier to Fielder, January 31, 1940, File 003.2 Indians of Porcupine and Red Shirt Table District, NARA-MDF.

63. Benjamin Reifel interviewed by Joseph H. Cash, summer 1967, in *The Plains Indians in the Twentieth Century*, ed. Peter Iverson (Norman: University of Oklahoma Press, 1985), 113.

64. Jensen to Social Worker Lucille Hamner, August 29, 1940, Box 141, File 003.2 Indians of Kyle District 1938–1944, NARA-MDF.

65. Fielder to Coulter, October 2, 1939, Box 141, File 003.2 Indians of Porcupine and Red Shirt Table District, NARA-MDF; Coulter to Educational Field Agent L.M. Keller, October 16, 1939, Box 141, File 003.2 Indians of Porcupine and Red Shirt Table District, NARA-MDF.

66. Teacher John C. Powless to Roberts, January 18, 1940, Box 141, File 003.2 Indians of Allen District, NARA-MDF.

67. Roberts to Jensen, August 10, 1940, Box 141, File 003.2 Indians of Kyle District, NARA-MDF; Jensen to Roberts, August 14, 1940, Box 141, File 003.2 Indians of Kyle District, NARA-MDF.

68. Private Joseph Hernandez to Farm Agent Willis J. Adams, June 21, 1944, Box 141, File 003.2 Kyle District, NARA-MDF; McKee to Adams, July 19, 1944, Box 141, File 003.2 Kyle District, NARA-MDF.

69. Midwest Collection Service to McKee, January 5, 1946, Box 141, File 003.2 Indians of Porcupine District, NARA-MDF; Midwest to McKee, January 22, 1946, Box 141, File 003.2 Indians of Porcupine District, NARA-MDF; Assistant Extension Agent Irvin E. Freiberg to Mrs. Oscar L. Jetley, August 7, 1942, Box 141, File 003.2 Indians of Wakpamni District, NARA-MDF.

70. Roberts to Fielder, March 19, 1943, Box 141, File 003.2 Indians of Porcupine District, NARA-MDF; Acting Agricultural Extension Agent J. J. Guyer to Principal J. W. Irving, January 20, 1943, Box 141, File 003.2 Indians of Porcupine and Red Shirt Table District, NARA-MDF.

71. Kildow to Field Aide Irvin E. Freiberg, April 11, 1944, Box 141, File 003.2 Indians of Oglala District, NARA-MDF; McKee to Roberts, Memorandum, July 17, 1944, Box 142, File 003.3 Superintendent, NARA-MDF.

72. Home Extension Agent Mamie Searles to Mr. John C. Powless, August 5, 1940, Box 141, File 003.2 Indians of Allen District, NARA-MDF.

73. Roberts to Joseph Rooks, May 31, 1939, Box 141, File 003.2 Indians of Kyle District, NARA-MDF; U.S. Representative Francis Case to Roberts, June 26, 1939 Box 141, File 003.2 Indians of Kyle District, NARA-MDF; Roberts to Case, July 11, 1939, Box 141, File 003.2 Indians of Kyle District, NARA-MDF.

74. Rooks to Kildow, January 22, 1940, Box 141, File 003.2 Indians of Kyle District, NARA-MDF; Jensen to Kildow, July 29, 1940, Box 141, File 003.2 Indians of Kyle District, NARA-MDF; Kildow to Jensen, August 2, 1940, Box 141, File 003.2 Indians of Kyle District, NARA-MDF; anonymous memo, U.S. Department of the Interior, Office of Indian Affairs, no date, Box 141, File 003.2 Indians of Kyle District, NARA-MDF.

75. Case to Roberts, December 13, 1940, Box 141, File 003.2 Indians of Porcupine and Red Shirt Table District, NARA-MDF; Roberts to Paul War Bonnet, January 22, 1941, Box 141, File 003.2 Indians of Porcupine and Red Shirt Table District, NARA-MDF; Frank A. Ecoffey to U.S. Senator Chan Gurney, May 24, 1942, Box 141, File 003.2 Indians of Wakpamni District, NARA-MDF; Assistant Commissioner of Indian Affairs Walter V. (illegible) to Senator Chan Gurney, June 6, 1942, Box 141, File 003.2 Indians of Wakpamni District, NARA-MDF.

76. John Collier quoted by Frank Fools Crow in Thomas E. Mails, *Fools Crow* (Garden City, NY: Doubleday, 1979; reprint ed., Lincoln: University of Nebraska Press, 1990), 147.

77. Roger Bromert, "The Sioux and the Indian New Deal, 1933–1944" (Ph.D. dissertation, University of Toledo, 1980), 174–75.

78. Noah Tall to Roberts, June 3, 1944, Box 141, File 003.2 Indians of Manderson District, NARA-MDF; Roberts to Tall, July 11, 1944, Box 141. File 003.2 Indians of Manderson District, NARA-MDF.

Chapter 4

1. Agnes Gildersleeve interviewed by John S. Painter, July 21, 1981. South Dakota Oral History Center, Institute of American Indian Studies, University of South Dakota, Vermillion, SD. American Indian Research Program [hereafter,

AIRP], 1961:9–10; Graham D. Taylor, *The New Deal and American Indian Tribalism: The Administration of the Indian Reorganization Act 1934–1945* (Lincoln: University of Nebraska Press, 1980), 90, 115.

2. Agnes Gildersleeve interviewed by Painter, AIRP, 1961:9–11, 14, 19–20; Benjamin Reifel interviewed by Thomas Biolsi, August 1984. AIRP, 1882:10, 14.

3. Agnes Gildersleeve interviewed by Painter, AIRP, 1961:9–11, 14, 19–20; Benjamin Reifel interviewed by Thomas Biolsi, August, 1984. AIRP, 1882:10, 14.

4. Agnes Gildersleeve interviewed by Painter, AIRP, 1961:9–11, 14, 19–20; Benjamin Reifel interviewed by Thomas Biolsi, June 1984. AIRP, 1882:10, 14.

5. Leonard Crow Dog with Richard Erdoes, *Crow Dog: Four Generations of Sioux Medicine Men* (New York: HerperPerennial, 1995), 8–10; James R. Walker, *Lakota Society*, Raymond J. DeMallie, ed. (Lincoln: University of Nebraska Press, 1982), 3–4.

6. John Collier, *From Every Zenith: A Memoir and Some Essays on Life and Thought* (Denver: Sage Books, 1963), 203, 216–26; John Collier, "Introduction" in Laura Thompson, *Personality and Government: Findings and Recommendations of the Indian Administration Research* (Mexico City: Ediciones de Insituto Indignenista InterAmericano, 1951), x–xi; Agnes Gildersleeve interviewed by Painter, AIRP, 1961:33–34.

7. Collier, *From Every Zenith*, 185–92.

8. Commissioner of Indian Affairs John Collier to Mr. James M. Stewart, c/o Mr. A. L. Hook, Land Field Agent, September 9, 1941, Box 143, File 003.7 Memoranda. Main Decimal File 1900–65, General Correspondence, General Records Pine Ridge Agency, Pine Ridge, South Dakota, Records of the Bureau of Indian Affairs, Record Group 75, National Archives and Records Administration-Kansas City, MO [hereafter NARA-MDF].

9. Superintendent W. O. Roberts, "For Indians at Work as the Editor sees fit," 1–2, no date, Box 149, File 011 Indian Office Publications, NARA-MDF.

10. Thompson, 88–9.

11. Benjamin Reifel interviewed by John Painter, October 8, 1980. AIRP, 1854:4; Reifel interviewed by Biolsi, August, 1984. AIRP, 1882:11; Roberts, 2–4; Graham D. Taylor, 90, 115; Thompson, 88–90.

12. Reifel interviewed by Painter, October 10, 1980, AIRP, 1854:38–9; Roberts, 2–4; Graham D. Taylor, 90, 115; Thompson, 88–90.

13. Graham D. Taylor, 135; Thompson, 88–91.

14. Roberts, 2–4.

15. Thomas Biolsi, *Organizing the Lakota: The Political Economy of the New Deal on the Pine Ridge and Rosebud Reservations* (Tucson: University of Arizona Press, 1992), 124; Thompson, 90.

16. Reifel interviewed by Painter, October 8, 1980. AIRP, 1854:38–47.

17. Graham D. Taylor, 115.

18. Biolsi, 146–47.

19. Reifel interviewed by Biolsi, August, 1984. AIRP, 1882:11, 15, 42–3; Reifel interviewed by Biolsi, August, 1984. AIRP, 1883:34; Benjamin Reifel interviewed by John Painter, May 29, 1979. AIRP, 1795:38–9.

20. Oglala Sioux Tribal Council, Ordinance no. 4, February 20, 1937, File 11 Ordinances 1936–1939, Records of the Oglala Sioux Tribal Government. Administrative Records and Ordinances, 1936–1939, General Records of the Oglala Sioux Tribal Government, General Records Pine Ridge Agency, Pine Ridge, South Dakota, Records of the Bureau of Indian Affairs, Record Group 75, National Archives and Records Administration–Kansas City, MO [hereafter NARA-AR].

21. Ibid.

22. Oglala Sioux Tribal Council, Resolutions no. 7, November 16, 1937; no. 16, January 15, 1938; no. 17, no date; no. 25, June 20, 1938; no. 27, June 21, 1938. File 11 Ordinances 1936–1939, Records of the Oglala Sioux Tribal Government, NARA-AR.

23. Thomas Conroy interviewed by Joseph H. Cash, Summer 1967. AIRP, 63:5–6; Johnson Holy Rock interviewed by Joseph H. Cash, Summer 1967. AIRP, 37:1; Reifel interviewed by Biolsi, August, 1984. AIRP, 1883:94.

24. Oglala Sioux Tribal Council, Resolution no. 1, May 1, 1936, File 11 Ordinances 1936–1939, Records of the Oglala Sioux Tribal Government, NARA-AR; Reifel interviewed by Painter, May 29, 1979. AIRP 1795:28.

25. Oglala Sioux Tribal Council, Ordinance no. 10, no date; no. 13, January 10, 1936; no. 14, January 11, 1938; no. 15, January 12, 1938; no. 19, no date; no. 20, 23–24, June 30, 1938; nos. 33, 36–37, July 14, 1938. File 11 Ordinances 1936–1939, Records of the Oglala Sioux Tribal Government, NARA-AR.

26. Oglala Sioux Tribal Council, Resolution no. 6, October 15, 1937; no. 15A, January 13, 1938. File 11 Ordinances 1936–1939, Records of the Oglala Sioux Tribal Government, NARA-AR; Oglala Sioux Tribal Council, Resolution no. 43, October 29, 1942, Box 13, Folder 5, Records of the Oglala Sioux Tribe, Oglala Lakota College, Kyle, Pine Ridge Reservation [hereafter OLC].

27. Oglala Sioux Tribal Council, Resolution no. 148, January 15, 1943; no. 149, February 17, 1943; no. 150, January 15, 1943, Box 16, Folder 2, OLC; Superintendent W. O. Roberts to Commissioner of Indian Affairs John Collier, March 6, 1943, Box 16, Folder 2, OLC.

28. Benjamin Reifel interviewed by Joseph H. Cash, Summer 1967 in *The Plains Indians in the Twentieth Century,* ed. Peter Iverson (Norman: University of Oklahoma Press, 1985), 110–111; Biolsi, 153–55, 162.

29. Reifel interviewed by Cash in Iverson, ed., 110–111; Edward Lazarus, *Black Hills/White Justice: The Sioux Nation Versus the United States, 1775 to the Present* (New York: HaperCollins Publishers, 1991), 162–63; Thompson, 90.

30. L. E. Clements, "Possibilities of Rehabilitating the Oglala Sioux (M.A. thesis, Colorado State College of Education, 1938), 16–17, 37, 48; Joe Starita, *The Dull Knifes of Pine Ridge: A Lakota Odyssey* (New York: Berkley, 1995), 247.

31. Reifel interviewed by Painter, October 10, 1980. AIRP, 1854:1–4, 12–16, 44; Reifel interviewed by Biolsi, August, 1984. AIRP, 1882:27; Reifel interviewed by Cash in Iverson, ed., 111–12; Paul M. Robertson, *The Power of the Land: Identity, Ethnicity, and Class among the Oglala Lakota* (New York: Routledge, 2002), 205–6; Graham D. Taylor, 89–90; Thompson, 175–76.

32. The districts with towns of OIA office sites parenthesized: Eagle Nest (Wanblee), Medicine Root (Kyle), White Clay (Oglala), Wounded Knee (Manderson), Pass Creek (Allen), Porcupine (Porcupine), Wakpamni (Pine Ridge).

33. Reifel interviewed by Cash in Iverson, ed., 111–112; Graham D. Taylor, 89–90; Thompson, 73–75; Robertson, 176.

34. Reifel interviewed by Painter, October 8, 1980, AIRP, 1854:22–23; Reifel interviewed by Biolsi, August, 1984. AIRP, 1883:51; Robertson, 65, 111–12.

35. Reifel interviewed by Biolsi, August, 1984. AIRP, 1882:83, 86; Reifel interviewed by Biolsi, August, 1984. AIRP, 1883:50; Biolsi 155–56, 159–60; Robertson, 173–74.

36. Oglala Sioux Tribal Council, Resolution no. 5, February 19, 1937, Box 13, Folder 3, OLC; Robertson, 202.

37. Oglala Sioux Tribal Council, Resolution no. 140, October 28, 1942, Box 16, Folder 1, OLC; Oglala Sioux Tribal Council, Resolution no. 170, July 15, 1943, Box 16, Folder 2, OLC; Oglala Sioux Tribal Council, Resolution no. 269, July 15, 1943, Box 16, Folder 3, OLC; Oglala Sioux Tribal Council, "Resolution of the Oglala Sioux Tribal Council Regarding the termination of the Tribal Buffalo Reserve and Proposing That the Area Be Utilized as a Part of the Livestock Breeding Program," July 12, 1944, Box 23, File 11, OLC; Walker, 28, 35, 52, 63, 97, 103–6.

38. Oglala Sioux Tribal Council, Ordinance no. 34, July 14, 1938; Resolution no. 26, June 21, 1938. File 11 Ordinances 1936–1939, Records of the Oglala Sioux Tribal Government, NARA-AR; Robertson, 175–76, 189.

39. Frank G. Wilson quoted in Robertson, 174.

40. Amos Red Owl to Commissioner of Indian Affair John Collier, May 11, 1938, quoted in Graham D. Taylor, 28.

41. Robertson, 189–90.

42. Ibid, 204.

43. Ibid, 136–84, 199; Graham D. Taylor, 115–16.44. Reifel interviewed by Biolsi, August, 1984. AIRP, 1883:53; Robertson, 187–89.

45. Reifel interviewed by Biolsi, August, 1984. AIRP, 1882:42–3.

46. Reifel interviewed by Painter, May 29, 1979. AIRP, 1795:22, 24–5; Reifel interviewed by Biolsi, August, 1984. AIRP, 1883:16, 18; Floyd Taylor interviewed by Joseph H. Cash, August 9, 1968. AIRP, 50:4.

47. Reifel interviewed by Painter, May 29, 1979. AIRP, 1795:22, 24–5; Reifel interviewed by Biolsi, August, 1984. AIRP, 1883:16, 18.

48. Thomas Conroy interviewed by Joseph H. Cash, Summer, 1967. AIRP, 63:1–2; Reifel interviewed by Painter, May 29, 1979. AIRP, 1795:22, 24–5; Reifel interviewed by Biolsi, August, 1984. AIRP, Tape 1883:16, 18; Floyd Taylor interviewed by Cash, August 9, 1968. AIRP, 50:4.

49. Biolsi, 159.

50. Ibid, 155–59; Reifel interviewed by Biolsi, August, 1984. AIRP, 1882:48–50; Roger Bromert, "The Sioux and the Indian New Deal, 1933–1944." Ph.D. dissertation, University of Toledo, 1980, 182–83.

51. Biolsi, 148–49.

52. Oglala Sioux Tribal Council, Resolution no. 34, February 18, 1942; Resolution no. 42, April 17, 1942, Box 13, Folder 5, OLC; Biolsi, 137–39.

53. Assistant Commissioner of Indian Affairs William Zimmerman, Jr., to Chairman Henry Jumping Eagle, August 5, 1942, Box 13, Folder 5, OLC.

54. Oglala Sioux Tribal Council, Ordinance no. 165, July 14, 1943, Box 16 Folder no. 2, OLC; Reifel interviewed by Painter, October 8, 1980. AIRP 1854, p. 27; Biolsi, 137–39.

55. Oglala Sioux Tribal Council, Resolution no. 234, January 12, 1945, Box 16, Folder no. 3, OLC; Biolsi, 146–47.

56. Oglala Sioux Tribal Council, Resolution no. 256, April 10–13, 1945, Box 16, Folder 3, OLC.

57. Oglala Sioux Tribal Council, Resolution no. 259, April 10–13, 1945, Box 16, Folder 3, OLC.

58. Oglala Sioux Tribal Council Secretary Matthew High Pine to CIA William H. Brophy, April 30, 1945, Box 16, Folder 4, OLC.

59. Reifel interviewed by Painter, May 29, 1979. AIRP, 1795:37; Graham D. Taylor, 115; Biolsi, 147.

60. Oglala Sioux Tribal Council, Resolution no. 317, February 20, 1946, Box 16, Folder 4, OLC; Biolsi, 146–47, Robertson, 187–90.

61. Oglala Sioux Tribal Council, Resolution no. 317, February 20, 1946, Box 16, Folder 4, OLC; *War Cry,* February 9, 1968 and June 28, 1968; Mary Crow Dog with Richard Erdoes, *Lakota Woman* (New York: HarperPerennial, 1991), 42–54;

Walter Karp, "I Remember Wounded Knee Between the Wars," *American Heritage* 25 (October 1973): 34–35.

62. Biolsi, 125.

63. Oglala Sioux Tribal Council Secretary Matthew High Pine to CIA William H. Brophy, April 30, 1945, Box 16, Folder 4, OLC; Biolsi, 57, 162–71; Robertson, 190.

64. Biolsi, 154; Robertson, 172–92.

65. Reifel interviewed by Biolsi, August 1984. AIRP, 1882:46–7.

66. Starita, 243–46, 296.

67. Sidney L. Harring, *Crow Dog's Case: American Indian Sovereignty, Tribal Law, and United States Law in the Nineteenth Century* (New York: Cambridge University Press, 1994), 147–48, 200; John R. Wunder, *"Retained by The People: A History of American Indians and the Bill of Rights* (New York: Oxford University Press, 1994), 39–41, 69–71.

68. Bromert, 174–75.

Chapter 5

1. For comprehensive analyses of termination, see Larry Burt, *Tribalism in Crisis: Federal Indian Policy, 1953–1961* (Albuquerque: University of New Mexico Press, 1982); "The Disastrous Policy of termination," in Vine Deloria, Jr., *Custer Died For Your Sins: An Indian Manifesto* (New York: Macmillan, 1969), 54–77; and Donald L. Fixico, *Termination and Relocation* (Albuquerque: University of New Mexico Press, 1986).

2. George McGovern, "Resolution for a New National Indian Policy," in *Red Power: The American Indians' Fight for Freedom*, ed. Alvin M. Josephy, (New York: McGraw-Hill, 1971), 60–63.

3. Ibid, 59, 63–65.

4. *War Cry* (Pine Ridge, South Dakota), March 1968; Robert M. Kvasnicka and Herman J. Viola, eds., *The Commissioners of Indian Affairs, 1824–1977* (Lincoln: University of Nebraska Press, 1979), 327; John R. Wunder, *"Retained by The People": A History of American Indians and the Bill of Rights* (New York: Oxford University Press, 1994), 159–60.

5. Phillip S. Deloria quoted in Kenneth R. Philp, ed., *Indian Self-Rule: First Hand Accounts of Indian-White Relations from Roosevelt to Reagan* (Salt Lake City: Howe Brothers, 1986), 193–94.

6. *War Cry* (Pine Ridge, South Dakota), November 28, 1968; Kvasnicka and Viola, eds., 334; Wunder, 160.

7. Phillip S. Deloria, "The Era of Indian Self-Determination: An Overview," in Philp, ed., 202; Kvasnicka and Viola, 334; Wunder, 160.

8. Kvasnicka and Viola, 335–36.

9. Ibid, 335–37.

10. Ibid, 336–37; Alexander McNabb in Philp, ed., 214.

11. Jake Herman interviewed by Joseph H. Cash, Summer 1967. South Dakota Oral History Center, Institute of American Indian Studies, University of South Dakota, Vermillion, SD. American Indian Research Program [hereafter AIRP], 38:4.

12. Many of Pine Ridge's roads are indescribably bad even today. It is difficult for this author to imagine them thirty-plus years ago. Describing the time period covered in the first part of this work, Vine Deloria, Jr., has said, "Dirt roads held the few mail routes together. One could easily get lost in the wild back country as roads turned into cowpaths without so much as a backward glance. Remote settlements such as Buzzard Basin and Cuny Table were nearly inaccessible. In the spring every bridge on the reservation would be washed out with the first rain and remain so until summer." Vine Deloria, Jr., "This Country Was A Lot Better Off When the Indians Were Running It," *New York Times Magazine,* March 8, 1970.

13. *War Cry* (Pine Ridge, South Dakota), August 1, 1968; Boise Cascade Center for Community Development, *Indian Economic Development, An Evaluation of EDA's Selected Indian Reservation Program: Individual Reservation Reports Prepared for the Economic Development Administration U. S. Department of Commerce* (Boise: Boise Cascade Center for Community Development, 1972), 2:211–15.

14. Hiram E. Olney to Wyman Babby, Director BIA Aberdeen Area, August 10, 1972, Box 21, Folder: Indian Law Enforcement Plans. Records of the Oglala Sioux Tribe, Oglala Lakota College Archives, Oglala Lakota College, Kyle, SD [hereafter OLC]; *The Oglala War Cry* (Pine Ridge, South Dakota), February 22, 1971, May 24, 1971.

15. *The Oglala War Cry* (Pine Ridge, South Dakota), February 22, 1971; Boise Cascade Center, 2:216.

16. Pine Ridge Realty Officer John F. Lewis interviewed by Joseph H. Cash, Summer 1967. AIRP, 62:10; Boise Cascade Center 2:211–13, 218–20.

17. Boise Cascade Center, 2:211–12, 218, 220–21.

18. Acting Superintendent Hiram E. Olney to Director of BIA Aberdeen Area, February 29, 1972. Folder Oglala Sioux Executive Letters, Box 2 Oglala Sioux Tribe 1970–1974 Projects, OLC; Boise Cascade Center, 2:215.

19. *War Cry* (Pine Ridge, South Dakota), August 1, 1968, September 26, 1968; *Oglala Lakota* (Pine Ridge, South Dakota), February 15, 1971; Lewis interviewed by Cash, Summer 1967. AIRP, 62:7–8; Kathleen Ann Pickering, *Lakota Culture, World Economy* (Lincoln: University of Nebraska Press, 2000), 3–5, 13.

20. *The War Cry* (Pine Ridge, South Dakota), September 26, 1968, October 24, 1968.

21. *The War Cry* (Pine Ridge, South Dakota), February 9, 1968.

22. Boise Cascade Center, 2:216.

23. Gerald One Feather interviewed by Joseph Cash, Summer 1967. AIRP, 36:1; Vine Deloria, Jr., *Behind the Trail of Broken Treaties* (New York: Delacorte Press, 1974), 70.

24. *War Cry* (Pine Ridge, South Dakota), September 6, 1968; *The Oglala War Cry* (Pine Ridge, South Dakota), September 21, 1970.

25. *The Oglala War Cry* (Pine Ridge, South Dakota), September 21, 1970.

26. Boise Cascade Center, 2:214–16.

27. *The Oglala War Cry* (Pine Ridge, South Dakota), September 7, 1970, September 21, 1970.

28. Gerald One Feather speaking at the 9th Annual Conference of the Institute of Indian Studies, June 1964. AIRP, 1275 (transcript pages not numbered); Gerald One Feather in Philp, ed., 255–57; *The Oglala Lakota* (Pine Ridge, South Dakota), August 28, 1970, February 15, 1971; Boise Cascade Center, 2:216.

29. Barbara Means-Adams interviewed by Akim D. Reinhardt, April 13, 1999, Kyle, South Dakota; Stanley David Lyman, *Wounded Knee 1973: A Personal Account* (Lincoln: University of Nebraska Press, 1991), 76; One Feather in Philp, 256–57.

30. *The Oglala Lakota* (Pine Ridge, South Dakota), February 15, 1971.

31. Ibid.

32. Mark Monroe, *An Indian in White America* (Philadelphia: Temple University Press, 1994), 17–25; Mary Crow Dog with Richard Erdoes, *Lakota Woman* (New York: HarperPerennial, 1991), 43–50, 60–61, 79–81; Russell Means with Marvin J. Wolf, *Where White Men Fear to Tread: The Autobiography of Russell Means* (New York: St. Martin's Press, 1995), 196–97, 239–42; "Conference Shines Light on Racism in Reservation Border Towns," Associated Press, April 6, 2006; Duane Martin, Sr., interviewed by Akim D. Reinhardt, July 6, 2004.

33. *The Gordon Journal*, February 23, 1972, March 1, 1972; Rolland Dewing, *Wounded Knee: The Meaning and Significance of the Second Incident* (New York: Irvington, 1985), 54–56.

34. *Oglala Nation News* (Pine Ridge, South Dakota), March 27, 1972; Leonard Crow Dog with Richard Erdoes, *Crow Dog: Four Generations of Sioux Medicine Men* (New York: HarperPerennial, 1996), 165.

35. *Oglala Nation News* (Pine Ridge, South Dakota), March 27, 1972.

36. Ibid; Akwesasne Notes, *Voices From Wounded Knee, 1973: In the Words of the Participants.* (Rooseveltown, NY: Akwesasne Notes, 1974), 13; Paul Chaat

Smith and Robert Allen Warrior, *Like A Hurricane: The Indian Movement from Alcatraz to Wounded Knee* (New York: New Press, 1996), 114.

37. Akwesasne Notes, 13; Dennis Banks with Richard Erdoes, *Ojibwa Warrior: Dennis Banks and the rise of the American Indian Movement* (Norman: University of Oklahoma Press, 2004), 115–16.

38. Akwesasne Notes, 13; Banks, 116–20; *The Gordon* (Nebraska) *Journal*, March 7, 1972; *Oglala Nation News* (Pine Ridge, South Dakota), March 27, 1972; *The Omaha World Herald*, February 27, 1972; Russell Means, 195; Dewing, 54–9.

39. *Oglala Nation News* (Pine Ridge, South Dakota), March 27, 1972.

40. Ibid.

41. Ibid.

42. Ibid; Lyman, xx–xi.

43. *Oglala Nation News* (Pine Ridge, South Dakota), February 27, 1972; Boise Cascade Center, 212.

44. Deloria, *Behind the Trail of Broken Treaties*, 70; Peter Matthiessen, *In the Spirit of Crazy Horse*, revised ed. (New York: Viking Press, 1991), 60–61.

45. Minutes of the Executive Committee Meetings, March 10, 1971, Box 21, Folder Executive Committee Meetings, OLC; Barbara Means-Adams interviewed by Reinhardt, April 13, 1999.

46. *War Cry* (Pine Ridge, South Dakota), September 6, 1968; Barbara Means-Adams interviewed by Reinhardt, April 13, 1999; Matthiessen, 60–1.

47. Means-Adams interviewed by Reinhardt, April 13, 1999; Matthiessen, 60–1.

48. Richard Wilson interviewed by Joseph Cash, July 17, 1973. AIRP, 918 (no transcript); Lyman, 69.

49. Mike Her Many Horses interviewed by Joseph H. Cash, July 18, 1973. AIRP, 915: side 2 (no transcript); Bessie Cornelius interviewed by Joseph H. Cash, July 17, 1973. AIRP, 917:22; *Oglala Nation News* (Pine Ridge, South Dakota), March 27, 1972; Thomas E. Mails, *Fools Crow* (Garden City, NY: Doubleday, 1979; revised ed., Lincoln: University of Nebraska Press, 1990), 199; Means-Adams interviewed by Reinhardt, April 13, 1999; Matthiessen, 60–1.

50. Russell Means, 196; Means-Adams interviewed by Reinhardt, April 13, 1999.

51. Akwesasne Notes, 14.

52. Wilson interviewed by Cash, July 17, 1973; Means-Adams interviewed by Reinhardt, April 13, 1999; Matthiessen, 60.

53. Bessie Cornelius interviewed by Cash, July 17, 1973. AIRP, 917:21–22; *Oglala Nation News* (Pine Ridge, South Dakota), March 27, 1972, April 17, 1972.

54. *Oglala Nation News* (Pine Ridge, South Dakota), April, 17, 1972.

55. Anonymous [name withheld by request] interviewed by Tom Short Bull, April 4, 1973. AIRP, 606 (no transcript) [copy of interview also in author's possession]; Deloria, *Behind the Trail of Broken Treaties,* 70; Matthiessen, 60–61; Means-Adams interviewed by Reinhardt, April 13, 1999.

56. Hobart Keith interviewed by Lewis Bad Wound, December, 1975. South Dakota Oral History Project, South Dakota Oral History Center, Institute of American Indian Studies, University of South Dakota, Vermillion, SD. American Indian Research Program [hereafter SDOHP], 1388 (no transcript); Minutes of the Oglala Sioux Tribal Council, April 11, 1972, Box 21, Folder Council Proceedings 1972, OLC.

57. Minutes of the Oglala Sioux Tribal Council, April 11, 1972, Box 21, Folder Council Proceedings 1972, OLC.

58. The prolonged efforts of full bloods and AIM supporters led to Pine Ridge getting its own radio station in 1983, KILI-FM ("Kili" is Lakota for "special"). Michael C. Keith, *Signals in the Air: Native Broadcasting in America* (Westport, CT: Praeger Publishers, 1995), 80–81.

59. *War Cry* (Pine Ridge, South Dakota), November 7, 1968.

60. Minutes of the Oglala Sioux Tribal Council, April 11, 1972, Box 21, Folder Council Proceedings 1972, OLC.

61. Minutes of the Oglala Sioux Tribal Council, July 18, 1972, Box 21, Folder Council Proceedings 1972, OLC; *Oglala Nation News* (Pine Ridge, South Dakota), August 3, 1972.

62. Minutes of the Oglala Sioux Tribal Council, July 25, 1972, Box 21, Folder Council Proceedings 1972, OLC.

63. Ibid; Oglala Sioux Tribal Council, Ordinance no. 072–04, August 17 1972, Box 12, Folder Council Proceedings 1972.

64. *Oglala Nation News* (Pine Ridge, South Dakota), August 3, 1972.

65. Oglala Sioux Tribal Council Executive Committee, Resolution no. 72–34XB, August 30, 1972, Box 21, Folder Executive Committee Resolutions 1972; Acting Superintendent Pine Ridge Reservation R.W. Penttila to BIA Director Aberdeen Area Wyman Babby, September 5, 1972, Box 21, Folder Executive Committee Resolutions 1972, OLC.

66. Ellen Moves Camp quoted in Akwesasne Notes, 14, 17.

67. Akwesasne Notes, 19.

Chapter 6

1. United States Department of Commerce, Bureau of the Census, *The Indian Population of the United States and Alaska, 1930* (Washington, DC: Government Printing Office, 1937), 8–9, 196–97; United States Department of Commerce,

Bureau of the Census, *Census of the Population, Subject Report: American Indians, 1970* (Washington, DC: Government Printing Office, 1973), 1, 138–40.

2. United States Congress, American Indian Policy Review Commission, Task Force Eight, *Report on Urban and Rural Non-Reservation Indians* (Washington, DC: Government Printing Office, 1976), 27–28; Elaine M. Neils, *Reservation to City* (Chicago: University of Chicago, Department of Geography, 1971), 46–47; Alison R. Bernstein, *American Indians and World War II* (Norman: University of Oklahoma Press, 1991), 40, 67–68; Alan L. Sorkin, *The Urban American Indian* (Lexington: D. C. Heath, 1978), 25.

3. LaVerne Madigan, *The American Indian Relocation Program* (New York: The Association of American Indian Affairs, Inc., 1956), 4–5; Larry W. Burt, "Roots of the Native American Urban Experience," *American Indian Quarterly* 10, no. 2 (1986): 88; U.S. Congress, *Report on Urban and Rural Non-Reservation Indians*, 28; Neils, 47, 50–51.

4. United States Department of the Interior, Bureau of Indian Affairs, *Planning in Action on the Navajo-Hopi Reservation* (Washington, DC: Government Printing Office, 1952), 28–32; Neils, 50–1; Burt, 88.

5. Donald L. Fixico, *Termination and Relocation* (Albuquerque: University of New Mexico Press, 1986), 137; Burt, 89.

6. Madigan, 4–6; Fixico, 137–38, 142; Neils, 55.

7. U.S. Congress, *Report on Urban and Rural Non-Farm Indians*, 32; United States Congress, House Committee on Interior and Insular Affairs, *Survey Report on the Bureau of Indian Affairs* (Washington, DC: Government Printing Office, 1954), 23; Burt, 89; Madigan, 10–11.

8. Madigan, 8–9.

9. Ibid, 5; Neils, 54–59; U.S. Dept. of Commerce, *The Indian Population of the United States and Alaska, 1930*, 8; U.S. Dept. of Commerce, *Subject Report: American Indians, 1970*, 1, part I:120; Sorkin, 25.

10. U.S. Dept. of Commerce, *The Indian Population of the United States and Alaska, 1930*, 8; U.S. Dept. of Commerce, *Subject Report: American Indians, 1970*, 1, part I:120; United States Department of Commerce, Bureau of the Census, *General Population and Housing Statistics, 1970*, vol. 1 (Washington, DC: Government Printing Office, 1970), part I:398–400.

11. A political confederacy of South Dakota's Siouan reservations, which was formed shortly after those tribes reorganized.

12. Gerald One Feather in Kenneth R. Philp, ed., *Indian Self-Rule: First-Hand Accounts of Indian White Relations from Roosevelt to Reagan* (Salt Lake City: Howe Brothers, 1986), 171.

13. Akwesasne Notes, *Voices From Wounded Knee, 1973* (Rooseveltown, NY:

Akwesasne Notes, 1974), 60; Rolland Dewing, *Wounded Knee: The Meaning and Significance of the Second Incident* (New York: Irvington, 1985), 44–48.

14. Akwesasne Notes, 60; Dewing, 44–48; Clyde Bellecourt quoted in Peter Matthiessen, *In the Spirit of Crazy Horse*, revised ed. (New York: Viking, 1991), 4.

15. Matthiessen, 34–35.

16. Dennis Banks, *Ojibwa Warrior: Dennis Banks and the Rise of the American Indian Movement* (Norman: University of Oklahoma Press, 2004), 12–31.

17. Ibid, 32–57.

18. Ibid, 58–61.

19. Ibid, 62–66; Akwesasne Notes, 60; Mary Crow Dog with Richard Erdoes, *Lakota Woman* (New York: HarperPerennial, 1990), 76; Paul Chaat Smith and Robert Allen Warrior, *Like A Hurricane: The Indian Movement from Alcatraz to Wounded Knee* (New York: New Press, 1996), 128.

20. Rachel A. Bonney, "The Role of AIM Leaders in Indian Nationalism," *American Indian Quarterly* 3 (autumn 1977): 212–15, 219–20; Russell Means with Marvin J. Wolf, *Where White Men Fear to Tread: The Autobiography of Russell Means* (New York St. Martin's Press, 1995), 536.

21. Vernon Bellecourt, "Interview: Vernon Bellecourt," *Penthouse International Magazine for Men* (July 1973): 59; Russell Means, 157; Dewing, 46–47.

22. Russell Means, 136–53; Wyman Babby interviewed by John S. Painter, January 2, 1982. AIRP, 1864:1–4, 18.

23. Vine Deloria, Jr., *Behind the Trail of Broken Treaties* (New York: Delacorte Press, 1974), 37–40; Troy R. Johnson, *The Occupation of Alcatraz Island* (Urbana: University of Illinois Press, 1996), 85, 130–46, 211–13; Smith and Warrior, 71; Dewing, 48–50. Note: The Alcatraz occupation is a seminal event from this era. For good accounts see Johnson; and Smith and Warrior, 1–111.

24. A largely-decentralized organization, AIM's local chapters were known as "(City) AIM."

25. Banks, 64, 105–25; Matthiessen, 51; Dewing, 46–47.

26. Raymond Yellow Thunder's sisters quoted in Akwesasne Notes, 13.

27. Ibid; Russell Means, 195–96; Banks, 115–16.

28. Leonard Crow Dog with Richard Erdoes, *Crow Dog: Four Generations of Sioux Medicine Men* (New York: HarperPerennial, 1995), 165–68; *The Gordon Journal* (Nebraska), March 7, 1972; Banks, 116–18; Means, 197–200; Smith and Warrior, 115–16.

29. Dewing, 57–59; Severt Young Bear quoted in Akwesasne Notes, 13.

30. Banks, 116; Leonard Crow Dog, 164. See also chapter 3.

31. Leonard Crow Dog, 171; Deloria, *Behind the Trail of Broken Treaties*, 46–47; Russell Means, 223–30; Smith and Warrior, 140–43.

32. "The 20-Points Position Paper," in *Legislative Review* 2 (November 1972): 57–64; Leonard Crow Dog, 171–72; Deloria, *Behind the Trail of Broken Treaties,* 65–66; Means, 223–30; Smith and Warrior, 144.

33. Leonard Crow Dog, 172–73; Deloria, *Behind the Trail of Broken Treaties,* 53–4; Russell Means, 230; Smith and Warrior, 146–50.

34. Russell Means, 230; Smith and Warrior, 153–54.

35. Leonard Crow Dog, 173; Mary Crow Dog, 86–87; Deloria, *Behind the Trail of Broken Treaties,* 53–54; Russell Means 230–31; Smith and Warrior, 154–55.

36. Leonard Crow Dog, 173–74; Mary Crow Dog, 89–91; Means, 231; Smith and Warrior, 155.

37. Robert M. Kvasnicka and Herman J. Viola, eds. *The Commissioners of Indian Affairs, 1824–1977* (Lincoln: University of Nebraska Press, 1979), 336–38; Means, 231; Smith and Warrior, 159, 174. See also chapter 5.

38. Leonard Crow Dog, 176; Deloria, *Behind the Trail of Broken Treaties,* 56; James V. Fenelon, *Culturicide, Resistance, and Survival of the Lakota ("Sioux Nation")* (New York: Garland Publishing, 1998), 239–40; Russell Means, 233–35; Smith and Warrior, 162–68.

39. Smith and Warrior, 160.

40. Ibid, 124–25, 181; Deloria, *Behind the Trail of Broken Treaties,* 56.

41. "By-Laws of the Oglala Sioux Tribe of the Pine Ridge Reservation of South Dakota," Article V, section 1; Akwesasne Notes, 15; Stanley David Lyman, *Wounded Knee 1973, A Personal Account* (Lincoln: University of Nebraska Press, 1991), xix.

42. Akwesasne Notes, 15; Bill Zimmerman, *Airlift to Wounded Knee* (Chicago: Swallow Press, 1976), 75.

43. Minutes of the Oglala Sioux Tribal Council, November 8, 1972, Box 12, Folder Council Proceedings 1972, Records of the Oglala Sioux Tribe, Oglala Lakota College Archives, Oglala Lakota College, Kyle, SD [hereafter OLC].

44. Minutes of the Oglala Sioux Tribal Council, November 10, 1972, Box 12, Folder Council Proceedings 1972, OLC.

45. Oglala Sioux Tribal Council, Resolution 072–55, November 10, 1972, Box 12, Folder Council Proceedings 1972. OLC.

46. Robert Burnette and John Koster, *The Road to Wounded Knee* (New York: Bantam, 1974), 220; the *Rapid City Journal* (Nebraska), February 28, 1973; Leonard Crow Dog, 179; Means, 239; Smith and Warrior, 191; Zimmerman, 76.

47. *Oglala Nation News* (Pine Ridge, South Dakota), February 23, 1973; Russell Means, 234, 236; Smith and Warrior 171–72, 177.

48. Russell Means, 236–37.

49. Ibid, 238; Michael C. Keith, *Signals in the Air: Native Broadcasting in America* (Westport, CT: Praeger Publishers, 1995), 137.

50. Barbara Means-Adams, interviewed by Akim D. Reinhardt, April 13, 1999, Kyle, South Dakota.

51. Throughout the 1970s, the Federal Bureau of Investigation illegally infiltrated, harassed, and sabotaged anti-establishment groups such as the American Indian Movement and the Black Panther Party. FBI files on AIM are available on microfilm: Federal Bureau of Investigation, United States, *The FBI Files on the American Indian Movement and Wounded Knee*, ed., by Rolland Dewing (Frederick, MD: University Publications of America, 1986). For a synthesis of events, see Ward Churchill and Jim Vander Wall, *Agents of Repression: The FBI's Secret Wars Against the Black Panther Party and the American Indian Movement* (Boston: South End Press, 1990), 103–352.

52. *Rapid City Journal*, February 28, 1973; Churchill and Vander Wall, 135; Deloria, *Behind the Trail of Broken Treaties*, 71; Rex Weyler, *Blood of the Land: The Government and Corporate War Against the American Indian Movement* (New York: Vintage Books, 1984), 70–71.

53. Matthiessen, 60–61; Zimmerman, 72–73.

54. Akwesasne Notes, 15–16; Zimmerman, 75.

55. Akwesasne Notes, 15–16; Zimmerman, 75.

56. Minutes of the Oglala Sioux Tribal Council, November 10, 1972, Box 12, Folder Council Proceedings 1972, OLC.

57. *Rapid City Journal* (Nebraska), February 28, 1973; Leonard Crow Dog, 179.

58. Leonard Crow Dog, 179; Matthiessen, 61.

59. Leonard Crow Dog, 179; Matthiessen, 61; Akwesasne Notes, 19; Churchill and Vander Wall, 136, 193; Russell Means, 237; Barbara Means-Adams interviewed by Reinhardt, April 13, 1999; Zimmerman, 75.

60. Bessie Cornelius interviewed by Joseph H. Cash, July 17, 1973. AIRP, 917:1, 3–4, 10–11 (partial transcript); Churchill and Vander Wall, 136.

61. Bessie Cornelius interviewed by Cash, July 17, 1973. AIRP, 917, tape 1, side 2 and tape 2, side 1 (partial transcript).

62. Dick Wilson quoted in Churchill and Vander Wall, 136.

63. Akwesasne Notes, 19.

64. Ibid., 19–21; Russel Adams interviewed by Herbert Hoover, May 8, 1972. AIRP, 821:6, 10; Churchill and Vander Wall, 192; *New York Times*, April 22, 1975.

65. Ellen Moves Camp quoted in Akwesasne Notes, 14.

66. Burnette and Koster, 225; Leonard Crow Dog, 179; Russell Means, 237; David Long quoted in *Rapid City Journal*, February 28, 1973.

67. Walter Gallagher interviewed by Anonymous, December 1, 1975. AIRP, 1795, no transcript.

68. Jake Herman interviewed by Joseph H. Cash, Summer 1967. AIRP, 38:10.

69. Mike Her Many Horses interviewed by Joseph H. Cash, July 18, 1973. AIRP, 915, side 1 (no transcript); Smith and Warrior, 136–36; Dennis Banks quoted in Leonard Crow Dog, 177.

70. Leonard Crow Dog, 11–13, 163–64, 177–78; Dennis Banks quoted in Leonard Crow Dog, 163.

71. Her Many Horses interviewed by Cash, AIRP, 915, side 1 (no transcript); Reverend Howard Orcutt interviewed by Herbert Hoover, July 3, 1974. South Dakota Oral History Project, South Dakota Oral History Center, Institute of American Indian Studies, University of South Dakota, Vermillion, SD [hereafter SDOHP], 1078 (no transcript); Mary Crow Dog, 28–41, 79–80.

72. Bessie Cornelius interviewed by Cash, AIRP, 917:10 (Partial transcript).

73. Orcutt interviewed Hoover, July 13, 1974, SDOHP, 1078 (no transcript).

74. See chapters 3 and 4.

75. Lyman, 86–87.

76. Ellen Moves Camp quoted in Akwesasne Notes, 14.

77. Marla N. Powers, *Oglala Women: Myth, Ritual, and Reality* (Chicago: University of Chicago Press, 1986), 150–51; Zimmerman, 141–60; Akwesasne Notes, 14–24; Mary Crow Dog, 80; Lyman, 13–14; Russell Means, 254.

78. Deloria, *Behind the Trail of Broken Treaties*, 41.

Chapter 7

1. Akwesasne Notes, *Voices From Wounded Knee, 1973: In the Words of the Participants* (Rooseveltown, NY: Akwesasne Notes, 1974), 16.

2. Minutes of the Oglala Sioux Tribal Council, December 12, 1972, Box 12, Folder Council Proceedings 1972, Records of the Oglala Sioux Tribe, Oglala Lakota College Archives, Oglala Lakota College, Kyle, SD [hereafter OLC]. See the previous discussion of Resolution 072–55 in chapter 6.

3. Ibid.

4. Ibid; Akwesasne Notes, 14–15; Ward Churchill and Jim Vander Wall, *Agents of Repression: The FBI's Secret Wars Against the Black Panther Party and the American Indian Movement* (Boston: South End Press, 1990), 281; Peter Matthiessen, *In the Spirit of Crazy Horse*, rev. ed. (New York: Viking Press, 1991), 37.

5. Minutes of the Oglala Sioux Tribal Council, December 12, 1972, Box 12, Folder Council Proceedings 1972, OLC.

6. Minutes of the Oglala Sioux Tribal Council, December 13, 1972, Box 12, Folder Council Proceedings 1972, OLC.

7. Minutes of the Oglala Sioux Tribal Council, December 14, 1972, Box 12, Folder Council Proceedings 1972, OLC.

8. Russell Means with Marvin J. Wolf, *Where White Men Fear to Tread: The Autobiography of Russell Means* (New York: St. Martin's's Press, 1995), 239–42; Paul Chaat Smith and Robert Allen Warrior, *Like A Hurricane: The Indian Movement from Alcatraz to Wounded Knee* (New York: New Press, 1996), 181–82.

9. Russell Means, 241–42.

10. *Omaha World Herald*, February 1, 1973; Leonard Crow Dog with Richard Erdoes, *Crow Dog: Four Generations of Sioux Medicine Men* (New York: Harper-Perennial, 1995), 181–82; Rolland Dewing, *Wounded Knee: The Meaning and Significance of the Second Incident* (New York: Irvington, 1985), 75–80; Matthiessen, 62; Russell Means, 243; Smith and Warrior, 183.

11. *Omaha World Herald*, February 1, 1973; Mary Crow Dog with Richard Erdoes, *Lakota Woman* (New York: HarperPerennial, 1990), 118. Leonard Crow Dog, 181–82; Dewing, 75–80; Matthiessen, 62; Russell Means, 243; Smith and Warrior, 183.

12. Dennis Banks with Richard Erdoes, *Ojibwa Warrior: Dennis Banks and the Rise of the American Indian Movement* (Norman: University of Oklahoma Press, 2004), 147–48; Leonard Crow Dog, 180; Russell Means, 242–43; Smith and Warrior, 178–81.

13. Leonard Crow Dog, 180–81; Russell Means, 242–43; Banks, 148–49; Smith and Warrior, 180, 182–83.

14. The counterintelligence programs conducted against AIM, the Black Panther Party, the Brown Berets, and other domestic protest organizations were later deemed to be illegal. For a record of FBI activities against AIM, see *The FBI Files on the American Indian Movement and Wounded Knee*, ed. Rolland Dewing, microfilm edition (Frederick, MD: University Publications of America, 1986) [hereafter *FBI Files*]. For a detailed analysis of the FBI's activities against AIM during this period, see Churchill and Vander Wall, 103–352; and Matthiessen, 103–126.

15. Mary Crow Dog, 118; Smith and Warrior, 181; Churchill and Vander Wall, 137.

16. Teletype, Acting Director of the Federal Bureau [ADFBI] of Investigation to Special Agents in Charge [SACs] Albuquerque et. al., February 5, 1973, doc. 397, File 105–203686, sec. 6, *FBI Files;* Teletype SAC Minneapolis to ADFBI, SACs Denver, Omaha, February 7, 1973, doc. 4, File 105–203686, sec. 6, *FBI Files;* Leonard Crow Dog, 183; Dewing, 82; Russell Means, 243–44; Banks, 152–53.

17. Mary Crow Dog, 118–19; Russell Means, 244–45; Smith and Warrior, 184.

18. *New York Times*, February 8, 1973; *Washington Post*, February 8, 1973; Russell Means, 244–46; Banks, 151–56; Leonard Crow Dog, 183–84; Mary Crow Dog, 119–21.

19. Mary Crow Dog, 116–18; Means, 246–48; Smith and Warrior, 185–90.

20. Minutes of the Oglala Sioux Tribal Council, February 5, 1973, Box 12, Folder Council Proceedings 1973, OLC; Minutes of the Oglala Sioux Tribal Council, February 7, 1973, Box 12, Folder Council Proceedings 1973, OLC.

21. Lou Bean quoted in Akwesasne Notes, 22.

22. *Oglala Nation News* (Pine Ridge, South Dakota), February 23, 1973; Stanley David Lyman, *Wounded Knee 1973: A Personal Account* (Lincoln: University of Nebraska Press, 1991), xxxvii.

23. Minutes of the Oglala Sioux Tribal Council, February 9, 1973, Box 12, Folder Council Proceedings 1973, OLC.

24. Ibid.

25. Ibid.

26. Akim D. Reinhardt, "Spontaneous Combustion: Prelude to Wounded Knee 1973," *South Dakota History* 29 (Fall 1999): 236–37; Akwesasne Notes, 22.

27. Anonymous [name withheld by request of informant] interviewed by Tom Short Bull, April 4, 1973. South Dakota Oral History Center, Institute of American Indian Studies, University of South Dakota, Vermillion, SD. American Indian Research Program [hereafter, AIRP], 606 (no transcript); Akwesasne Notes, 20, 22; Lyman 19–20; Bill Zimmerman, *Airlift to Wounded Knee* (Chicago: Swallow Press, 1976), 79.

28. Marla N. Powers, *Oglala Women: Myth, Ritual, and Reality* (Chicago: University of Chicago Press, 1986), 150–54.

29. Akwesasne Notes, 15, 20; Gladys Bissonette quoted in Zimmerman, 76–77.

30. Zimmerman, 76–78.

31. Lyman, 19–20, 33, 54–5, 77.

32. Ibid. Ironically, Lyman's disenchantment with the marshals during the siege of Wounded Knee grew from their unwillingness to act according to the ideals of Nixon's self-determination policy. Once the siege was underway, federal authorities all but ignored the Oglala Sioux Tribe and treated Chairman Wilson as little more than nuisance, shunting him aside.

33. Ibid, 3.

34. Wilson quoted in Zimmerman, 77.

35. Teletype, SAC Minneapolis to ADFBI, February 14, 1973, Doc. 413, *FBI Files;* Airtel, SAC Dallas to ADFBI, February 14, 1973, Doc. 420, *FBI Files;* Teletype, SAC Chicago to ADFBI, SACs Buffalo, Minneapolis, February 14, 1973, Doc. 421, *FBI Files;* Smith and Warrior, 191–92; Lou Bean quoted in Akwesasne Notes, 23.

36. *Oglala Nation News* (Pine Ridge, South Dakota), February 23, 1973; Akwesasne Notes, 22–23.

37. Akwesasne Notes, 24–25.

38. Reinhardt, 237–39; Banks, 157–58.

39. Lyman, 5 [emphasis original].

40. Stanley Lyman interviewed by Harry Dowell Smith in Harry Dowell Smith, "Old Cars and Social Productions Among the Teton Lakota." Ph.D. dissertation, University of Colorado, 1973, 212–17, 219, 221–25, 229–32, 236–40.

41. Russell Means, 251.

42. Akwesasne Notes, 23; Lyman, 6.

43. Lyman, 4–5; Mary Crow Dog, 122.

44. Minutes of the Oglala Sioux Tribal Council, February 22, 1973, Box 12, Folder Council Proceedings 1973, OLC; *Rapid City Journal,* February 28, 1973; Smith and Warrior, 192; Akwesasne Notes, 25–6

45. Minutes of the Oglala Sioux Tribal Council, February 22, 1973, Box 12, Folder Council Proceedings 1973, OLC; Akwesasne Notes, 26.

46. Pedro Bissonette: 650 in Akwesasne Notes, 26; Stanley Lyman: "not more than seven hundred people," in Lyman, 6; Bill Zimmerman: "Over 500" in Zimmerman, 78.

47. Minutes of the Oglala Sioux Tribal Council, February 22, 1973, Box 12, Folder Council Proceedings 1973, OLC.

48. Ibid.

49. Ibid.

50. Ibid.

51. Ibid.

52. Ibid.

53. Ibid.

54. Ibid.

55. Ibid.

56. Ibid; Akwesasne Notes, 26; Lyman, 6–7.

57. Minutes of the Oglala Sioux Tribal Council, February 22, 1973, Box 12, Folder Council Proceedings 1973, OLC; Lyman, 7; Dick Wilson quoted in *Oglala Nation News* (Pine Ridge, South Dakota), February 23, 1973 and Akwesasne Notes, 26.

58. Lyman, 8.

59. Minutes of the Oglala Sioux Tribal Council, February 23, 1973, Box 12, Folder Council Proceedings 1973, OLC; Thomas E. Mails, *Frank Fools Crow* (Garden City, NY: Doubleday, 1979; reprint ed. Lincoln: University of Nebraska Press, 1990), 190–91.

60. *Oglala Nation News* (Pine Ridge, South Dakota), February 23, 1973; Lyman, 8.

61. Minutes of the Oglala Sioux Tribal Council, February 23, 1973, Box 12, Folder Council Proceedings 1973, OLC; Akwesasne Notes, 26; Lyman, 9; Dick Wilson quoted in Akwesasne Notes, 47.

62. Minutes of the Oglala Sioux Tribal Council, February 23, 1973, Box 12, Folder Council Proceedings 1973, OLC; Akwesasne Notes, 26; Lyman, 9.

63. Minutes of the Oglala Sioux Tribal Council, February 23, 1973, Box 12, Folder Council Proceedings 1973, OLC; Lyman, 10–11.

64. Lyman, 11.

65. Minutes of the Oglala Sioux Tribal Council, February 23, 1973, Box 12, Folder Council Proceedings 1973, OLC; *Oglala Nation News* (Pine Ridge, South Dakota), February 23, 1973; Akwesasne Notes, 26; Russell Means, 250–51; Zimmerman, 78–9; C. Hobart Keith quoted in Akwesasne Notes, 26.

66. Lyman, 12.

67. Minutes of the Oglala Sioux Tribal Council, February 23, 1973, Box 12, Folder Council Proceedings 1973, OLC; *Oglala Nation News* (Pine Ridge, South Dakota), February 27, 1973.

68. Minutes of the Oglala Sioux Tribal Council, February 23, 1973, Box 12, Folder Council Proceedings 1973, OLC; Lyman, 12–13.

69. Minutes of the Oglala Sioux Tribal Council, February 23, 1973, Box 12, Folder Council Proceedings 1973, OLC.

70. Ibid.

71. Lyman looking out a window: "a hundred folks" in Lyman, 13; Pedro Bissonette: 650 in Akwesasne Notes, 26; *Oglala Nation News:* 150 in *Oglala Nation News* (Pine Ridge, South Dakota), February 23, 1973.

72. *Oglala Nation News* (Pine Ridge, South Dakota), February 23, 1973.

73. Lyman, 13–15.

74. *Oglala Nation News* (Pine Ridge, South Dakota), February 23, 1973; Lyman, 13–17.

75. Akwesasne Notes, 26, 28; Leonard Crow Dog, 187; Mary Crow Dog, 122; Lyman, 14; Zimmerman, 79.

76. Lyman, 11–12.

77. Akwesasne Notes, 4, 31, 36; Leonard Crow Dog, 187–88; Mary Crow Dog, 123; Mails, 191; Russell Means, 252; Zimmerman, 79.

78. Akwesasne Notes, 28, Zimmerman, 79.

79. Reinhardt, 237–44.

80. Teletype, SAC Minneapolis to ADFBI, February 25, 1973, Doc. 486, File 105–203686, sec. 7, *FBI Files;* Akwesasne Notes, 28; Zimmerman, 79, 148.

81. Akwesasne Notes, 31; Churchill and Vander Wall, 141; Vine Deloria, Jr., *God is Red: A Native View of Religion* (Golden, CO: Fulcrum Publishing, 1994), 245; Zimmerman, 79–80, 124–25, 148; Ellen Moves Camp quoted in Akwesasne Notes, 31; Banks, 157–58.

82. *The New York Times*, February 25, 1973; Smith and Warrior, 192–93; Lyman, xxii; John G. Neihardt, *Black Elk Speaks: Being the Life Story of a Holy Man of the Oglala Sioux*, with an Introduction by Vine Deloria, Jr., (New York: William Morrow and Company, 1932; reprint ed., Lincoln: University of Nebraska Press, 1979).

83. Akwesasne Notes, 29, 32; Lyman xxii; Zimmerman, 124–25.

84. Akwesasne Notes, 31–32; Vine Deloria, Jr., *Behind the Trail of Broken Treaties* (New York: Delacorte Press, 1974), 21; Leonard Crow Dog, 187–88; Russell Means, 252–53, 257.

85. ADFBI to SACs Minneapolis, Oklahoma City, February 28, 1973, Doc. 461, File 105–203686, Sec. 7, *FBI Files*; Akwesasne Notes, 32–9; Leonard Crow Dog, 188–89; Mary Crow Dog, 125, 128–30; Russell Means, 257–58; Zimmerman, 126–27. Mary Crow Dog quoted in Mary Crow Dog, 122.

Chapter 8

1. Alice Kehoe, *The Ghost Dance: Ethnohistory and Reviatlization* (New York: Holt, Winston, Rinehart, 1989); Robert M. Utley, *The Lance and the Shield: The Life and Times of Sitting Bull* (New York: Henry Holt, 1993), 281–83.

2. Utley, 282–83; John G. Neihardt, *Black Elk Speaks: Being the Life Story of a Holy Man of the Oglala Sioux*, with an Introduction by Vine Deloria, Jr., (New York: William Morrow, 1932; reprint ed., Lincoln: University of Nebraska Press, 1979), 231–36.

3. Gary C. Anderson, *Sitting Bull and the Paradox of Lakota Nationhood* (New York: Longman, 1996), 157–61; Utley, 284–285.

4. James McLaughlin, *My Friend the Indian*, with an introduction by Robert M. Utley (New York: Houghton Mifflin, 1910; reprint ed., Lincoln: University of Nebraska Press, 1989), 180; Neihardt, 248.

5. McLaughlin, 183–84; Neihardt, 248; Utley, 285–90.

6. McLaughlin, 184–85, 190–222; Utley, 284–90, 293–305.

7. Anderson, 172–73; Ralph K. Andrist, *The Long Death: The Last Days of the Plains Indians* (New York: Macmillan, 1964), 345–52; Neihardt, 253–62.

8. Anderson, 172–73; Andrist, 351–53; Neihardt, 253–62.

9. Dee Brown, *Bury My Heart at Wounded Knee: An Indian History of the American West* (New York: Holt, Winston, Rinehart, 1971).

10. Raymond J. DeMallie, "Pine Ridge Economy: Cultural and Historical Per-

spectives," in *World Anthropology: American Indian Economic Development,* ed. Sam Stanley (The Hague: Mouton Press, 1978), 305; Francis Paul Prucha, *The Great Father: The United States Government and the American Indians,* 2 vols. (Lincoln: University of Nebraska Press, 1984), 2:1119; Paul Chaat Smith and Robert Allen Warrior, *Like A Hurricane: The Indian Movement from Alcatraz to Wounded Knee* (New York: New Press, 1996), 191.

11. See also Akim D. Reinhardt, "Spontaneous Combustion: Prelude to Wounded Knee 1973," *South Dakota History* 29 (fall 1999): 229–44.

12. Leonard Crow Dog with Richard Erdoes, *Crow Dog: Four Generations of Medicine Men* (New York: HarperPerennial, 1995), 185–87; Akim D. Reinhardt, "Spontaneous Combustion: Prelude to Wounded Knee 1973," *South Dakota History* 29 (fall 1999): 229–44.

13. Clive Gildersleeve interviewed by John S. Painter, July 24, 1981. South Dakota Oral History Center, Institute of American Indian Studies, University of South Dakota, Vermillion, SD. American Indian Research Program [hereafter, AIRP], 1862:1–4, 7; C.A. Gildersleeve interviewed by Gerald Wolff, August 23, 1972. AIRP, 876:6. Note: Gildersleeve's first name is misspelled as "Clyde" in the transcript of interview 876.

14. C.A. Gildersleeve interviewed by Gerald Wolff, August 23, 1972. AIRP, 876:4–6; Clive Gildersleeve interviewed by Painter, AIRP, 1862:5–6, 9–11.

15. C.A. Gildersleeve interviewed by Wolff. AIRP, 876 2–5; Clive Gildersleeve interviewed by Painter. AIRP: 1862:13–14; Dewing, 103.

16. United States Department of the Interior, *Statistical Supplement to the Annual Report of the Commissioner of Indian Affairs* (Washington DC: Government Printing Office, 1939), 76; Ward Churchill and Jim Vander Wall, *Agents of Repression: The FBI's Secret War Against the Black Panther Party and the American Indian Movement* (Boston: South End Press, 1990), 143; Leonard Crow Dog,189; Mary Crow Dog with Richard Erdoes, *Lakota Woman* (New York: HarperPerennial, 1990), 128–29; Russell Means with Marvin J. Wolf (New York: St. Martin's Press, 1995), 202–3; *Oglala Nation News* (Pine Ridge, South Dakota), March 27, 1972; Paul Chaat Smith and Robert Allen Warrior, *Like A Hurricane: The Indian Movement from Alcatraz to Wounded Knee* (New York: New Press, 1996), 118.

17. C.A. Gildersleeve interviewed by Wolff, August 23, 1972. AIRP, 876:22.

18. *Oglala Nation News* (Pine Ridge, South Dakota), March 27, 1972; Steve Talbot, "The Meaning of Wounded Knee, 1973: Indian Self-Government and the Role of Anthropology," in *World Anthropology: The Politics of Anthropology: From Colonialism and Sexism Toward a View From Below* (The Hague: Mouton Press, 1979), 235; Leonard Crow Dog,189; Mary Crow Dog, 128–29; Means, 202–3; Smith and Warrior, 118; Churchill and Vander Wall, 143.

19. C.A. Gildersleeve interviewed by Wolff, August 23, 1972. AIRP, 876:2–3, 5.

20. Ibid, 3–4.

21. Bessie Cornelius interviewed by Joseph H. Cash, July 17, 1973. AIRP, 917:15 (partial transcript).

22. C.A. Gildersleeve interviewed by Wolff, August 23, 1972. AIRP, 876:32–4.

23. Ibid, 1; John Burrows, "The Pine Ridge Murders," in *New York Review of Books* 30, no. 14 (September 29, 1983).

24. Modern scholars are nearly unanimous in their condemnation of the policy. For thorough discussions of termination, see Donald L. Fixico, *Termination and Relocation: Federal Indian Policy 1945–1960* (Albuquerque: University of New Mexico Press, 1986), and Larry W. Burt *Tribalism in Crisis: Federal Indian Policy, 1953–1961* (Albuquerque: University of New Mexico Press, 1982).

25. C. A. Gildersleeve interviewed by Wolff, August 23, 1972. AIRP, 876:23–6.

26. For a discussion of Relocation see: Fixico; Larry W. Burt, "Roots of the Native American Urban Experience" *American Indian Quarterly* 10, no. 2 (1986): 85–99; Kenneth R. Philp, "Stride Toward Freedom: The Relocation of Indians to Cities, 1958–1960," *Western Historical Quarterly* 16, no. 2 (April 1985).

27. C.A. Gildersleeve interviewed by Wolff, August 23, 1972. AIRP, 876:26–28.

28. Ibid, 27–28. Gildersleeve named neither the rancher nor his employee in his interview, but he did assert that a variety of swindles transpired in which Lakotas were defrauded out of their wealth. Also hampering economic development were various inept federal programs.

29. Ibid, 21.

30. Cornelius interviewed by Cash, July 17, 1973. AIRP, 917:14 (partial transcript).

31. John G. Neihardt, *Black Elk Speaks: Being the Life Story of a Holy Man of the Oglala Sioux*, with an introduction by Vine Deloria, Jr. (New York: William Morrow and Company, 1932; reprint ed., Lincoln: University of Nebraska Press, 1979).

32. Burrows, "The Pine Ridge Murders"; Tim Giago, "The Memory of Wounded Knee Still Bleeds," *The Star Telegram*, December 26, 2003. Online edition http://www.dfw.com/mld.dfw.news.opinion/7569872.htm?1c: (accessed March 21, 2004); Cook-Lynn and Gonzalez, 139; John G. Neihardt interviewed by Mybelle Wilcox November 14, 1970. South Dakota Oral History Project, South Dakota Oral History Center, Institute of American Indian Studies, University of South Dakota, Vermillion, SD, 2178 Tape 1 Side 1 (no transcript).

33. C. A. Gildersleeve interviewed by Wolff, August 23, 1972. AIRP, 876:4; Dewing, 103.

34. *Oglala Nation News*, March 27, 1972; Gonzalez and Cook-Lynn, 75, 93. Claudia Iron Hawk Sully quoted in Gonzalez and Cook-Lynn, 135.

35. *Oglala Nation News*, March 27, 1972.

36. Ibid.

37. *Oglala Nation News,* March 27, 1972; C. A. Gildersleeve interviewed by Wolff, August 23, 1972. AIRP, 876:4; Smith and Warrior, 188; Dewing, 61.

38. *Oglala Nation News,* March 27, 1972; C. A. Gildersleeve interviewed by Wolff, August 23, 1972. AIRP, 876:4.

39. C. A. Gildersleeve interviewed by Wolff, August 23, 1972. AIRP, 876:10.

40. *Oglala Nation News,* March 27, 1972.

41. Akwesasne Notes, *Voices From Wounded Knee, 1973: In the Words of the Participants* (Rooseveltown, NY: Akwesasne Notes, 1974), 55; *New York Times,* March 12, 1973.

42. Minutes of the Oglala Sioux Tribal Council Special Session, March 13, 1973, Box 21, Folder Council Proceedings 1973, Records of the Oglala Sioux Tribe, Oglala Lakota College Archives, Oglala Lakota College, Kyle, SD [hereafter OLC]; Stanley David Lyman, *Wounded Knee 1973: A Personal Account* (Lincoln: University of Nebraska Press, 1991), 154.

43. Lyman, *Wounded Knee 1973,* 13–14, 80–1, 89–90; Stanley Lyman interviewed by Gerald Woloff, August 23, 1972. South Dakota Oral History Center, Institute of American Indian Studies, University of South Dakota, Vermillion, SD. American Indian Research Program [hereafter, AIRP], 877 (no transcript).

44. President Richard Nixon quoted by Alexander "Sandy" MacNabb in Kennth R. Philp, ed., *Indian Self-Rule: First-Hand Accounts of Indian-White Relations from Roosevelt to Reagan* (Salt Lake City: Howe Brothers, 1986), 215.

45. Minutes of the Oglala Sioux Tribe Special Session, March 17, 1973, Box 21, Folder Council Proceedings 1973, OLC; Minutes of the Oglala Sioux Tribal Council, April 4–6, 16, 1973, Box 21, Folder Council Proceedings, 1973, OLC; Lyman, *Wounded Knee 1973,* 66, 154.

46. Minutes of the Oglala Sioux Tribal Council, April 4–6, 16, 1973, Box 21, Folder Council Proceedings 1973, OLC.

47. Smith and Warrior, 263–65.

48. Thomas E. Mails, *Fools Crow* (Garden City, NY: Doubleday, 1979; reprint ed. Lincoln: University of Nebraska Press, 1990), 9–10, 190–91, 198–200, 216.

49. Ward Churchill and Jim Vander Wall, *Agents of Repression: The FBI's Secret Wars Against the Black Panther Party and the American Indian Movement* (Boston: South End Press, 1990), 175, 200–3; Peter Matthiessen, *In the Spirit of Crazy Horse,* revised ed. (New York: Viking Press, 1991), 100–102, 128–29; for a detailed analysis of the Pine Ridge civil war, see Churchill and Vander Wall, 175–217 and Matthiessen, 103–149.

50. For a complete evaluation of the Peltier case, see Matthiessen, 153–535 and Churchill and Vander Wall, 235–327.

51. United States Congress, Committee on Interior and Insular Affairs, Sub-

committee on Indian Affairs. Touche, Ross and Co., *Occupation of Wounded Knee: Hearings Before the Subcommittee on Indian Affairs* (Washington, DC: Government Printing Office, 1976), 2–3.

52. Ibid, part II, sec. A, 10–28, 387–95, 401.

53. Mike Her Many Horses interviewed by Joseph H. Cash, July 18, 1973. AIRP, 915 (no transcript); Joseph Cash, Field Notes, July 17, 1973. AIRP, 920:1; Joseph Cash, Field Notes, July 19, 1973. AIRP,924:5–6.

54. Russell Means speech read by Lewis Bad Wound interviewed by Joe Rock Boy, June 12, 1973. AIRP, 902, side 1 (no transcript).

55. Edison Ward interviewed by Herbert Hoover, July 3, 1974. South Dakota Oral History Project, South Dakota Oral History Center, Institute of American Indian Studies, University of South Dakota, Vermillion, SD. American Indian Research Program [hereafter SDOHP], 1076:16.

56. Mona Montgomery interviewed by Herbert Hoover, May 16, 1972. AIRP, 820:21–2; Her Many Horses interviewed by Cash, July 18, 1973. AIRP, 915 (no transcript).

57. United States Commission on Civil Rights, Staff Report, *Report of Investigation: Oglala Sioux Tribal Election, 1974* (Washington, DC: Government Printing Office, 1974), 1; Her Many Horses interviewed by Cash, AIRP, 915 (no transcript); Phillip D. Roos et al., "The Impact of AIM on the Pine Ridge Reservation," *Phylon* 41 (March, 1980): 95.

58. U.S. Commission on Civil Rights, iii, 1, 2–34, 28; Roos et al., 95.

59. Verna Larvie interviewed by Herbert Hoover, August 17, 1974. SDOHP, 1172:11–12; U.S. Commission on Civil Rights, 18–20, 24, 28.

60. *Means v. Wilson,* 383 F. Supp. 378 (1974); *Means v. Wilson,* 522 F. 2d 833 (1975).

61. Mails, 199, 215–16; Matthiessen, 419–20; Roos, et al., 99; Lewis Bad Wound interviewed by Mary Pat Cuney Rambo at the Kyle Community Center, September 24, 1974. AIRP, 1039:4; Frank Fools Crow quoted in Talbot, 252.

62. Mails, 200; Matthiessen, 581.

63. Lawrence M. Hauptman, "The Indian Reorganization Act," in Sandra L Cadwalder and Vine Deloria, Jr., eds., *The Aggressions of Civilization* (Philadelphia: Temple University Press, 1984), 143; Tom Holm, "The Crisis in Tribal Government," in Vine Deloria, Jr., ed., *American Indian Policy in the Twentieth Century* (Norman: University of Oklahoma Press, 1985), 135; Paul M. Robertson, *The Power of the Land: Identity, Ethnicity and Class Among the Oglala Lakota* (New York: Routledge, 2002), 172–73.

64. Marla N. Powers, *Oglala Women: Myth, Ritual, and Reality* (Chicago: University of Chicago Press, 1986), 147.

65. Grace Black Elk and Gladys Bissonette quoted in Akwesasne Notes, 57.

66. Mails, 147.

67. Mary Crow Dog with Richard Erdoes, *Lakota Woman* (New York: Harper-Perennial, 1990), 118; Leonard Crow Dog, 114.

68. Powers, 144; Taiaiake Alfred, *Peace, Power, Righteousness: An Indigenous Manifesto* (Don Mills, Ontario: Oxford University Press, 1999), 2, 30.

69. Mails, 211–12.

70. Grass Roots Oyate, "Chronology–The Awakening of Our Tribe," in *Fire on Prairie*, February 27, 2000, http://www.fireonprairie.org/Oglala%20takeover%20 chronology.html (accessed July 1, 2000); Robertson, 241–45.

71. *Sioux Falls Argus Leader*, March 24, 2000; Robertson, 241–45.

72. Assistant Secretary for Indian Affairs Kevin Glover to Akim D. Reinhardt, November 12, 2006, email letter; 2006 *Sioux Falls Argus Leader*, March 24, 2000.

73. Peter Harriman,"Fire Thunder Tries to Regain Power," *Argus Leader*, July 19, 2006; Peter Harriman, "Ousted Leader Not Giving Up," *Argus Leader*, August 4, 2006; David Melmer, "Fire Thunder Reinstated," *Indian Country Today*, July 18, 2006; "Janis Appointed to Oglala Post," *Argus Leader*, August 1, 2006.

74. Harriman, "Fire Thunder Tries to Regain Power"; Harriman, "Ousted Leader Not Giving Up"; Melmer, "Fire Thunder Reinstated"; "Janis Appointed to Oglala Post."

75. Harriman, "Fire Thunder Tries to Regain Power"; Harriman, "Ousted Leader Not Giving Up"; Melmer, "Fire Thunder Reinstated"; "Janis Appointed to Oglala Post."

76. "Cherokee Tribe Elects New Leadership," Associated Press, September 4, 2003; Becky Bohrer, "Judge Sentences Former Crow Chairman, Stays Decision," September 12, 2003; James Parker, "Conflict of Interest Alleged in Setup of Tobacco Shop," *Star Phoenix* (Saskatoon), August 16, 2003.

77. Loretta Fowler, *Arapaho Politics, 1851–1978: Symbols in Crises of Authority* (Lincoln: University of Nebraska Press, 1982); Paul C. Rosier, *Rebirth of the Blackfeet Nation: 1912–1954* (Lincoln: University of Nebraska Press, 2001), 282.

78. Dick Wilson interviewed by Joseph Cash, July 17, 1973. AIRP, 918 (no transcript).

Bibliography

Unpublished Primary Sources

American Indian Research Program. South Dakota Oral History Center. Institute of American Indian Studies. University of South Dakota, Vermillion, SD.

Main Decimal File 1900–1965, General Correspondence. General Records Pine Ridge Agency, Pine Ridge, South Dakota. Records of the Bureau of Indian Affairs, Record Group 75, National Archives and Records Administration, Kansas City, MO.

Ordinances, 1936–1939, Administrative Records. General Records of the Oglala Sioux Tribal Government, General Records Pine Ridge Agency, Pine Ridge, South Dakota. Records of the Bureau of Indian Affairs, Record Group 75, National Archives and Records Administration, Kansas City, MO.

Records of the Oglala Sioux Tribe. Oglala Lakota College Archives, Oglala Lakota College, Kyle, SD.

South Dakota Oral History Project. South Dakota Oral History Center. Institute of American Indian Studies. University of South Dakota, Vermillion, SD.

Published Primary Sources

Akwesasne Notes. *Voices From Wounded Knee, 1973: In the Words of the Participants.* Rooseveltown, NY: Akwesasne Notes, 1974.

Banks, Dennis, with Richard Erdoes. *Ojibwa Warrior: Dennis Banks and the Rise of the American Indian Movement.* Norman: University of Oklahoma Press, 2004.

Bellecourt, Vernon. "Interview: Vernon Bellecourt," *Penthouse International Magazine for Men* (July 1973): 59–64, 122, 131–32.

Boise Cascade Center for Community Development. *Individual Reservation Reports.* Vol. 2 of *Indian Economic Development: An Evaluation of EDA's Selected Indian Reservation Program: Prepared for the Economic Development Administration U. S. Department of Commerce.* Boise: Boise Cascade Center for Community Development, 1972.

Burnett, Robert, and John Koster. *The Road to Wounded Knee.* New York: Bantam, 1974.

Collier, John. *From Every Zenith: A Memoir and Some Essays on Life and Thought.* Denver: Sage Books, 1963.

Crow Dog, Leonard, with Richard Erdoes. *Crow Dog: Four Generations of Sioux Medicine Men.* New York: HarperPerennial, 1995.

Crow Dog, Mary with Richard Erdoes. *Lakota Woman.* New York: HarperPerennial, 1990.

Deloria, Vine, Jr., ed. *The Indian Reorganization Act: Congresses and Bills.* Norman: University of Oklahoma Press, 2002.

Iverson, Peter, ed. *The Plains Indians of the Twentieth Century.* Norman: University of Oklahoma Press, 1985.

Kappler, Charles J., ed. *Indian Treaties 1778–1883.* 3rd ed. Washington, DC: Government Printing Office, 1904; reprint ed., New York: Interland Publishing, 1972.

Lautenschlager, Virginia Irene (Kain). *A History of Cuny Table, South Dakota 1890–2002,* edited by Katherine Bahr. Chadron, NE: Chadron State College, n.d.

Lyman, Stanley David. *Wounded Knee 1973: A Personal Account,* edited by Floyd A. O'Neil, June K. Lyman, and Susan McKay. Lincoln: University of Nebraska Press, 1991.

Mails, Thomas E. *Fools Crow.* Lincoln: Garden City, NY: Doubleday, 1979; reprint ed. Lincoln: University of Nebraska Press, 1990.

Means, Russell, with Marvin J. Wolf. *Where White Men Fear to Tread.* New York: St. Martin's Press, 1995.

Philp, Kenneth R., ed. *Indian Self-Rule: First-Hand Accounts of Indian-White Relations from Roosevelt to Reagan.* Salt Lake City: Howe Brothers, 1986.

Roberts, W. O. "The Pine Ridge Reservation Land Program." *Indians at Work Magazine* 4 (May 1937): 8–11.

United States. Commission on Civil Rights. Staff Report. *Report of Investigation: Oglala Sioux Tribal Election, 1974.* Washington, DC: Government Printing Office, 1974.

———. Federal Bureau of Investigation. *The FBI Files on the American Indian Movement and Wounded Knee,* edited by Rolland Dewing. Frederick, MD: University Publications of America, 1986.

Bibliography

———. Senate Subcommittee on Indian Affairs. *Occupation of Wounded Knee, Hearings Before the Subcommittee on Indian Affairs.* Washington, DC: Government Printing Office, 1976.

Walker, James R., *Lakota Society,* edited by Raymond J. DeMallie Lincoln: University of Nebraska Press, 1982.

Wilson, Dick. "Real Indians Condemn AIM." In *Contemporary Native American Address,* edited by John R. Maestas Provo: Brigham Young University Press, 1976, 63–65.

Zimmerman, Bill. *Airlift to Wounded Knee.* Chicago: Swallow Press, 1976.

Newspapers

The Gordon (NE) Journal, 1972.

The New York Times, 1972–1973.

Oglala Lakota (Pine Ridge, SD), 1971–1972.

Oglala Nation News (Pine Ridge, SD), 1972–1973.

The Oglala War Cry (Pine Ridge, SD), 1970–1971.

Omaha World-Herald, 1972–1973.

Rapid City (SD) Journal, 1972–1973.

The Washington Post, 1972–1973.

War Cry (Pine Ridge, SD), 1968.

Unpublished Secondary Sources

Clements, Leon Eugene. "Possibilities of Rehabilitating the Oglala Sioux." M.A. thesis, Colorado State College of Education, 1938.

D'Arcus, Bruce. "The Wounded Knee Occupation and the Politics of Scale: Marginal Protest and Central Authority in a Media Age." Ph.D. dissertation, Syracuse University, 2001.

Smith, Harry Dowell. "Old Cars and Social Productions Among the Teton Lakota." Ph.D. dissertation, University of Colorado, 1973.

Washburn, Francis Arline. "Beauty of Word and Meaning: An Analysis of Lakota Oral Tradition." Ph.D. dissertation, University of New Mexico, 2003.

Books

Alfred, Taiaiake. *Heeding the Voices of our Ancestors: Kahnawake Mohawk Politics and the Rise of Native Nationalism.* Don Mills, Ontario: Oxford University Press, 1995.

Anderson, Terry L. *Sovereign Nations or Reservations: An Economic History of American Indians.* San Francisco: Pacific Research Institute for Public Policy, 1995.

Biolsi, Thomas. *Organizing the Lakota: The Political Economy of the New Deal on the Pine Ridge and Rosebud Reservations.* Tucson: University of Arizona Press, 1992.

Castile, George Pierre, *To Show Heart: Native American Self-Determination and Federal Indian Policy, 1960–1975.* Tucson: University of Arizona Press, 1998.

Cornell, Stephen. *The Return of the Native: American Indian Political Resurgence.* New York: Oxford University Press, 1988.

Cornell, Stephen, and Joseph P. Kalt. *Sovereignty and Nation-Building: The Development Challenge in Indian Country Today.* Cambridge, MA: Harvard Project on American Indian Economic Development, 2003.

Churchill, Ward, and Jim Vander Wall. *Agents of Repression: The FBI's Secret Wars Against the Black Panther Party and the American Indian.* Boston: South End Press, 1990.

Deloria, Vine, Jr., *Custer Died For Your Sins: An Indian Manifesto.* New York: Macmillan Company, 1969.

———. *Behind the Trail of Broken Treaties.* New York: Delacorte Press, 1974.

Deloria, Vine, Jr., and Clifford Lytle. *The Nations Within: The Past and Future of American Indian Sovereignty.* New York: Pantheon Books, 1984.

Dewing, Rolland. *Wounded Knee: The Meaning and Significance of the Second Incident.* New York: Irvington, 1985.

Fenelon, James V. *Culturicide, Resistance, and the Survival of the Lakota ("Sioux Nation").* New York: Garland, 1998.

Fowler, Loretta. *Arapahoe Politics, 1851–1978: Symbols in Crises of Authority.* Lincoln: University of Nebraska Press, 1982.

———. *Tribal Sovereignty and the Historical Imagination: Cheyenne-Arapaho Politics.* Lincoln: University of Nebraska Press, 2002.

Gibbon, Guy. *The Sioux: The Dakota and Lakota Nations.* Malden, MA: Blackwell Publishing, 2003.

Gonzalez, Mario, and Elizabeth Cook-Lynn. *The Politics of Hallowed Ground: Wounded Knee and the Struggle for Indian Sovereignty.* Urbana: University of Illinois Press, 1999.

Hecht, Robert A. *The Occupation of Wounded Knee.* Charlotteville, NY: Sum Har Press, 1981.

Harring, Sidney L. *Crow Dog's Case: American Indian Sovereignty, Tribal Law, and United States Law in the Nineteenth Century.* New York: Cambridge University Press, 1994.

Lazarus, Edward. *Black Hills White Justice: The Sioux Nation Versus the United States, 1775 to the Present.* New York: HarperCollins Publishers, 1991.

Lopach, James J., Margery Hunter, and Richmond L. Clow. *Tribal Government*

Today: Politics on Montana Indian Reservations. Boulder: Westview Press, 1990.

Matthiessen, Peter. *In the Spirit of Crazy Horse.* Rev. ed. New York: Viking, 1991.

Mekeel, H. S. *Economy of a Modern Teton-Dakota Community.* New Haven: Yale University Press, 1936.

Nabokov, Peter. *A Forest of Time: American Indian Ways of History.* New York: Cambridge University Press, 2002.

Ortiz, Roxanne Dunbar. *The Great Sioux Nation: Sitting in Judgement on America.* San Francisco: American Indian Treaty Council Information Center/ Moon Books, 1977.

Parman, Donald L. *The Navajos and the New Deal.* Cambridge: Cambridge University Press, 1970.

Peroff, Nicholas. *Menominee Drums: Tribal Termination and Restoration, 1954–1974.* Norman: University of Oklahoma Press, 1982.

Pickering, Kathleen Ann. *Lakota Culture, World Economy.* Lincoln: University of Nebraska Press, 2000.

Powers, Marla N. *Oglala Women: Myth, Ritual, and Reality.* Chicago: University of Chicago Press, 1986.

Rosier, Paul C. *Rebirth of the Blackfeet Nation, 1912–1954.* Lincoln: University of Nebraska Press, 2001.

Robertson, Paul R. *The Power of the Land: Identity, Ethnicity and Class Among the Oglala Lakota.* New York: Routledge, 2002.

Rusco, Elmer R. *A Fateful Time: The Background and Legislative History of the Indian Reorganization Act.* Reno: University of Nevada Press, 2000.

Sayer, John William. *Ghost Dancing the Law: The Wounded Knee Trials.* Cambridge, MA: Harvard University Press, 1997.

Smith, Paul Chaat, and Robert Allen Warrior. *Like A Hurricane: The Indian Movement to Wounded Knee.* New York: The New Press,1996.

Starita, Joe. *The Dull Knifes of Pine Ridge: A Lakota Odyssey.* New York: Berkley Books, 1995.

Taylor, Graham D. *The New Deal and American Indian Tribalism: The Administration of the Indian Reorganization Act, 1934–1945.* Lincoln: University of Nebraska Press, 1980.

Thompson, Laura. *Personality and Government: Findings and Recommendations of the Indian Administration Research.* Mexico City: Ediciones del Instituto Indigenista Interamericana, 1951.

Tuhiwai Smith, Linda. *Decolonizing Methodologies: Research and Indigenous Peoples.* London: Zed Books, 1999.

Bibliography

Weyler, Rex. *Blood of the Land: The Government and Corporate War Against the American Indian Movement.* New York: Vintage Books, 1984.

Wilkins, David E. *American Indian Politics and the American Political System.* Lanham, MD: Rowman & Littlefield, 2002.

Wunder, John R. *"Retained by The People": A History of American Indians and the Bill of Rights.* New York: Oxford University Press, 1994.

Articles

Bromert, Roger. "The Sioux and the Indian-CCC," *South Dakota History* 8 (winter 1978): 340–356.

Clements, Leon Eugene. "Red Shirt Table, A Community Working Toward Self-Support." *Indians at Work Magazine* 4 (June 1937): 36–38.

Clow, Richmond. "The Indian Reorganization Act and the Loss of Tribal Sovereignty: Constitutions on the Rosebud and Pine Ridge Reservations." *Great Plains Quarterly* 7 (spring 1987): 125–134.

———. "Tribal Populations in Transition: Sioux Reservations and Federal Policy, 1934–1965," *South Dakota History* 19 (winter 1989): 362–391.

DeMallie, Raymond J. "Pine Ridge Economy: Cultural and Historical Perspectives." In *World Anthropology: American Indian Economic Development,* edited by Sam Stanley. The Hague: Mouton Press, 1978, pp. 237–312.

Dewing, Rolland. "South Dakota Newspaper Coverage of the 1973 Occupation of Wounded Knee." *South Dakota History* 12, no. 1 (1982): 48–64.

Elbert, Ted. "Wounded Knee: A Struggle for Self-Determination." *Christian Century* 90 (March 28, 1973): 356–357.

Hauptman, Lawrence M. "The Indian Reorganization Act." In *The Aggressions of Civilization,* edited by Sandra L. Cadwalder and Vine Deloria, Jr., Philadelphia: Temple University Press, 1984, pp. 141–59.

Holm, Tom. "The Crisis in Tribal Government." In *American Indian Policy in the Twentieth Century,* edited by Vine Deloria, Jr., Norman: University of Oklahoma Press, 1985, pp. 135–154.

Kelly, Lawrence C. "The Indian Reorganization Act: The Dream and the Reality." *Pacific Historical Review* 44, no. 3 (August 1975): 291–312.

Lewis, David Rich. "Reservation Leadership and the Progressive-Traditional Dichotomy: William Wash and the Northern Utes, 1865–1928." *Ethnohistory* 38, no. 2 (spring 1991): 124–48.

Lonowski, Delmer "A Return to Tradition: Proportional Representation in Tribal Government." *American Indian Culture and Research Journal* 18, no. 1 (winter 1994): 147–163.

Metcalf, Richard P. "Who Should Rule at Home? Native American Politics and

Indian-White Relations." *Journal of American History* 61 (December 1974): 651–665.

Philp, Kenneth R. "Stride Toward Freedom: The Relocation of Indians to Cities, 1952–1960." *Western Historical Quarterly* 16, no. 2 (April 1985).

Reinhardt, Akim D. "Spontaneous Combustion: Prelude to Wounded Knee 1973." *South Dakota History* 29 (fall 1999): 229–244.

———. "A Crude Replacement: The Indian New Deal, Indirect Colonialism, and Pine Ridge Reservation." *The Journal of Colonialism and Colonial History* 6, no. 1 (spring 2005).

Roos, Phillip D., et al. "The Impact of the American Indian Movement on the Pine Ridge Indian Reservation." *Phylon* 41 (March 1980): 89–99.

Schultz, Terri. "Bamboozle Me Not at Wounded Knee: The Making of a Media Event that Had Everything But the Truth." *Harper's* (June 1973): 46–56.

Skopek, Tracy A., Rich Engstrom, and Kenneth Hansen. "All That Glitters . . . The Rise of American Indian Tribes in State Political Behavior. *American Indian Culture and Research Journal* 29, no. 4 (2005).

Talbert, Carol. "Experiences at Wounded Knee." *Human Organization* 33, no. 2 (1974): 215–17.

Talbot, Steve. "The Meaning of Wounded Knee, 1973: Indian Self-Government and the Role of Anthropology." In *World Anthropology: The Politics of Anthropology: From Colonialism and Sexism to Toward a View from Below,* edited by Sam Stanley. The Hague: Mouton Press, 1978, pp. 227–58.

Taylor, Graham D. "The Tribal Alternative to Bureaucracy: The Indian's New Deal: 1933–1945," *Journal of the West* 12 (January 1974): 128–42.

Tilsen, Kenneth E. "U. S. Courts and Native Americans at Wounded Knee." *Gild Practitioner* 31 (spring 1974): 61–69.

Thomas, Robert K. "Powerless Politics." Washington, DC: Department of the Interior, 1966; *New University Thought.* University of Chicago (winter 1966–1967).

Wirth, Rex Sylvester, and Stefanie Wickstrom. "Competing Views: Indian Nations and Sovereignty in the Intergovernmental System of the United States," *American Indian Quarterly* 26, no.4 (fall 2002).

Index